# The Book
# of Music and
# Nature

Terra Nova Books aim to show
how environmental issues are relevant
not only in scientific and political spheres; they
also resonate at the cultural and artistic level.
The books combine essays, reportage, fiction, art,
and poetry to reveal the complex and paradoxical
ways the natural and the human are continually
redefining one another.

Other Terra Nova Books:
THE NEW EARTH READER
THE WORLD AND THE WILD
WRITING ON WATER
WRITING ON AIR
WRITING THE FUTURE
WRITING THE WORLD

TERRA NOVA
New Jersey Institute of Technology
Newark, NJ 07102
www.terranovabooks.org

—————————

Music/Culture
A series from Wesleyan University Press

# The Book of Music and Nature

*An Anthology of Sounds, Words, Thoughts*

EDITED BY DAVID ROTHENBERG & MARTA ULVAEUS

A TERRA NOVA BOOK

Wesleyan University Press    Middletown, Connecticut

Published by Wesleyan University Press, Middletown, CT 06459
www.wesleyan.edu/wespress

©2001 by Wesleyan University Press
All rights reserved

Second edition 2009
ISBN for the Second Edition: 978-0-8195-6935-6

*The Disc of Music and Nature* is a virtual CD available at
http://www.wesleyan.edu/wespress/musicandnaturecd

Printed in the United States of America
5   4   3

Wesleyan University Press is a member of the Green Press Initiative. The paper
used in this book meets their minimum requirement for recycled paper.


*The Library of Congress has cataloged the original edition as follows:*
Library of Congress Cataloging-in-Publication Data
The book of music and nature : an anthology of sounds, words, thoughts /
edited by David Rothenberg & Marta Ulvaeus.
p. cm. — (Music/culture)
Based on special issue of Terra nova (summer 1997, vol. 2, no. 3).
"A Terra nova book."
Includes index.
ISBN 0-8195-6407-9 (cloth) — ISBN 0-8195-6408-7 (pbk.)
1. Music — Philosophy and aesthetics.   2. Music, Influence of.
3. Environment (Aesthetics)   I. Rothenberg, David, 1962–   II. Ulvaeus, Marta.
III. Terra nova (Cambridge, Mass.)   IV. Series.
ML3845.B614 2001
781.1'7 — dc21      00-51327

# CONTENTS

## IV. *Many Natures, Many Cultures*

## V. *The Disc of Music and Nature*     231

*The Disc of Music and Nature* is now a virtual CD available at
http://www.wesleyan.edu/wespress/musicandnaturecd

# LIST OF ILLUSTRATIONS

## ACKNOWLEDGMENTS

First and foremost, we would like to acknowledge all of our contributors to this book and CD, who agreed to be part of this project for little or no money. Second, the project would never have begun without the tireless work of Sabine Hrechdakian putting together the "Music from Nature" issue of *Terra Nova* (Summer 1997, vol. 2, no. 3), which was the genesis of this present work. We also acknowledge the support of her partner the late Mark Sandman and express deep sympathy over his early and tragic death.

Over the years many musicians and music aficionados have helped us refine how music can be a part of ecology, including Charlie Keil, Michael Pestel, Malcolm Goldstein, Chris Watson, Andra McCartney, Jim Cummings, Sarah Peebles, René van Peer, Peter Warshall, Gayle Young, Jason Reinier, Ben Neill, Charlie Morrow, Jim Metzner, David Abram, Jim Motavalli, Ellen Kushner, Jukka Mikkola, Hans Ulrich Werner, Walter Tilgner, Norman Lowrey, Philip Bimstein, Richard Teitelbaum, Annea Lockwood, Paul Winter, Dave Aftandilian, Oliver Lowenstein, Lisa Garrison, Alexandra Christy, Scott McVay, Jennifer Sahn, Laney Harrison, Paul Pannhuysen, David Hykes, Paul Godwin, Steve Gorn, David Jaffe, and Jeffrey Goldberg.

Thanks to the New Jersey Institute of Technology for giving us a place to call home, to the Geraldine R. Dodge Foundation for supporting our initial efforts on this topic, and to the KEOH Foundation for a grant to support the preparation of this book. Finally, deepest gratitude to Mia Söderlund and Matthew Ebinger for their invaluable assistance in putting this together.

Go outside, keep listening. There's always more to hear.

## NOTE TO THE SECOND EDITION

*The Disc of Music and Nature* is now a virtual CD available at
http://www.wesleyan.edu/wespress/musicandnaturecd

Pentimento
op 92, no.
DUH
DUH
DUH
DUH
UH
UH
UH
UH
UH
UH
GLASS
GLASS
DUH
UH
UH
GLASS
GLASS
DUH
UH
UH

DAVID ROTHENBERG

# Introduction
## Does Nature Understand Music?

Some say music is the universal language. This couldn't possibly be true. Not everyone speaks it; not all understand it. And even those who do cannot explain what it says. No one knows how music speaks, what tales it tells, how it tugs at our emotions with its mixture of tones, one after another, above and below.

You can be moved by music and have absolutely no idea what is going on. Language is not like that. You must be able to speak a language to know what is being said. Music is only in part a language, that part you understand when you learn its rules and how to bend those rules. But the rest of it may move us even though we are unable to explain why.

Nature is one such place. It can mean the place we came from, some original home where, as Nalungiaq the Netsilik Eskimo reminds us, "people and animals spoke the same language." Not only have we lost that language, we can barely imagine what it might be. Words are not the way to talk to animals. They'd rather sing with us — if we learn their tunes without making them conform to ours. Music could be a model for learning to perceive the surrounding world by listening, not only by naming or explaining.

For to know and to feel the meaning of music are two different things. We may not know the reason why the coyote is howling, or have any idea why the brown thrasher sings nearly two thousand songs. (Scientists haven't a clue why this one bird needs to know so many more tunes than any other.) With only a little effort, the whole world can be heard as music. We can hear sounds whose meanings are not intended for us as if they were music and soon call them beautiful. This is part of music's power.

This book considers the many ways music can engage and define nature. Music here becomes a form of knowledge, if you will, that links us more closely to the reverberations of the surrounding world. As soon as you begin to pay attention, the borders become less clear. On the enclosed disc you will hear an Australian bird that sounds as controlled in its singing as a human composing a tune on a flute. You will hear compositions that mirror the workings of nature in their manner of operation, an aesthetic dream most often attributed to John Cage. Cage learned of it from art historian Ananda Coomaraswamy, who had extracted it from Aristotle's vision of *techne* — a word that once meant both "art" and "tool." Addressing nature as a manner of operation, we complete processes that have been left unfinished, leaving a place for the ingenuity that so marks human presence on the earth.

But no music can exist without the given ways that sound behaves, with or without the human impulse to organize and perceive it. At the same time, music seems to be about little else beside itself — the play of tones up and away, the game of noise and silence.

Once I rode east, from Reykjavik, on a jacked-up bus with huge balloon tires, over moraines and outflows beneath a great glacier in southern Iceland. My companion, Elias Davidsson, was a former orchestral composer who now makes music by banging on stones collected from the far corners of his country. "Many people collect stones," he remarked, "but usually they choose those that look or feel a certain way. I instead go for the *sound*. I hold the rock up in the air. I suspend it from wires or strings. Then I strike it with mallets or with other stones, building xylophones of strange complexity. This is the music I make out of this country."

A party was under way when we arrived at the tiny stone hut in which we would live for several days. Twenty farmers and their families had walked over the glacier from the other side, a journey of several days. They were members of a choir that had been formed in a remote community by one of the farmers who had become crippled years ago and could no longer work the land. So a while back he had started this singing group and brought music to this isolated village. Now the group had carried him over the mountains to this hut to celebrate their tenth anniversary.

The music was loud, boisterous, and billowing with a unique joy. The sun never went down, and never came up; rushing clouds and fog that blew steadily off the ice filled the constantly gray sky. I pulled out my clarinet — the instrument that comes with me wherever I go — and the reason for carrying it everywhere suddenly became clear. There is music all over the world, resounding from inside mountain shacks, echoing off melting ice and tumultuous rivers. I don't consider all of it good, but this was one of those moments worth traveling so far to hear.

The music I yearn for comes out of nature but sounds as if from a world far from home. There is a virtue in finding a song that moves from the familiar into the unfamiliar. This way miracles arise out of the everyday. I once heard Indian *santur* master Shivkumar Sharma play in a vast auditorium. The sound system went dead, and because his instrument, a refined hammer dulcimer, is very quiet, the huge crowd had to sit in utter silence just to pick up the faintest strains of his raga improvisations. The drums and the drone became so imperceptibly soft, we all dared not move, since the slightest noise might obscure the sudden beautiful sound experiments.

Sitting as quietly as possible, listening carefully for faint expressions, the whole audience had learned suddenly to hear in a new way. The music had released us into hearing nature for what it is: a vast unstoppable music — what Murray Schafer named a *soundscape* — as inescapable for us as the landscapes that enable us to stand out from and also be a part of them. Sounds define us, hold us in, lead us away. They announce themselves to us; they call from all over the world. We cannot close our ears.

It is no great challenge to hear all sounds as music — the whole history of music in our time has pointed the way toward this. Classical musicians broke down the rules of harmony in this century to welcome chance as well as noise into the mix of organized sound. Popular musicians, seeking ever more variation within accessible constraints, have sampled beats, noises, whirrs, and chirps from all available sources. And jazz musicians have improvised over sound changes as well as chord changes. If music is progressing anywhere, it is toward a blurring of boundaries, toward what Steven Feld calls a *schizophonia*, which makes it impossible to know where any sound is coming from or what it might musically mean.

The eighteenth-century composer Vivaldi wrote a "Goldfinch" concerto in which the flutists are supposed to play just a little bit like a goldfinch. And in our century, Olivier Messiaen meticulously transcribed birdsongs and required that the orchestra play them note for note. Today we might jam with the birds or play their sounds directly out of inscrutable black-box machines. Modernity in music has really prepared us to accept sound merely as sound, as harmonic rules have been bent and twisted so much that they finally fall away. This is no culmination, only a beginning of a cross-cultural journey that will in no time have us concerting with kookaburras and flamingos as a matter of course.

Our contributors have found music in natural sounds, or made music out of wild material, or made music that sounds as if it came straight out of nature, even if the source of the songs might be wholly artificial. The writings consist of musings by composers on their own work, reports of wild sound-gatherings, and tales where music and nature surprisingly converge.

When you have finished reading and listening to this clamorous collection, we hope you will be so riveted by the sound of the whole world that you will be unable to turn away from it no matter how much our regular lives encourage us to think of no one but human beings like ourselves. Life sings and improvises from molecules to galaxies. Sound speaks to us yet has nothing specific to tell. The melodies of the world are what they are. Nothing less, nothing more. You should never be afraid to *listen*.

*Terra Nova* put out a special "Music from Nature" issue in the summer of 1997, vol. 2, no. 3. This issue was a great critical success, and because of its inherently ephemeral nature, we decided to expand the project into a book that might have a chance of staying around longer. No anthology of writings and sounds of music and nature has ever before been published, and we think it's high time for one. Nature has always been a part of human music, and although humanity may have forgotten how to pay attention over the years, we have always been intrigued by the sounds that surround us.

In expanding the issue into a book, we thought it important to include what we consider classic texts in the field, pieces written by Pauline Oliveros, John Cage, R. Murray Schafer, and others. We decided to include fictional outbursts only between the sections of essays and reports, although we could easily have found many more. Stories such as Junichiro Tanizaki's wonderful parable of the wild nightingale brought into the city teach us much about the juncture of music and nature: the songbird cannot sing the same song it sings in the wilds, for it takes more than the native tongue to evoke wilderness inside the heart of civilization. The nightingale must be trained carefully to translate the wild into the parlor rooms of the elite.

But nature need not be the nightingale stuck in a cage who will only sing if a cloth is drawn around its bars. We will not survive as artists or as species if we cannot become a part of the world that surrounds us. There should be no duality between music and nature. Natural sound is never so clearly separable from human sound. The moment we decide to listen, to seek out meaning, we start to change the world. We cannot preserve that sound world apart from our listening, and we cannot make any kind of music without sensing its resonance in an environment, be it a concert hall, a bedroom, a car, a bar, or a windy bluff out in the rain like the Oregon concert David James Duncan describes so well.

For our first CD we chose pieces that we thought would amaze and surprise, would touch and lure in the most skeptical of listeners, from the butcherbird that sounds astonishingly like a human making up a song in a meadow to the Beethoven excerpt that Russell Sherman so aptly argues is a piece out of nature as well. There were no pure soundscapes, and no assaultive avant-garde cacophonies (much as we personally enjoy such things), and we shied away from the sanguine sweetness of New Age tinkles with loon calls (although a few transformed loons did make it on there in the end).

On this new disc, we responded to some of our critics: too many birds! Birds are melodious, but theirs is the music most easily found in nature. This

CD has music based more on the sounds of rivers, deserts, insects, and the forest floor. The pieces are a bit longer, more experimental, and there are more words in the mix.

Bernie Krause is right on when he says that no recording technology can "capture" nature in any sense of the word. The microphone is a tool for making artifacts out of sound. These, like our visual images, respond to what they face but are immediately transformed into something human. In his fine book *No Nature*, Gary Snyder reminds us that "we do not easily know nature." But there is no humanity without the surrounding nature that has made us possible. We imagine we have free will, but there is an environment that is necessary for our survival. We are bounded, enjoyed, devoured, by the world. We owe it respect and involvement.

One aesthetic idea that deserves more scrutiny is the notion that music might imitate nature, not by sounding like nature but by working like nature, part of an art not literally mimetic but like nature only "in manner of operation." Many of us are attracted to that idea but are unclear about just what it means. Perhaps we are drawn to it because as artists many of us want our works to be perfect or integrated enough to approach the *necessity* that is nature, a nature that might not be perfect but is something that seems essential, fitting into the world exactly as it is. If we create a work that becomes something the world could not possibly do without, then we have somehow succeeded in being necessary to the world around us. This might be easy for other living creatures, but it is paradoxically difficult for human beings.

For, while we are created from nature, we are somehow cast out by our wily, civilized ways. And that is why there is a perennial aesthetic pull of the earthy, the natural, the green, the living.

Many of the musicians in this book speak of the desire to have their works sound as if they live, as breathing, pulsing beings, which, while they might be made from instruments and machines, at their best achieve a life of their own, sailing beyond their creators and contexts. When could one think that a work might be alive? If it moves and surprises, teaches the listener, player, or composer something new with every change; if it seems to have not only its own intelligence but also an inner ability to move or transform in unexpected ways.

Of course nature is more than life. It is death, eternity, calamity, softness, and devastation. Some say there is no evil in nature, that all violence is tempered by some kind of endless balance. But there are others who maintain that humanity finds what it wishes in the malleable environment, that a naturalistic aesthetics is only a matter of projection. I disagree. There are real powers out there inside a birdsong or thunderclap. It may mean nothing to hear a chirp and be able to identify its avian source. That's just order and classification. It takes much more dwelling inside an ecology to know the significance of a wayward sound. To hear each melody as a piece of a vast composition or improvisation, the ever building soundscape that makes up this world, is the final task of the attentive listener. Once trained to listen, you will let the sounds and their significance find you, not just hear what you are listening for.

We cannot close our ears, and we let sounds tweak them to give their place and position rather than adjusting our hearing, the way we refocus our gaze with our eyes. This is why music might be an avenue toward taking in the ecology, as visual acuity has trained the human look outward upon the world we claim. If we treat each sound we hear as a part of a potentially meaningful sonic world, then the environment might have a place for us humans after all.

So what, then, is the difference between a human sound and a natural one? Is there one? I used to think it was easy to discern the whoom of a machine from the call of an animal. But once I heard the monotonous even-toned "ping" of the northern saw-whet owl — a high, tinny note that can repeat evenly for hours high in cold Canadian winter forests — I knew that a living creature could sound like a living machine.

Living or nonliving, though, there still can be sonic images that help us work like nature. Sound shapes are never exact, only suggestive; they are not fixed but are always subtly moving. There are sudden noises, but they have a natural fullness, a richness that surpasses the bleeps of machines. There may be a repetitive minimalism, but it ebbs and flows; it is rarely pounding and incessant but is rocking, varying, never the same.

This is not to say that learning to expertly record and appreciate the sounds of nature is the same as making music out of nature. Some ways of combining sounds seem to make living, breathing artworks, whereas in others different aesthetics are at work. Not all music moves close to nature, and not all natural sound is music.

Well, what kind is, and what kind isn't? Music is in a great sense in the ear of the beholder. If you listen well enough, then any series of sounds can have the organization and quality necessary for it to be knowable and lovable as music. That's what abstraction in the arts has offered us in the twentieth century — openness to the beauty of the world in so many newly direct ways.

Music in nature is any series of sounds that can be appreciated for their depth, beauty, and artistry. These include wind voices and whale songs, as well as people playing in forests, canyons, acoustically massaged concert halls, and stairwells. Any music that fits into its place is an environmental music, one that is enhanced by its surroundings and not fighting against them as it plays. But the sound out there is music only if you can hear it as a beautiful form that can be enjoyed in itself apart from its purpose in the world.

Poet David Ignatow's most famous lines are "I wish I could look at a mountain for what it is and not as a comment on my life." Those words have haunted me for years, and they suddenly come back right now as I wonder what the sound of, say, the crashing waves on a fine Pacific sand beach really are — just a wash of water that comes to land again and again, or unbelievably sweet music that has no beginning and will never end? Which is the comment on *my* life? Which is the world in itself? This is the classic question of the phenomenologist, the seeker looking so hard for what Wallace Stevens called "things as they are, not on the blue guitar."

You cannot perfectly record that beach sound. Emulations like Mendelssohn's "Fingal's Cave" overture do not capture it — "da da dade dah dom" played over and over again in a manner to suggest the magnificence of the wavy sea. But you can learn to hear it as music, to welcome the surf into your realm of possible musics, and work with it, learn from it, build on it. There are few rules in music today, but there are many pressures to which it can easily succumb: tradition, avant-gardism, commercialism, professionalism, elitism. And it is equally hard to escape from music. It flows as ceaselessly from machines as it pours out of the natural world.

We have too much of everything we have made and not enough of the source material from which we and all other life emerge. That's all quickly fading away into the hush that remains only after our own noises have died down. Which brings up another important way music could connect to nature: how might it help us increase our concern for the earth and its fate?

In putting together this project, we have not addressed the important role that music can and does play as propaganda for nature: people recording and performing songs that praise nature and protest what humanity is doing to the environment. While this is one very important role that music plays, emphasizing it obscures the more nebulous aesthetic challenges of looking for nature right in the music and music right in the midst of nature.

Music can be instrumental in human transformation, though the good it does there can easily be construed as being the music's quality. How dare one say something bad about any music that's clearly done so much for a good cause? It's an unpopular critical position to take, that's for sure. But if we are afraid to talk about what we consider good or not good in a work of art, then we are afraid to take it seriously enough to figure out what possible standards there might be against which we could measure it. This is not to recommend incessant evaluation but to encourage us to ask what is good and what is not good in the music that takes a stand for nature. The melody and rhythm can bring the message alive, keep it moving and current, and the best of this music transforms that message into something that can be carried no other way.

As the environmental crisis perpetuated by humanity intensifies, all artists, including musicians and composers, ought to take some responsibility for finding ways of linking excellence in their work with making constructive contributions to the solutions of the world's problems. It is not only the plea of an aesthete to want better music that draws from more-than-human sounds and their structures. Those of us who want our species to pay more attention to the environment will not achieve our goal by only stating scary facts and harboring inadequate feelings of guilt at the damage we have wrought. We're used to *seeing* humanity's devastating effects on nature, from the sludging of rivers to the smogging of the sky. But you can just as easily *hear* what's awry: where are all of those songbirds that are supposed to live here? How hard it is to find any place free from the droning sounds of human creation. All over the planet, peace is soon disrupted by a distant jet or a nearby chainsaw. That's simply the way we live.

But music didn't cause all this trouble; music is an art that moves stealthily onward, tying humanity to the rhythms of the world. Despite our emphasis here on making art out of sound — cutting and pasting, making works on tape and on disc, virtual sound-pictures recording events that never happened — it is much more important to get out there and jam, to play with the world and let the world play with us. That's so much more direct than extracting bits of nature in order to insert precious effects into our own artificial sound worlds. If we use nature, we must really listen to what we use and put it to use in a way that respects its own life and integrity — if that is at all possible.

There is much music that seems to *live* just by the way it moves and by the way it draws the listeners and players so much closer together around a common, organic pulse. Charles Keil calls this the *groove* and has written that the best music grooves take us up into their world, holding a part of us there even after the sound has ceased. It's the thrum of life, the beat that is catchy, the pattern that the drummer and woodpecker can share.

More and more people dance to machine-generated beats and swear these new sounds are more hypnotic than what people can play on acoustic instruments. Maybe so, maybe so. It is true that the long history of human-made musical instruments may make up the best of our machines. From drums and didgeridoos to euphoniums and theremins, the enhancement of human expression is surely one of our great achievements.

Buckminster Fuller was fond of pointing out that every few years, pop music seemed to get faster and faster, and people still were able to keep dancing to it. There has always been room for both the quick and the languorous in the way people can move to a beat. Is earlier music any more natural because the tools that made it are simpler? It's tempting to view that old musical life of gathering together, playing together, making art together outside in the fields as being closer to nature. But the expanding of our listening acceptance and the imitative powers of our machines have led some people to claim that electronic music is closer to the whirr and thrum of the world in process than anything humans could make previously.

At least this supports the currency of the aesthetic principle that something can be good if it *sounds like* nature. And if it's especially good, it will change the way we hear nature, define nature, and then live in nature. Hopefully the trajectory of Western culture has taught us to hear more, not less, and to hear enough to make us question the whole course of that culture. By listening, by dancing, by grooving, music itself can become an agent for change.

That aspect of music that is poised for the uncertainties of life and is able to change its direction in unexpected situations calls attention to the inadequacy of inflexible human plans. Evan Eisenberg has written in *The Ecology of Eden* of an "earth jazz" that is more a philosophy of living than it is a music: improvising with nature, offering designs like chord changes, suggested structures that may be bent by new opportunities offered by circumstance. The gist of his advice is that if we jam with the world with the same intelligence and awareness of a skilled jazz musician, then we stand a chance of learning a way into the great improvised complexity of the natural world, a concert so endless and immense that we may never be humble enough to accept our small part in it.

We will always be but a small part of the world's music. The more attentively we listen, the more we will hear. There are still many more structures and forms for us to discover and learn inside this vast melee of sound. These structures serve only to guide aural experience, not to replace it. Music plays on wherever you find it. You can love and be touched by it even if you have no idea what is going on musically. That's why calling music a language captures only a small part of its power.

So does nature understand music? Nature is full of beings who listen along with us, and sharing music with all of them can profoundly deepen the sense of exaltation and well-being that leads humans to listen and play. We people have invented so many categories to explain the bounds and extent of our world, yet we can do so only because we have been offered a place in a natural world, an enveloping place that always sounds a little different when we listen differently. There is a "natural" harmonic series that came from the overtones of wind in the trees before it became properties that a few thousand years ago Pythagoras could mark down on a single plucked chord. It's a small step from there to octaves, fifths, fourths, and in-between thirds, and then a leap to the many possible scales that provide step-by-step pitches for melodies to be picked out and recalled. It took a few thousand years of tinkering to figure these out.

But is there anything inherently natural about the "natural" harmonic series? Or do we just call it natural because it is simpler, more grounded in the physics of resonances, less massaged by musical rules? This series is not arbitrary but a confluence of the way sound behaves and the range of the human ear; our physical properties bind us inextricably to nature. It comes from the way we hear the wind in the trees. Other biological beings might come up with musics that we are unable to hear. There might be different entire ranges of music in nature. We can only hope to discover what ours is meant to be, but we can expand the range of our hearing and magnify sounds we might otherwise never hear. Amplification can be a tool for increasing sensitivity, as long as we don't abuse or overuse it.

Music is not just bound by natural limits; it can help us discover the limits of nature by putting forth newly creative ways of fitting into a surrounding world. This is why there are so many kinds of music that could be called "environmental" — those musics that create worlds, places to move into. Brian Eno wants his music "not to evoke landscape, but to *be* landscape." His are pieces with no beginning or end, worlds you can enter and then leave when you wish. The piece works if it has as much integrity as a landscape, and as much necessity. It's a good landscape if you want to spend more time inside it, exploring, walking, living in it like you belong there.

Is that asking for too much placidity in a real world? Nature can be frightening, dangerous, and unbearable too. Do we want only sweet soundscapes? Of course not. But we probably want sound worlds that seem intelligent, infinitely various, endlessly interesting. As listeners you will always be able to choose. So look for ways to assess this new kind of music with new criteria. Don't accept it uncritically.

That's the human plight all over again: to come from nature and yet to have to work so hard to get back there. It's an endless adventure. It keeps our species alive, but also dangerous.

There is music in nature and nature in music. What may be most wonderful is that we can love and be immersed in both without needing to understand how the two are forever intertwined.

DAVID ROTHENBERG

# I

## Roots of the Listening

# The Music of the Spheres

By this title I do not wish to encourage any superstition, or any ideas that might attract people into the fields of curiosity; but through this subject I wish to direct the attention of those, who search for truth, towards the law of music which is working throughout the whole universe and which, in other words, may be called the law of life, the sense of proportion, the law of harmony, the law which brings about balance, the law which is hidden behind all aspects of life, which holds this universe intact, and works out its destiny throughout the whole universe, fulfilling its purpose.

Music as we know it in our everyday language is only a miniature: that which our intelligence has grasped from that music or harmony of the whole universe which is working behind us. The music of the universe is the background of the little picture which we call music. Our sense of music, our attraction to music, shows that music is in the depth of our being. Music is behind the working of the whole universe. Music is not only life's greatest object, but music is life itself.

Hafiz, our great and wonderful poet of Persia, says: "Many say that life entered the human body by the help of music, but the truth is that life itself is music." I should like to tell you what made him say this. There exists in the East a legend which relates that God made a statue of clay in His own image, and asked the soul to enter into it. But the soul refused to enter into this prison, for its nature is to fly about freely, and not be limited and bound to any sort of captivity. The soul did not wish in the least to enter this prison. Then God asked the angels to play their music and, as the angels played, the soul was moved to ecstasy. Through that ecstasy — in order to make this music more clear to itself — it entered this body.

It is a beautiful legend, and much more so is its mystery. The interpretation of this legend explains to us two great laws. One is that freedom is the nature of the soul, and for the soul the whole tragedy of life is the absence of that freedom which belongs to its original nature. The next mystery that this legend reveals to us is that the only reason why the soul has entered the body of clay or matter is to experience the music of life, and to make this music clear to itself.

And when we sum up these two great mysteries, the third mystery, which is the mystery of all mysteries, comes to our mind: that the unlimited part of ourselves becomes limited and earthbound for the purpose of making this life, which is the outward life, more intelligible. Therefore there is one loss and one gain. The loss is the loss of freedom, and the gain is the experience of life which is fully gained by coming to this limitation of life which we call the life of an individual.

What makes us feel drawn to music is that our whole being is music: our mind, our body, the nature in which we live, the nature that has made us, all that is beneath and around us — it is all music. As we are close to all this music and live and move and have our being in music, it therefore interests us. It attracts our attention and gives us pleasure, for it corresponds with the rhythm and tone which are keeping the mechanism of our whole being intact. What pleases us in any of our arts, whether drawing, painting, carving, architecture, or sculpture, and what interests us in poetry, is the harmony behind them which is music. It is music that poetry suggests to us: the rhythm in the poetry, or the harmony of ideas and phrases.

Besides this, in painting and in drawing it is our sense of proportion and our sense of harmony which give us all the pleasure we gain in admiring art. What appeals to us in being near to nature is nature's music, and nature's music is more perfect than that of art. It gives us a sense of exaltation to be moving about in the woods, to be looking at the green, to be standing near the running water which has its rhythm, its tone and its harmony. The swinging of the branches in the forest, the rising and falling of the waves — all has its music. Once we contemplate and become one with nature, our hearts open to its music. We say: "I enjoy nature," and what is it in nature that we enjoy? It is its music. Something in us has been touched by the rhythmic movement, by the perfect harmony which is so seldom found in this artificial life of ours. It lifts one up and makes one feel that it is this which is the real temple, the true religion. One moment standing in the midst of nature with open heart is a whole lifetime, if one is in tune with nature.

When one looks at the cosmos, the movements of the stars and planets, the laws of vibration and rhythm — all perfect and unchanging — it shows that the cosmic system is working by the law of music, the law of harmony. Whenever that harmony in the cosmic system is lacking in any way, then in proportion disasters come about in the world, and its influence is seen in many destructive forces which manifest in the world. If there is any principle upon which the whole of astrological law is based — and the science of magic and mysticism behind it — it is music.

Therefore, for the most illuminated souls who have ever lived in this world, as for the greatest of all the prophets of India — their whole life was music.

HAZRAT INAYAT KHAN

From the miniature music which we understand, they expanded themselves to the whole universe of music, and in that way they were able to inspire. The one who finds the key to the music of the whole working of life — it is he who becomes intuitive; it is he who has inspiration; it is he to whom revelations manifest, for then his language becomes music. Every object we see is revealing. In what form? It tells us its character, nature and secret. Every person who comes to us tells us his past, present and future. In what way? Every presence explains to us all that it contains. In what manner? In the form of music — if only we can hear it. There is no other language: it is rhythm, it is tone. We hear it, but we do not hear it with our ears. A friendly person shows harmony in his voice, his words, his movements and manner. An unfriendly person, in all his movements, in his glance and expression, in his walk, in everything, will show disharmony — if only one can see it. I used to amuse myself in India with a friend who became cross very easily. Sometimes when he visited me I would say: "Are you cross to-day?" He would ask: "Now how do you know that I am cross to-day?" I replied: "Your turban tells me. The way you tie your turban does not show harmony."

One's every action shows a harmonious or inharmonious attitude. There are many things you can perceive in handwriting, but the principal thing in reading handwriting is the harmonious or inharmonious curves. It almost speaks to you, and tells you the mood in which the person wrote. Handwriting tells you many things: the grade of evolution of the writer, his attitude towards life, his character. You do not need to read the letter, you only have to see his handwriting; for line and curve will show him either to be harmonious or inharmonious — if only you can see it.

In every living being you can see this, and if you look with an open insight into the nature of things, you will read even in the tree — the tree that bears fruit or flower — what music it expresses.

You can see from the attitude of a person whether that person will prove to be your friend, or will end in being your enemy. You need not wait until the end, you can see at the first glance whether he is friendly inclined or not, because every person is music, perpetual music, continually going on day and night. Your intuitive faculty can hear that music, and that is the reason why one person is repellent and the other attracts you so much: it is the music he expresses. His whole atmosphere is charged with it.

There is a story of Umar, the well-known *khalif* of Arabia. Someone who wanted to harm Umar was looking for him, and he heard that Umar did not live in palaces — although he was a king — but that he spent most of his time with nature. This man was very glad to think that now he would have every opportunity to accomplish his objective. As he approached the place where Umar was sitting, the nearer he came, the more his attitude changed, until in the end he dropped the dagger which was in his hand, and said: "I cannot harm you. Tell me, what is the power in you that keeps me from accomplishing the objective which I came to carry out?" Umar answered: "My at-one-ment with God." No doubt this is a religious term, but what does that at-one-ment with God mean? It is being in tune with the Infinite, in harmony with the whole universe. In plain words, Umar was the receptacle of the music of the whole universe.

The great charm that the personality of the holy ones has shown in all ages has been their responsiveness to the music of the Whole Being. That has been the secret of how they became the friends of their worst enemies. But this is not only the power of the holy ones; this manifests in every person to a greater or lesser degree. Everyone shows harmony or disharmony according to how open he is to the music of the universe. The more he is open to all that is beautiful and harmonious, the more his life is tuned to that universal harmony, and the more he will show a friendly attitude towards everyone he meets, his very atmosphere will create music around him.

The difference between the material and the spiritual point of view is that the material point of view sees matter as the first thing, from which intelligence, beauty and all else evolved afterwards. From the spiritual point of view we see the intelligence and beauty first, and from them comes all that exists. From a spiritual point of view we see that what one considers last is the same as first. Therefore in the essence of this Whole Being — as its basis — there is music, as one can see that in the essence of the seed of the rose there is the rose itself, its fragrance, form and beauty. Although in the seed it is not manifest, at the same time it is there in essence. The one who tunes himself not only to the external but also to the inner being and to the essence of all things, gets an insight into the essence of the Whole Being, and therefore he can find and enjoy that fragrance and flower which he sees in the rose, to the same extent even in the seed.

The great error of this age is that activity has increased so much that there is little margin left in one's everyday life for repose. Repose is the secret of all contemplation and meditation, the secret of getting in tune with that aspect of life which is the essence of all things. When one is not accustomed to take repose, one does not know what is behind one's being. This condition is experienced by first preparing the body, and also the mind, by means of purification. And by making the senses finer one is able to tune one's soul with the Whole Being.

It seems complex, and yet it is so simple. When one is open to one's tried friend in life, one knows so much about him. It is only the opening of the heart; it is only at-one-ment with one's friend; we know his faults and his merits. We know how to experience and to enjoy friendship. Where there is hatred and prejudice and bitterness, there is loss of understanding. The deeper the person, the more friends he has. It is smallness, narrowness, lack of spiritual development which makes a person exclusive, distant and different from others. He feels superior, greater and better than others; his friendly attitude seems to have been lost. In that way he cuts himself apart from others, and in this lies his tragedy. That person is never happy.

The one who is happy is he who is ready to be friends with all. His outlook on life is friendly. He is not only friendly to persons, but also to objects and conditions. It is by this attitude of friendship that man expands and breaks down those walls which keep him in prison. And by breaking down those walls he experiences at-one-ment with the Absolute. This at-one-ment with the Absolute manifests as the music of the spheres, and this he experiences on all sides: beauties of nature, color of flowers, everything he sees, everyone he meets. In the hours of contemplation and solitude, and in the hours when he is in the midst of the world, always the music is there, always he is enjoying the harmony.

There are many in this world who look for wonders. If one only noticed how much there is in this world which is all phenomena! The deeper one sees into life, the wider life opens itself to one, and then every moment of one's life becomes full of wonders and full of splendors. What we call music in everyday language is only a miniature of that which is behind this all, and which has been the source and origin of this nature. It is therefore that the wise of all ages have considered music to be a sacred art; for in music the seer can see the picture of the whole universe, and in the realm of music the wise can interpret the secret and nature of the working of the whole universe.

This idea is not a new idea; at the same time it is always new. Nothing is as old as the truth, and nothing is as new as the truth. Man's desire to search for something traditional, for something original, and man's desire for something new — all these tendencies can be satisfied in the knowledge of truth.

In the *Vedas* of the Hindus we read: *Nada Brahma* — sound, being the Creator. In the works of the wise of ancient India we read: "First song, then Vedas or wisdom." When we come to the Bible, we find: "First was the word, and the word was God," and when we come to the Qur'an we read that the word was pronounced, and all creation was manifest. This shows that the origin of the whole creation is sound.

No doubt the word, in the way it is used in our everyday language, is a limitation of that sound which is suggested by these Scriptures. Language is made up of names of comparable objects, and that which cannot be compared has no name. Truth is that which can never be spoken and, what the wise of all ages have spoken, is what they have tried their best to express, little as they were able to do so.

There is in Persian literature a poem by Hafiz who tells us that, when God commanded the soul to enter the human body, which is made of clay, the soul refused. Then angels were asked to sing and on hearing the angels sing the soul entered the body which it had feared to be a prison. It is a philosophy which is poetically expressed in this story. Hafiz remarked: "People say that on hearing the song the soul entered into the body, but in reality the soul itself was song."

Those who have probed the depth of material science as far as modern science can reach, do not deny the fact that the origin of the whole creation is in movement, in other words: in vibration. It is this original state of the existence of life which is called in the ancient tradition sound, or the word. The first manifestation of this sound is therefore audible, the next manifestation visible. In the forms of expression of life, life has expressed itself first as sound, next as light. This is supported by the Bible where it is said that first was the word, and then came light. Again one finds in a *Sura* of the Qur'an: "God is the light of the heaven and the earth."

The nature of the creation is the doubling of one, and it is this doubling aspect which is the cause of all duality in life. This doubling aspect represents one positive part, the other part being negative; one expressive, the other responsive. Therefore, in this creation of duality, spirit and nature stand face to face. And as there is the first aspect, which I have called sound, and the next, which I have called light, at first in these opposite nature aspects, or responsive aspects, only the light works, and if the creation goes still deeper there is sound. In nature, which is face to face with spirit, what is first expressed is light — or what man first responds to is light, and what man responds to next is what touches him deeper: it is sound.

The human body is a vehicle of the spirit, a finished vehicle which experiences all the different aspects of creation. This does not mean that all other forms and names that exist in the world — some as objects, others as creatures — are not responsive to the expression of the spirit. Really speaking, every object is responsive to the spirit and to the work of the spirit which is active in all aspects, in all names and forms of this universe. One reads in the great work of Maulana Rumi, a Persian poet and mystic, that earth, water, fire and air before man are objects, but before God are living beings: they work at His command — as man understands living beings working under the command of a master.

If the whole creation can be well explained, it is by the phases of sound or vibration, which have manifested in different grades in all their various forms in life. Objects and names and forms are but the expression of vibrations in dif-

HAZRAT INAYAT KHAN

ferent aspects. Even all that we call matter or substance, and all that does not seem to speak or sound — it is all in reality vibration.

The beauty of the whole creation is this, that creation has worked in two ways; in one way it has expressed, and in the other way it has made itself a mold in order to respond. For instance, there is substance — matter to touch — and there is a sense to feel touch. There is a sound, and at the same time there is the sense of hearing to perceive the sound. There is light, there is form, there are colors, and at the same time there are eyes to see them.

What man calls beauty is the harmony of all he experiences. What after all is music? What we call music is the harmony of the audible notes. In reality there is music in color, there is music in lines, there is music in the forest where there is a variety of trees and plants, in the way in which they correspond with each other. The more widely one observes nature, the more it appeals to one's soul. Why? Because there is a music there. And to the extent to which one sees more deeply into life and observes life more widely, one listens to more and more music — the music which answers the whole universe.

But the one whose heart is open — he need not go as far as the forest; in the midst of the crowd he can find music. At this time human ideas are so changed, owing to materialism, that there is no distinction of personality. But if one studies human nature one finds that even a piano of a thousand octaves cannot produce the variety that human nature represents: how people agree with one another, how they disagree; some become friends after a contact of one moment, and some in thousand years cannot become friends. If one could only see to what pitch the different souls are tuned, in what octave different people speak, what standards different people have! Sometimes there are two persons who disagree, and there comes a third person and all unite together. Is this not the nature of music? The more one studies the harmony of music, and then studies human nature — how people agree, and how they disagree, how there is attraction and repulsion — the more one sees that it is all music.

But now there is another question to be understood. What man knows is generally the world that he sees around himself. Very few people trouble to think that there is something beyond that which they realize around themselves. To many it is a story, when they hear that there are two worlds. But if one looks deep within oneself, there are not only two worlds, there are so many worlds that it is beyond expression. That part of one's being which is receptive is mostly closed in the average man. What he knows is to express outwardly and to receive from this same sphere as much as he can receive by himself. For instance, the difference between a simple man and a thinking person with deeper understanding is that, when the simple person has received a word only in his ears, the thinking person has received the same word as far as his mind. So the same word has reached the ears of the one, and the heart of the other. This man whose ears the word has touched has only seen the word, but he whose heart the word has touched has seen deeper. If this simple example is true, it can be understood that one person lives only in the external world, while another lives in two worlds, and a third person may live in many worlds at the same time. When one asks: Where are those worlds? Are they above the sky, or down below the earth? — the answer is: All these worlds are in the same place as we are. As a poet has said: "The heart of man, if once expanded, becomes larger than all the heavens."

The deep thinkers of all ages have therefore held one principle of awakening to life, and that principle is: emptying the self. In other words, making oneself a clearer and fuller accommodation in order to accommodate all experiences more clearly and more fully. All the tragedy of life, all its sorrows and pains belong mostly to the surface of the life in the world. If one were fully awake to life, if one could respond to life, if one could perceive life, one would not need to look for wonders, one would not need to communicate with spirits; for every atom in this world is a wonder for the one who sees with open eyes.

In answer to the question: What is the experience of those who dive deep into life, and who touch the depth within? — there is a verse in Persian by Hafiz who has said: "It is not known how far is the destination, but so much I know: that music from afar is coming to my ears." The music of the spheres, according to the point of view of the mystic, is like the lighthouse in the port that a man sees from the sea; it promises him that he is coming nearer to the destination.

Now one may say: What music may this be? If there were no harmony in the essence of life, life would not have created harmony in this world of variety. Man would not have longed for something which was not already in his spirit. Everything in this world which seems to lack harmony is in reality the limitation of man's own vision. The wider the horizon of his observation becomes, the more harmony of life he enjoys. In the very depth of man's being the harmony of the working of the whole universe sums up in a perfect music. Therefore, the music which is the source of creation, the music which is found near the goal of creation, is the music of the spheres. And it is heard and enjoyed by those who touch the very depth of their own lives.

HAZRAT INAYAT KHAN

# Primal Sound

It must have been when I was a boy at school that the phonograph was invented. At any rate it was at that time a chief object of public wonder; this was probably the reason why our science master, a man given to busying himself with all kinds of handiwork, encouraged us to try our skill in making one of these instruments from the material that lay nearest to hand. Nothing more was needed than a piece of pliable cardboard bent to the shape of a funnel, on the narrower round orifice of which was stuck a piece of impermeable paper of the kind used to seal bottled fruit. This provided a vibrating membrane, in the middle of which we then stuck a bristle from a coarse clothes brush at right angles to its surface. With these few things one part of the mysterious machine was made, receiver and reproducer were complete. It now only remained to construct the receiving cylinder, which could be moved close to the needle marking the sounds by means of a small rotating handle. I do not now remember what we made it of; there was some kind of cylinder which we covered with a thin coating of candlewax to the best of our ability. Our impatience, brought to a pitch by the excitement of sticking and fitting the parts, as we jostled one another over it, was such that the wax had scarcely cooled and hardened before we put our work to the test.

How this was done can easily be imagined. When someone spoke or sang into the funnel, the needle in the parchment transferred the sound-waves to the receptive surface of the roll turning slowly beneath it, and then, when the moving needle was made to retrace its path (which had been fixed in the meantime with a coat of varnish), the sound which had been ours came back to us tremblingly, haltingly from the paper funnel, uncertain, infinitely soft and hesitating and fading out altogether in places. Each time the effect was complete. Our class was not exactly one of the quietest, and there can have been few moments in its history when it had been able as a body to achieve such a degree of silence. The phenomenon, on every repetition of it, remained astonishing, indeed positively staggering. We were confronting, as it were, a new and infinitely delicate point in the texture of reality, from which something far greater than ourselves, yet indescribably immature, seemed to be appealing to us as if seeking help. At the time and all through the intervening years I believed that that independent sound, taken from us and preserved outside us, would be unforgettable. That it turned out otherwise is the cause of my writing the present account. As will be seen, what impressed itself on my memory most deeply was not the sound from the funnel but the markings traced on the cylinder; these made a most definite impression.

I first became aware of this some fourteen or fifteen years after my schooldays were past. It was during my first stay in Paris. At that time I was attending the anatomy lectures in the École des Beaux-Arts with considerable enthusiasm. It was not so much the manifold interlacing of the muscles and sinews nor the complete agreement of the inner organs one with another that appealed to me, but rather the bare skeleton, the restrained energy and elasticity of which I had already noticed when studying the drawings of Leonardo. However much I puzzled over the structure of the whole, it was more than I could deal with; my attention always reverted to the study of the skull, which seemed to me to constitute the utmost achievement, as it were, of which this chalky element was capable; it was as if it had been persuaded to make just in this part a special effort to render a decisive service by providing a most solid protection for the most daring feature of all, for something which, although itself narrowly confined, had a field of activity which was boundless. The fascination which this particular structure had for me reached such a pitch finally, that I procured a skull in order to spend many hours of the night with it; and, as always happens with me and things, it was not only the moments of deliberate attention which made this ambiguous object really mine: I owe my familiarity with it, beyond doubt, in part to that passing glance, with which we involuntarily examine and perceive our daily environment, when there exists any relationship at all between it and us. It was a passing glance of this kind which I suddenly checked in its course, making it exact and attentive. By candlelight — which is often so peculiarly alive and challenging — the coronal suture had become strikingly visible, and I knew at once what it reminded me of: one of those unforgotten grooves, which had been scratched in a little wax cylinder by the point of a bristle!

And now I do not know: is it due to a rhythmic peculiarity of my imagination, that ever since, often after the lapse of years, I repeatedly feel the impulse to make that spontaneously perceived similarity the starting point for a whole series of unheard of experiments? I frankly confess that I have always treated this desire, whenever it made itself felt, with the most unrelenting mistrust — if proof be needed, let it be found in the fact that only now, after more than a decade and a half, have I resolved to make a cautious statement concerning it. Furthermore, there is nothing I can cite in favour of my idea beyond its obstinate recurrence, a recurrence which has taken me by surprise in all sorts of places, divorced from any connexion with what I might be doing.

*What* is it that repeatedly presents itself to my mind? It is this:

The coronal suture of the skull (this would first have to be investigated) has — let us assume — a certain similarity to the closely wavy line which the needle of a phonograph engraves on the receiving, rotating cylinder of the apparatus. What if one changed the needle and directed it on its return journey along a tracing which was not derived from the graphic translation of a sound, but existed of itself naturally — well: to put it plainly, along the coronal suture, for example. What would happen? A sound would necessarily result, a series of sounds, music . . .

Feelings — which? Incredulity, timidity, fear, awe — which of all the feelings here possible prevents me from suggesting a name for the primal sound which would then make its appearance in the world . . .

Leaving that side for the moment: what variety of lines then, occurring anywhere, could one not put under the needle and try out? Is there any contour that one could not, in a sense, complete in this way and then experience it, as it makes itself felt, thus transformed, in another field of sense?

At one period, when I began to interest myself in Arabic poems, which seem to owe their existence to the simultaneous and equal contributions from all five senses, it struck me for the first time, that the modern European poet makes use of these contributors singly and in very varying degree, only one of them — sight overladen with the seen world — seeming to dominate him constantly; how slight, by contrast, is the contribution he receives from inattentive hearing, not to speak of the indifference of the other senses, which are active only on the periphery of consciousness and with many interruptions within the limited spheres of their practical activity. And yet the perfect poem can only materialize on condition that the world, acted upon by all five levers simultaneously, is seen, under a definite aspect, on the supernatural plane, which is, in fact, the plane of the poem.

A lady, to whom this was mentioned in conversation, exclaimed that this wonderful and simultaneous capacity and achievement of all the senses was surely nothing but the presence of mind and grace of love — incidentally she thereby bore her own witness to the sublime reality of the poem. But the lover is in such splendid danger just because he must depend upon the coordination of his senses, for he knows that they must meet in that unique and risky centre, in which, renouncing all extension, they come together and have no permanence.

As I write this, I have before me the diagram which I have always used as a ready help whenever ideas of this kind have demanded attention. If the world's whole field of experience, including those spheres which are beyond our knowledge, be represented by a complete circle, it will be immediately evident that, when the black sectors, denoting that which we are incapable of experiencing, are measured against the lesser, light sections, corresponding to what is illuminated by the senses, the former are very much greater.

Now the position of the lover is this, that he feels himself unexpectedly placed in the centre of the circle, that is to say, at the point where the known and the incomprehensible, coming forcibly together at one single point, become complete and simply a possession, losing thereby, it is true, all individual character. This position would not serve the poet, for individual variety must be constantly present for him, he is compelled to use the sense sectors to their full extent, as it must also be his aim to extend each of them as far as possible, so that his lively delight, girt for the attempt, may be able to pass through the five gardens in one leap.

As the lover's danger consists in the nonspatial character of his standpoint, so the poet's lies in his awareness of the abysses which divide the one order to sense experience from the other: in truth they are sufficiently wide and engulfing to sweep away from before us the greater part of the world — who knows how many worlds?

The question arises here, as to whether the extent of these sectors on the plane assumed by us can be enlarged to any vital degree by the work of research. The achievements of the microscope, of the telescope, and of so many devices which increase the range of the senses upwards and downwards, do they not lie in another sphere altogether, since most of the increase thus achieved cannot be interpenetrated by the senses, cannot be "experienced" in any real sense? It is, perhaps, not premature to suppose that the artist, who develops the five-fingered hand of his senses (if one may put it so) to ever more active and more spiritual capacity, contributes more decisively than anyone else to an extension of the several sense fields, only the achievement which gives proof of this does not permit of his entering his personal extension of territory in the general map before us, since it is only possible, in the last resort, by a miracle.

But if we are looking for a way by which to establish the connection so urgently needed between the different provinces now so strangely separated from one another, what could be more promising than the experiment suggested earlier in this record? If the writer ends by recommending it once again, he may be given a certain amount of credit for withstanding the temptation to give free rein to his fancy in imagining the results of the assumptions which he has suggested.

*Soglio. On the day of the Assumption of the Blessed Virgin, 1919.*

JOHN CAGE

# Happy New Ears

Max Ernst, around 1950, speaking at the Arts Club on Eighth Street in New York City, said that significant changes in the arts formerly occurred every three hundred years, whereas now they take place every twenty minutes.

Such changes happen first in the arts which, like plants, are fixed to particular points in space: architecture, painting, and sculpture. They happen afterward in the performance arts, music and theater, which require, as animals do, the passing of time for their realization.

In literature, as with the myxomycetes and similar organisms which are classified sometimes as plants and sometimes as animals, changes take place both early and late. This art, if it is understood as printed material, has the characteristics of objects in space; but, understood as a performance, it takes on the aspects of processes in time.

I have for many years accepted, and I still do, the doctrine about Art, occidental and oriental, set forth by Ananda K. Coomaraswamy in his book *The Transformation of Nature in Art*, that the function of Art is to imitate Nature in her manner of operation. Our understanding of "her manner of operation" changes according to advances in the sciences. These advances in this century have brought the term "space-time" into our vocabulary. Thus, the distinctions made above between the space and the time arts are at present an oversimplification.

Observe that the enjoyment of a modern painting carries one's attention not to a center of interest but all over the canvas and not following any particular path. Each point on the canvas may be used as a beginning, continuing, or ending of one's observation of it. This is the case also with those works which are symmetrical, for then the observer's attention is made mobile by the rapidity with which he drops the problem of understanding structure. Whether or not a painting or sculpture lacks a center of interest may be determined by observing whether or not it is destroyed by the effects of shadows. (Intrusions of the environment are effects of time. But they are welcomed by a painting which makes no attempt to focus the observer's attention.) Observe also those

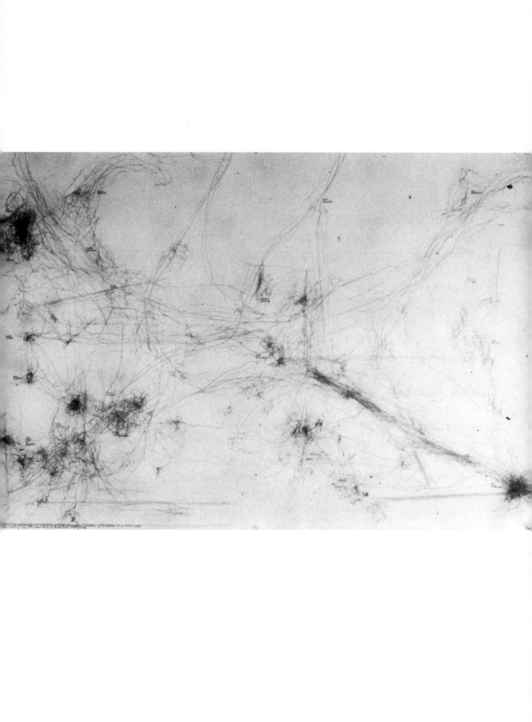

works of painting, sculpture, and architecture which, employing transparent materials, become inseparable from their changing environments.

The tardiness of music with respect to the arts just mentioned is its good fortune. It is able to make deductions from their experiences and to combine these with necessarily different experiences which arise from its special nature. First of all, then, a composer at this moment frees his music of a single overwhelming climax. Seeking an interpenetration and non-obstruction of sounds, he renounces harmony and its effect of fusing sounds in a fixed relationship. Giving up the notion of *Hauptstimme* his "counterpoints" are superimpositions, events that are related to one another only because they take place at the same time. If he maintains in his work aspects of structure, they are symmetrical in character, canonic or enjoying an equal importance of parts, either those that are present at one instant, or those that succeed one another in time. His music is not interrupted by the sounds of the environment, and to make this a fact he either includes silences in his work or gives to his continuity the very nature of silence (absence of intention).

In addition, musicians, since they are several people rather than one person as a painter or sculptor is, are now able to be independent each from another. A composer writes at this moment indeterminately. The performers are no longer his servants but are freemen. A composer writes parts but, leaving their relationship unfixed, he writes no score. Sound sources are at a multiplicity of points in space with respect to the audience so that each listener's experience is his own. The mobiles of modern sculpture come to mind, but the parts they have are not as free as those of a musical composition since they share a common suspension means and follow the law of gravity. In architecture, where labor is divided as it is in music, music's freedom is not yet to be observed. Pinned to the earth, a building well made does not fall apart. Perhaps, though, when the dreams of Buckminster Fuller become actualities, houses, for example, that are dropped from the air instead of bombs, architecture, through flexible means unfamiliar to us now, will initiate a wholly new series of changes in the arts.

Changes in music precede equivalent ones in theater, and changes in theater precede general changes in the lives of people. Theater is obligatory eventually because it resembles life more closely than the other arts do, requiring for its appreciation the use of both eyes and ears, space and time. "An ear alone is not a being." Thus, more and more, we encounter works of art, visual or audible, which are not strictly speaking either paintings or music. In New York City they are called "Happenings." Just as shadows no longer destroy paintings, nor ambient sounds music, so environmental activities do not ruin a happening. They rather add to the fun of it. The result, coming to the instance of daily life, is that our lives are not ruined by the interruptions that other people and things continually provide.

I have attempted briefly here to set forth a view of the arts which does not separate them from the rest of life, but rather confuses the difference between Art and Life, just as it diminishes the distinctions between space and time. Many of the ideas involved come from the Orient, particularly China and Japan. However, what with the printing press, the airplane, telegraphy, and nowadays Telstar, the distinctions between Occident and Orient are fast disappearing. We live in one world. Likewise the distinctions between self and other are being forgotten. Throughout the world people cooperate to effect an action. Hearing of anonymity, one can imagine the absence of competition.

Can anyone say how many artists will be born in the next twenty minutes? We are aware of the great changes taking place each instant in the numbers of people on this planet. And we know of the equally great changes in practicality — what, that is, through technology, people are able to do. Great numbers of men will bring about the future works of art. And these will go in more directions than history records. We no longer have to lull ourselves expecting the advent of some one artist who will satisfy all our aesthetic needs. There will rather be an increase in the amount and kinds of art which will be both bewildering and productive of joy.

Last April in Hawaii, I asked Toru Takemitsu what Maki (his three-year-old daughter) thought of the United States. He said: She thinks it's another part of Japan. Visiting Hamada in Machiko, I expected there, off the beaten track, to see things specifically Japanese. Hamada showed pots, objects, and furniture from all over the world — Spain, Mexico, China, Arizona. The situation music finds itself in in the United States and Europe, it also finds itself in in Japan. We live in a global village (Buckminster Fuller, H. Marshall McLuhan). Maki is right.

One of the things we nowadays know is that something that happens (anything) can be experienced by means of technique (electronic) as some other (any other) thing (happening). For instance, people getting in and out of elevators and the elevators moving from one floor to another: this "information" can activate circuits that bring to our ears a concatenation of sounds (music). Perhaps you wouldn't agree that what you heard was music. But in that case another transformation had intervened: what you heard had set your mind to repeating the definitions of art and music that are found in out-of-date dictionaries. (Even if you didn't think it was music, you'd admit that you took it in through your ears, not through your eyes, nor did you feel it with your hands or walk around inside it. Perhaps you did walk around inside it: the architecturality of music is now a technical possibility and a poetic fact.)

If this elevator-originated music had been heard, what modern Japanese music would it have been? Who among the following would have made this possibility an actuality (a music which we will soon hear whether we happen to be in Tokyo, New York, Berlin, or Bombay)? Yori-aki Matsudaira? Yuji Takahashi? Joji Yuasa? Toru Takemitsu? Takehisa Kosugi? Toshi Ichiyanagi?

Toshi Ichiyanagi. During my recent visit to Japan I listened to tape recordings of music by all the composers I mention except Kosugi. Kosugi's work I saw at Sogetsu Art Center. (His music is taking the clothes of theater and wearing them in a way that redignifies both arts.) And in April at the East-West Center in Hawaii I was with Takemitsu. All these composers interest me, and more than European ones because they give me more freedom to do my own listening. They don't use sound to push me where I don't want to listen. However, they all connect themselves (their ideas, their feelings, the accident that they're Japanese) with the sounds they make. Except Ichiyanagi. Ichiyanagi has found several efficient ways to free his music from the impediment of his imagination. In a piece called *Distance* he requires the performers to climb above the audience to a net from which they activate instruments which are placed below on the theater floor. This physical separation brings about an unusual playing technique that brings the sounds together in the natural way they are together whether in the fields, in the streets, or in the homes and buildings. In a string quartet called *Nagaoka*, Ichiyanagi requires the players to bow where they usually finger and finger where they normally bow. This is miraculous, producing a music that does not make the air it is in any heavier than it already was. And with the assistance of Junosuke Okuyama (who if the Lord knew His business would be multiplied and placed in every electronic music studio in the world) Ichiyanagi has made a number of useful works: *Life Music, Mixture on Tinguely, Pratyahara*. These pieces (I heard only the first two recently) are as outrageous and interminable as Buddhist services and meditations. But like other unpleasant things and experiences, they are good for us. Why? Because, if we don't pamper ourselves but actually put up with the experience of them, we find our ears and our lives changing, not in a way that obliges us to go through Ichiyanagi (or Japan for that matter) to have our daily beauty but which fits us each moment (no matter where we live) to do our music ourselves. (I am speaking of nothing special, just an open ear and an open mind and the enjoyment of daily noises.)

In this changing musical world Japan is no less centrally placed than any other country. Having the composers and technical assistance it has, it is more fortunately populated than most.

# Diary
## Emma Lake Music Workshop 1965

August 15.     The role of the composer is other than it was.     Teaching, too, is no longer transmission of a body of useful information, but's conversation, alone, together, whether in a place appointed or not in that place, whether with those concerned or those unaware of what is being said.     We talk, moving from one idea to another as though we were hunters.     *Christopher Lake Line Four Ring Two-One.     Operator doesn't answer.*     Everyone who's coming's still coming, others leaving for a day.     (By music we mean sound; but what's time?     Certainly not that something begins and ends.)     August 16.     This is the day the workshop opens, but due to circumstances — a concert in Saskatoon — it opened yesterday.     Tomorrow?     (Hunted mushrooms in muskeg nearby.     Got lost.)     (Missed lunch.)     *Correspondence.*     Listening to music, what do I do?     Those musical conventions assume I recognize relationships.     They give no exercise to my faculty to reach the impossibility of sufficient auditory memory to transfer from one like event to another the memory imprint (Duchamp paraphrased).     I managed in the case of Mozart to listen enthusiastically to the held clarinet tones.     They *reminded* me of feedback.     August 17.     Plan: to meet as a group every day at four in the afternoon for discussion of my current concern: music without measurements, sound passing through circumstances.     ¶The room where we meet is a biological laboratory.     There's a piano and an oven for drying fungi.     We leave our music on tables there (each in the group has access to whom, as musicians, the others are).     *Each person is free to bring me his work, to discuss it with me privately.     What else that happens happens freely: going to get a pail of water at the pump, I pass by the lab; two of them are in there talking about Vivaldi.*     August 18.     First student was easy to teach: i.e., don't consider your composition finished until you've heard it performed.     (Today we had the second group meeting.     During the first I had described *Variations V* for which I've not yet made a "score." This involved me in a brief history of electronic music and finally a description of the antennae, photoelectric devices, etc., which enabled dance movements to trigger sound sources.)     Two more students visited: one with a poem and sense of drama. The other's young. Is he also gifted? August 19. (The geologist leaves tomorrow. Our talks involved him in computer music; there's a computer in his office in Calgary. He had written symphonic music which no orchestra ever played. Now he sees music as programming.) It seems a wild goose chase: examining the fact of musical composition in the light of *Variations V*, seeing composition as activity of a sound system, whether made up of electronic components or of comparable "components" (scales, intervalic controls, etc.) in the mind of a man. *Five more people in the workshop today.* August 20. Today's yesterday. What happened? Hunted fungi; lunch; took notes on *Leccinum* species; discussed their work with two composers; continued component inquiry — discussing Young, Brown, Kagel; dinner — food's getting serious: no green vegetables; Alloway lecture on pop and op; boat ride after midnight: "Wow!" *Started exhibit of mushrooms in dining room, giving Latin names and remarks about edibility.* There's a convincing young poet here (his physical stance, his energy of spirit, his face). He wants his poetry to be useful, to improve society. Will he only make matters worse (Kwang-Tse)? August 21. [He knows about canon and permutations. Does he need to know about variation (Alloway's talk about op and systematic art)?] It's the place, the people, the land and air with its mosquitoes and all, more than that it's music and painting: zoologists, poets, potter, they too are with it. *Buckminster Fuller: the practicality of living* here *or there.* A teacher should do something other than filling in the gaps. (Gave my lecture *Where Are We Going? and What Are We Doing?* — four texts superimposed. Seems to me the life has just about gone out of it.) *Questions.* No tundra, nevertheless a northern sense of heightened well-being. ¶Another farewell. August 22. Lindner invited several of us to see his paintings: observation of nature — stumps with moss and lichen; skilful rendering of what he sees. His devotion is to his foregrounds; the backgrounds are best when he doesn't do them at all: just leaves the surface unpainted. Viennese, he settled in Saskatchewan. Self-taught, he spent his life teaching others in the high schools here. *Gathered wild raspberries.* Alloway informed, intelligent, sympathetic; Godwin straight-forward: conversation re Godwin's paintings. (Diary.) Rick Miller and I gathered many *boletes.* Plan: to cook them, say, for twenty people. But which twenty? The people have become a family. Fortunately, there were enough mushrooms for everyone (everyone who dared eat them). August 23. The one with the poem is getting along well, given structure, writing parts, score later. *Posted dried fungi with notes and spore-prints to Smith.* Several after lunch off to Lindner's muskeg. Found a large stand of *Hydnum repandum.* When others left for a nearby lake, refused to leave. Arranged to meet on road at 4:00. 3:30 started back 4:00 hurried.    6:30 lost.    Yelling, startled moose.    8:00 darkness, soaked sneakers; settled for the night on squirrel's midden.    (Family of birds; wind in the trees, tree against tree; woodpecker.)    Fire.    ¶Roasted *L. aurantiacum*.    Rationed cigarettes (one every three hours: they'd last 'till noon).    Thought about direction (no stars).    Where is north?    6-ft. radius.    August 24.    5:30 sky overcast.    6:00 aiming for solid dry spots, angry (7:00): full circle back again (checked that fire was out).    Goal: walk in one direction.    *Mushrooms.*    Lost cigarettes and wax paper.    Recognized path connecting two lakes.    Visiting the larger one, passed by *Amanita virosa*.    9:00 heard horn.    Shouted.    Received reply!    Don Reichert and Rick Shaller picked me up.    Friendship vs nature: St. Ives denim, ham sandwiches and canoe.    (Distinguished between sounds and relationship of them: no sounds.)    *Cooked hydnums.    Gave reading.* Search organized by Jack Sures, potter.    DNR men.    Fifty people, mostly artists.    Helicopter.    Dog.    Jeep.    At night, searchlights, shouts, horns.    That night also: loss of mind, cabin destroyed by fire, Mrs. Kaldor hospitalized.    August 25.    Discussion: fugue.    (The question remains unanswered.)    Hearing several recordings of his music, was struck by difference between sections, no transitions.    Suggested carrying this to extreme (Satie, McLuhan, newspaper): not bothering with cadences.    ¶Made no effort ("Unperformed work isn't finished.") towards workshop concert. Therefore it happened and skilfully: piano solos by Ted Bourré, setting of Duncan poem (two voices — singing, speaking, two pianos and percussion) by Martin Bartlett.    Music by Jack Behrens, Boyd McDonald, and myself also heard.    (Having missed poetry-reading, heard recording of it.    Gerry Gilbert spoke of poetry as voice instead of words on page.    Like a dance: human by nature.)    August 26.    *Art McKay.*    What we learn isn't what we're taught nor what we study.    We don't know we're learning.    Something about society?    That if what happens here (Emma Lake) happened there (New York City), such things as rights and riots, unexplained oriental wars wouldn't arise.    Something about art?    That it's experience shared? That we must have had the experience before we have the art?    (Rock 'n Roll.    Two couples servicing north with amplifiers, loud-speakers, the ladies dressed in silver.)    *Self-education.*    [Seminar (last day): answered questions re graphic notation.] Dining room turned into dance-hall.    August 27. Cree Indians formerly found a fungus underground, in books called Indian Bread.    The Montreal Lake Indians I spoke to, some of them on in years, had never heard of it.    Authentic Indian designs are no longer geometric: they're floral.    *If they ask you to write some music and tell you what to write, how long etc. (a commission) do all they ask, I told him, and whatever else, besides, you can.*    (Departures at all hours; people arriving, leaving, and coming back;

difference of directions; Mrs. Kaldor, who baked the pies, blueberry and saskatoon, still in the hospital.     Shopped for moccasins.)     August 28.     He'd written a piece in one style and was fulfilling a commission in another. What did I think?     O.K.     (The one-hundred-year project at Regina: artificial mountain (slides away), artificial lake (weeds grow over), university. The land is flat.     How excellent if it could remain so, the people living underground, ready for daily amazement of coming to the surface!)     Why did we leave ahead of time?     Circumstances?     The distances to travel?     The fact of weekend?     We'd gotten together and so could separate?     ¶There had been a robbery.     None of the paintings taken, only the coin collection.

*Saskatchewan*.

TIM HODGKINSON

# An Interview with Pierre Schaeffer

*Introduction: What Is Musique Concrète?*

Musique concrète is music made of raw sounds: thunderstorms, steam-engines, waterfalls, steel foundries. The sounds are not produced by traditional acoustic musical instruments; they are captured on tape (originally, before tape, on disk) and manipulated to form sound-structures.

The work method is therefore empirical. It starts from the concrete sounds and moves toward a structure. In contrast, traditional classical music starts from an abstract musical schema. This is then notated and only expressed in concrete sound as a last stage, when it is performed.

Musique concrète emerged in Paris in 1948 at the RTF (Radio Television Français). Its originator, leading researcher, and articulate spokesman was Pierre Schaeffer — at that time working as an electroacoustic engineer with the RTF.

Almost immediately, musique concrète found itself locked in mortal combat not only with its opponents within traditionally notated music but also with electronic music, which emerged in Cologne in 1950 at the NWDR (Nord West Deutscher Rundfunk). Electronic music involved the use of precisely controllable electronic equipment to generate the sound material — for example, the oscillator, which can produce any desired wave-form, which can then be shaped, modulated, etc.

At the time, the antagonism between musique concrète and electronic music seemed to revolve largely around the difference in sound material. Over the decades, this difference has become less important, so that what we now call "electroacoustic music" is less concerned with the origin of the sound material than with what is done with it afterward.

On the other hand it would be facile to allow the category of electroacoustic music to absorb everything just on the basis of shared technology. For there are underlying choices to be made about the nature of the whole project. The hands-on listening-based approach of concrète — its curiosity about the actual nature of listening — suggests that the way forward in aesthetic terms will be a process of thoughtful but direct engagement with sound materials rather than the usual ritual of submission to the technical possibilities.

We have to admit that today this is still a radical idea. In other words, concrète is still here to remind us of the project of actually making music, as opposed to demonstrating equipment or putting systems through their paces. The new musicians are not only not in the conservatory; they are not in the laboratories of IRCAM (Institut de recherche et coordination acoustique/ musique) or at Sony either.

Tim Hodgkinson: You are a writer, a thinker, and a radio sound-engineer. This makes you, from the point of view of "Music" with a capital "M" — something of an outsider. Do you think that, in moments of crisis, the non-specialist has a particular and important role to play? I don't know whether this is entirely correct, but I sense that, at the moment when you came into music, around 1948, you were a nonspecialist of this kind.

Pierre Schaeffer: Yes. But chance alone doesn't explain why a nonspecialist gets involved in an area he doesn't know about. In my case there were double circumstances. First of all, I'm not completely unknowledgeable about music, because I come from a family of musicians: my father was a violinist and my mother was a singer. I did study well — theory, piano, cello, etcetera, so I'm not completely untrained. Secondly, I was an electroacoustic engineer working for the French radio, so I was led to study sound and what's called "high fidelity" in sound. Thirdly, after the war, in the '45 to '48 period, we had driven back the German invasion but we hadn't driven back the invasion of Austrian music, twelve-tone music. We had liberated ourselves politically, but music was still under an occupying foreign power, the music of the Vienna school.

So these were the three circumstances that compelled me to experiment in music: I was involved in music; I was working with turntables (then with tape-recorders); I was horrified by modern twelve-tone music. I said to myself, "Maybe I can find something different; maybe salvation, liberation, is possible." Seeing that no one knew what to do anymore with DoReMi, maybe we had to look outside that. Unfortunately it took me forty years to conclude that nothing is possible outside DoReMi. In other words, I wasted my life.

Hodgkinson: We'll certainly have to come back to that. Right now, I want to ask you if you think that there is an inherent connection between what seem to be simultaneous developments; that, on the one hand, there is the crisis of traditional music — twelve-tone and so forth — and on the other, there are the new possibilities offered by technology, possibilities of opening up new continents of sound. Sometimes this seems to me to be merely a matter of luck. At other times it seems that there must be an inherent reason.

Schaeffer: I would answer that this luck is deceptive. First, it doesn't surprise me that traditional music has experienced a kind of exhaustion in the twentieth century — not forgetting that many musicians started to look outside the traditional structures of tonality. Debussy was looking at six-note scales, Bartok was exploring mode; tonality seemed to be exhausted. The impressionists, Debussy, Fauré, in France, did take a few steps forward. Then, after the impressionists, we have a period of rigor, of barbarity, a period seeking to re-establish something more solid. This is epitomized in the Vienna school. At this point the Vienna school was also inspired by scientific ideas, by a rigor coming from a discipline which wasn't music but an algebraic equation.

So it seems that one of two things can happen in a period of high technology: either technology itself seems to come to the rescue of art — which is in a state of collapse — (that was my starting point, musique concrète with the tape-recorder, now electronic music, etcetera), or it's the ideas of technology, ideas from mathematics, ideas with a scientific aura, or real scientific ideas given an unreal relevance to an art which is seeking its discipline — its ordering principles — outside itself instead of within the source of its own inspiration. This coincidence of a music which is debilitated and failing and a glorious, all-conquering science is what really characterizes the twentieth-century condition.

What did I try to do, in this context, in 1948? As Boulez said, extremely snidely (he's a pretentious boy, a kind of musical Stalinist. I'm an anarchist myself), it was a case of *bricolage*.[1] I retain this term not as an insult but as something very interesting. After all, how did music originate? Through bricolage, with calabashes, with fibres, as in Africa. (I'm familiar with African instruments). Then people made violin strings out of the intestines of cats. And of course the tempered scale is a compromise and also a bricolage. And this bricolage, which is the development of music, is a process that is shaped by the human, the human ear, and not the machine, the mathematical system.

Hodgkinson: It seems to me that there are several possible attitudes to the machine. There is something which we can trace to a kind of puritan tradition, where the machine represents a kind of purification, or perfection, which we in ourselves cannot achieve, and is therefore an escape from the human. Then there is another point of view which retains a humanist perspective and sometimes a kind of projection of human qualities onto the machine,

TIM HODGKINSON

and which is in any case a more complex and a more doubting relationship. I would place the Futurists, for example, in this second point of view. Looking at the history of musique concrète, there sometimes seems to be a symmetry, with sound on one side and system on the other, with musique concrète taking the side of sound. Within this duality, would you agree that musique concrète embodies a more humanist position?

Schaeffer: Yes, of course. You mention symmetry, and I would like to take this term as a very good way of looking at this. But what symmetry? I think we are speaking of a symmetry between the sound world and the music world. The sound world is natural — in the sense where this includes sound made by sound-producing instruments — the Rumori generators, concrète, etcetera — the sound of the voice, the sounds of nature, of wind and thunder, and so forth. So there is, within the human ear, as it developed over millions of years, a great capacity for hearing all this sound. Sound is the vocabulary of nature. When we hear the wind, the wind says, "I'm blowing." When we hear water, the water says, "I'm running," and so forth. Noises have generally been thought of as indistinct, but this is not true. In the seventeenth century people thought of noises as unpleasant — but noises are as well articulated as the words in a dictionary. Opposing this world of sound is the world of music, the world of musical entities, of what I have called "musical objects." These occur when sounds bear musical value. Take a sound from whatever source, a note on a violin, a scream, a moan, a creaking door, and there is always this symmetry between the sound basis, which is complex and has numerous characteristics which emerge through a process of comparison within our perception. If you hear a door creak and a cat mew, you can start to compare them — perhaps by duration, or by pitch, or by timbre. Thus, while we are used to hearing sounds by reference to their instrumental causes, the sound-producing bodies, we are used to hearing musical sounds for their musical value. We give the same value to sounds emanating from quite different sources. So the process of comparing a cat's mew to a door creak is different from the process of comparing a violin note to a trumpet note, where you might say they have the same pitch and duration but different timbre. This is the symmetry between the world of sound and the world of musical values.

Hodgkinson: What is musical value for you exactly?

Schaeffer: The best analogy is with language — since we talk of musical languages. People who share the same language, French or Chinese or whatever, have the same vocal cords and emit sounds which are basically the same, as they come from the same throats and lungs. So this is a sound world. But the same sounds have linguistic values and this makes them different. These linguistic values derive from their role within a system. In the same way, musical value is inseparable from the idea of system.

But how does this bear on the question of the machine in our contemporary world — which is really a different question from the question of symmetry? We could say that the machine has had two quite different, even antagonistic, impacts on our modern world. There is the romantic, romanesque, illusionist tendency which proposes a biology of the machine, which is rather what the Italians (Futurists) were about; it goes back to the storms and the murmuring forests of romanticism, the pastoral symphony, the representation of nature in music. But of course as machines now constitute nature, music now needs machines to represent this nature; our forests and countrysides *are* machines. But there is another, quite opposite, tendency, which sees machines as the means not only of producing sound but also of musical values themselves. Many researchers, well understanding the preeminent importance of musical value, turned to the physicists. Their values were now frequencies, decibels, harmonic spectra. With electronics they could get direct access to all this and have really precise and objective musical values. But then — another symmetry, this time a really disturbing one. When you build a farcical machine for Rumori with things rubbing against each other — like the Italians — lead shot in a drum, etcetera, you don't hurt a fly, it lasts ten, twenty years — it's circus, quite harmless little sound effects. But when you stick generations of young musicians, as is happening today, in front of synthesizers — I don't mean the ones for commercial music, but the really precise ones, where you have one control for the frequency, another for the decibels, another for the harmonic spectrum — then you're really in the shit . . . [laughter].

Hodgkinson: What then should one want to do with music? Accepting the need for musical values is one thing, but how do you choose?

Schaeffer: You have to remind musicians of what Dante wrote over the Gates of Hell: Abandon hope all ye who enter here.

Hodgkinson: But if you stay outside?

Schaeffer: Well then you don't have any music. If you enter, if you want to make music, you must abandon hope. Of what? Of making a new music.

Hodgkinson: So new music is impossible?

Schaeffer: Yes, a music which is new because it comes from new instruments, new theories, new languages. So what's left? Baroque music. Has it struck you that the music which is regarded as the most sublime in western civilization, which is the music of Bach, is called baroque?[2] Bizarre. Even its contemporaries called it baroque. Bach lived in a moment of synthesis, in terms of the instruments, the theory — tempered scale, etcetera — and was putting everything together. He was taking from the Middle Ages, from the new developments in the instruments of his time, from the Italians, and he made a music which was so clearly made up of bits and pieces that it called itself baroque. Simultaneously traditional and new. And this applies today; it will be when our contemporary researchers abandon their ludicrous technologies and systems and "new" musical languages and realize that there's no way out of traditional music, that we can get down to a baroque music for the twenty-first century.

Such a music has been prefigured in popular music — not that I rate it very highly. Jazz, rock, etcetera, the music of "mass" culture, and I'm not talking about good jazz, the marvelous negro spirituals which are completely traditional, but the kind of utility-music which is widely used for dancing, making love, etcetera; this is a baroque music, a mixture of electricity and DoReMi.

Hodgkinson: So there is nothing essentially relevant in the fact that the world we live in is changing and that we might need to express new or different things about it?

Schaeffer: The answer is that the world doesn't change.

Hodgkinson: There is no progress?

Schaeffer: There is no progress. The world changes materially. Science makes advances in technology and understanding. But the world of humanity doesn't change. Morally, the world is both better and worse than it was. We are worse off than in the Middle Ages, or the seventeenth and eighteenth centuries, in that we have the atomic menace. It's ridiculous that time and time again we need a radioactive cloud coming out of a nuclear power-station to remind us that atomic energy is extraordinarily dangerous. So this shows the imbecility, the stupidity of mankind. Why should a civilization which so misuses its power have, or deserve, a normal music?

Hodgkinson: Well, if you are committed to music, you try to reach, to encourage, the good in people, whatever that is.

Schaeffer: That could be wishful thinking. I'll bring in Lévi-Strauss, who has said again and again that it's only things that change; the structures, the structures of humanity, stay the same — and the uses we make of these things. On this level we are just like the caveman who makes a tool out of a flint, a tool for survival, but also a deadly weapon: we haven't changed at all. The world has just got more dangerous because the things we use have got more dangerous. In music there are new things — synthesizers, tape-recorders, etcetera — but we still have our sensibilities, our ears, the old harmonic structures in our heads. We're still born into DoReMi — it's not up to us to decide. Probably the only variations are ethnological. There are the different musical cultures, the music of ancient Greece, for example, insofar as we can know it, the music coming from the Hebrews into the

Gregorian chant, the music of India, China, Africa, these are the variations, and it's all DoReMi.

Hodgkinson: Are you pessimistic about the future of this variation — in the sense that there is a cultural imperialism which is destroying the local musics of the world and replacing them by a kind of central music which is driven forward by industrial and political power?

Schaeffer: I'm very aware of what you're talking about as I was involved with the radio in Africa in the same period as I was doing concrète — I was doing both at the same time. I was deeply afraid that these vulnerable musical cultures — lacking notation, recording, cataloging, and with the approximative nature of their instruments — would be lost. I and my colleagues were beginning to collect African music. At the radio there is a small department run by Mr. Toureille, who has very courageously for seventeen years systematically sent out expeditions to gather authentic African musics and released them on record.

Hodgkinson: The problem is that the records are bought in Europe and not in Africa. It's hard to see how you can regenerate the music in its own context. In fact, we can accuse ourselves of appropriating it. There is this ambiguity in that we are in a meta-cultural position with the entire cultural geography and history of the world laid out for our pleasure. Do you think this situation brings about a lack of a sense of the real value of culture and cultural artifacts? Many people listen to ethnic musics from all over the place. Does this leaping about in space and time affect the quality of the listening?

Schaeffer: Well I don't think we can answer this question of value ultimately, but we can recognize the fact that civilizations are mortal. In music there are, unfortunately, two principles at work. There's the principle of barbarity. The fact that western civilization invaded these autochthonous people entwined with their ancient local cultures — this was certainly barbarous, if not entirely heedless. Barbarians always think of themselves as the bringers of civilization. The western barbarity was turntables, the radio, etcetera.

Then there's the principle of economics which is that bad money gets thrown after good. So if barbarity is the triumph of force, bad money is the triumph of economy — in a metaphoric sense.

Hodgkinson: I'd like to turn now to the idea that, scattered all over the world, probably in tiny garrets rather than in expensive state-of-the-art studios, there are people busily cutting up bits of tape, making loops, experimenting with tape-recorders, and I would like to ask you if you have anything you would specially want to say to these people.

Schaeffer: Well, first I can't pass the buck to them. I started all that. I think they have the great satisfaction of discovering the world of sound. The world of music is probably contained within DoReMi, yes; but I'm saying that the world of sound is much larger than that. Let's take a spatial analogy. Painters and sculptors are concerned with spaces, volumes, colors, etcetera, but not with language. That's the writer's concern. The same thing is true with sound. Musique concrète, in its work of assembling sound, produces sound-works, sound-structures, but not music. We have to not call music things which are simply sound-structures.

Hodgkinson: Is it not enough for a sound-work to have system, for it to become music?

Schaeffer: The whole problem of the sound-work is distancing oneself from the dramatic. I hear a bird sing, I hear a door creak, I hear the sounds of battle; you start to get away from that. You find a neutral zone. Just as a painter or sculptor moves away from a model, stops representing a horse, or a wounded warrior, and arrives at the abstract. A beautiful sculptural form, as beautiful as an egg, a greenhouse, a star. And if you continue this abstracting movement, you get to the graphics of the forms of letters in written language. And in music you get to music. There's thus a gradation between the domain of raw sound, which starts by being imitative, like the representational plastic arts, and the domain of language. Between, there's a zone of gradation which is the area of "abstract" in the plastic arts, and which is neither language nor model, but a play of forms and materials.

There are many people working with sound. It's often boring, but not necessarily ugly. It contains dynamic and kinaesthetic impressions. But it's not music.

Hodgkinson: But what is the exact moment at which something becomes music?

Schaeffer: This is a difficult question. If you had the complete answer you'd be a prophet. The traditional testimony is that a musical schema lent itself to being expressed in sound in more than one way. An example is that Bach sometimes composed without specifying the instruments: he wasn't interested in the sound of his music. That's music, a schema capable of several realizations in sound. The moment at which music reveals its true nature is contained in the ancient exercise of the theme with variations. The complete mystery of music is explained right there. Thus a second, a third, a fourth variation were possible, which all kept the single idea of the theme. This is the evidence that with one musical idea you can have different realizations.

Hodgkinson: Do you listen to rock music?

Schaeffer: My eighteen-year-old daughter listens a lot downstairs, so I hear what comes under her door. It's enough.

Hodgkinson: I was thinking that rock music is also a music that's essentially engaged with technologies, in the sense that it grew up with the recording technology and the means of mass-producing discs.

Schaeffer: What strikes me is the violence of the sound, a violence which seems to be designed to reach not only the ear but also the gut. In a certain way this seems to function as a drug. Real music is a sublime drug, but you can't really call it a drug because it doesn't brutalize, it elevates. These two characteristics of rock, the violence of the sound and the drug-function, revolve on the basis of a musical formula which is impoverished. This doesn't interest me. I feel rather that it indicates a nostalgia among today's young people, a desire to revert to savagery, to recover the primitive. At this time, who can blame them? The primitive is also a source of life. But the musical means seem sad and rather morbid. It's a dishonest primitive because it's reached through technological sophistication. It's a cheat.

Hodgkinson: But do you recognize in it the techniques of concrète, for example in the idea of production, as the term is used in the recording industry, this conceptualization of the difference between sound source and process, between source and manipulation — where the producer can regard the recorded sound as simply raw material for a process of radical transformation, but of course, more often than not, with the aim of making a successful commodity? Would you allow any kind of humanist potential where the empiricism, the bricolage of rock, is not totally subordinated to commerce?

Schaeffer: Well we've already mentioned pessimism, and I must say that I do judge these times to be bad times. We seem to be afflicted by ideologies — often, entirely incompatible ones. Thus, the ideology of scientific rigor and at the same time the ideology of chance; ideologies of power, technology, improvisation, and facility — technology with which to replace inspiration. If I compare that to jazz for example in its historically fecund period, the extraordinary fruition of American music at the point where the European DoReMi was suddenly seized upon by the blacks for the production of expressive forms; this was sublime. Now if you think that, decades later, this bloated, avaricious, and barbarous culture, brutalized by money and machines and advertising, is still living off this precious vein. Well, you have to admit that some periods are simply vile, disgusting, and that this is one of them. The only hope is that our civilization will collapse at a certain point, as always happens in history. Then, out of barbarity, a renaissance.

Hodgkinson: Some of what you were saying about rock music reminded me of Adorno's essay on jazz, the regressive, nostalgic function, and so forth. Yet you find jazz, in its great period, sublime.

Schaeffer: But primitive American jazz was very rich, it wasn't very learned, but it was richly inventive, in ways of expressing into sound, in its voicings; what I really admired, when I was there the first time, after the liberation, in the '50s, were the operettas — Carmen Jones, excellent music, I can't remember the titles, but great music — Gershwin of course.

Hodgkinson: I have the impression that in the '40s and '50s you were optimistic about the outcomes of your musical project. Was there a particular moment when you underwent a general change in your relationship to this project?

Schaeffer: I must say honestly that this is the most important question you have asked me. I fought like a demon throughout all the years of discovery and exploration in musique concrète; I fought against electronic music, which was another approach, a systemic approach, when I preferred an experimental approach actually working directly, empirically with sound. But at the same time, as I defended the music I was working on, I was personally horrified at what I was doing. I felt extremely guilty. As my father, the violinist, used to say, indulgently, What are you up to, my little chap? When are you going to make music? And I used to say — I'm doing what I can, but I can't do that. I was always deeply unhappy at what I was doing. I was happy at overcoming great difficulties — my first difficulties with the turntables when I was working on "Symphonie pour un homme seul"; my first difficulties with the tape-recorders when I was doing "Étude aux objets" — that was good work, I did what I set out to do — my work on the "Solfege." It's not that I disown everything I did — it was a lot of hard work. But each time I was to experience the disappointment of not arriving at music. I couldn't get to music — what I call music. I think of myself as an explorer struggling to find a way through in the far north, but I wasn't finding a way through.

Hodgkinson: So you did discover that there was no way through.

Schaeffer: There is no way through. The way through is behind us.

Hodgkinson: So it's in that context that we should understand your relatively small output as a composer after those early years?

Schaeffer: I was very well received. I had no social problems. These successes added to my burden of doubt. I'm the opposite of the persecuted musician. In fact I don't consider myself a real musician. I'm in the dictionary as a musician. It makes me laugh. A good researcher is what I am.

Hodgkinson: Did your time in Africa have any particular relevance to changes in your attitudes to music?

Schaeffer: No. I had always been very interested in music from Asia, Africa, America. I considered that music should be tracked down over the whole surface of the planet.

Hodgkinson: I think we've said enough.

Schaeffer: Yes, I think we've said a lot.

## *Notes*

The interview took place in 1986 at the house of Pierre Schaeffer. It was conducted in French and was translated by Tim Hodgkinson.

1. The French noun *bricolage* has no direct equivalent in English, but it is close to the adjective "makeshift" and the idea of improvising new uses for things originally meant for something else.

2. In the French language, the term "baroque" has the meaning "roughly put together" as well as the meaning we have in English of the theatrical, excessive, late-Renaissance style.

TIM HODGKINSON

EVAN EISENBERG

# Deus ex Machina

Is music about human feelings, or is it something more?

The best case for the first alternative is made by Suzanne Langer in her classic study of symbolism, *Philosophy in a New Key*. Music, she argues, is not self-expression in the usual sense. Instead, "it expresses primarily the composer's *knowledge of human feeling*. . . ?" It is not precisely a language of emotion, as it has no vocabulary; but though denotation is lacking there is connotation to burn, the mark of true symbolism. Notes are not interchangeable with words like "anger" or "love" because "*music articulates forms which language cannot set forth.*" Naturally a melody admits of widely differing interpretations, "for *what music can actually express is only the morphology of feeling*; and it is quite plausible that some sad and some happy conditions may have a very similar morphology." In music there is no fixed denotation, but rather "a transient play of contents" much truer to our inner experience.

Anyone in the market for an emotive theory of music can stop right here. But though the wisdom of centuries supports it, I am uncomfortable with this special status of music. It has to cramp the Muse, confining her to the inner world while her sisters range the inner and outer at will. "Music is our myth of the inner life," says Langer. Aren't all myths myths of the inner life, as well as the outer? They would hardly hold us as they do if they did not penetrate to the inner life. And they would not hold us, either, if they had no concrete contents (the plural is important) for us to hold on to.

There is something prissy and insulting in making the musician a species of psychologist. Dante was that, but he was also an astronomer, theologian, historian, political polemicist, metaphysician. Can we say less of Beethoven?

It is true that Western music reached its summit at a time and place of obsessive inwardness — Germany and Austria in the eighteenth and nineteenth centuries. Social life was stuck in its tracks, so people explored their insides. But alongside music it was not psychology that flourished (that happened later, when music was disintegrating); it was history, geography, natural science, and philosophy, above all metaphysics. There is another clue. Metaphysics grew from myth. Both grope for a layer of existence that is the foun-

dation of every other, lending its deep structures to every other realm — the physical, the biological, the emotional, the social, the artistic.

Schopenhauer's theory of music, to which the argument now leads us, was the lintel of a great metaphysical structure full of damp corridors that no one visits anymore. It was popular at one time for its weight and gloom, which answered a *fin de siècle* need, and for its odd but compelling explanation of the way one feels when listening to music. Nietzsche and Wagner both altered the theory to fit the supercharged music they favored. But it is only now, with the help of the phonograph, that we can clearly hear what Schopenhauer heard.

According to Schopenhauer, the world I perceive is merely a representation — *Vorstellung*, which has the physical sense of placing a picture before the mind. The world is something I construct with the aid of certain innate, automatic mental tools. These are "categories" modeled on those of Kant (although for Schopenhauer the category of causality includes all the others). Behind this picture show is the thing-in-itself, which according to Kant is unknowable; but according to Schopenhauer the thing-in-itself is known, and at first hand. It is the will, which I feel in myself and recognize by analogy in all other objects, quick and inanimate. The will is the raging, aimless river that runs through me and through everything else. It is refracted through the Platonic Ideas, reaching various stages of objectification in the rock, the oak, the rabbit, the man. These Ideas or perfect forms are refracted in turn through the principle of individuation — time, space, causality — into the numberless rocks, oaks, rabbits, and men that I perceive.

In this way the will becomes an object to me, the subject. Even the will within me, which I know directly, can be an object to me: this happens whenever I explain my behavior in terms of motives, goals, emotions, or character. These are illusions, but so, in a deeper sense, is my direct experience of the will — namely, my feeling of free will. In harsh fact I am a puppet of the will, locked in a death struggle against all its other puppets. ". . . The will must live on itself, since nothing exists besides it, and it is a hungry will. Hence arise pursuit, hunting, anxiety, and suffering." Does all this turmoil add up to anything, as it might for Nietzsche or Darwin? No. The will remains a worm, hungry and blind. In its refractions it battles against itself like the ant-lion that has been cut in two.

Is there any escape? Only the saint escapes permanently, by denying the will to live. But a temporary respite, a "Sabbath of the penal servitude of willing," can be found in art. The artist's perception is not chained to his will. He looks upon an apple tree not as something to eat from or build with, but as something to look upon. So it is no longer an individual object useful or useless to him as an individual creature; it has become the Idea of its species. Art is a copy of that Idea (not, as Plato alleged, a copy of a copy). As artists "we *lose* ourselves entirely in this object, to use a pregnant expression; in other words, we forget our individuality, our will, and continue to exist only as pure subject, as "pure mirror of the object. . . ."

Like most mimetic theories of art, this one seems to leave music out in the cold. If no Idea leaves its imprint in music, some still deeper track must be there; for of all the arts music speaks most powerfully. Schopenhauer reasons that it must be like the other arts, only more so — that "its imitative reference to the world must be very profound."

Now, having devoted his mind "to the impression of music in its many different forms," he reaches this stunning conclusion: ". . . Music, since it passes over the Ideas, is also quite independent of the phenomenal world, positively ignores it, and, to a certain extent, could still exist even if there were no world at all, which cannot be said of the other arts. Thus music is as *immediate* an objectification and copy of the whole *will* as the world itself is, indeed as the ideas are. . . ."

Music could exist *even if there were no world at all*. These words pull the earth from under us, as music itself often does: that metaphysical shiver we feel in Carnegie Hall, as if the red carpet had slipped away and left us hanging over the abyss, has nothing to do with the faint rumblings of the N and R trains.

Both music and the Ideas are objectifications of the will. Although there is no resemblance between them, there must be a parallel. The deep bass, Schopenhauer says, is analogous to the lowest grade of Ideas, the brute mass of the planet from which everything else is generated. Between bass and soprano fall the ripieno or harmony parts, representing the intermediate grades of the will's objectification — minerals, vegetables, animals. And the melody is man: "It relates the most secret history of the intellectually enlightened will, portrays every agitation, every effort, every movement of the intellectually enlightened will, everything which the faculty of reason summarizes under the wide and negative concept of feeling." So music does express feelings, as everyone says it does; but it expresses "their essential nature, without any accessories, and so also without the motives for them."

Of all the parts only the melody is a significant whole, since only man has the connected consciousness that gives a life shape. As the shape of man's life is a restless transition from want to satisfaction, then back to another want, so the shape of melody is "a constant digression and deviation from the keynote in a thousand ways." Yet music gives us solace. It "floats to us as from a paradise quite familiar and yet eternally remote"; for "it reproduces all the emotions of our innermost being, but entirely without reality and remote from its pain." In real life, by contrast, "we ourselves are now the vibrating string that is stretched and plucked."

Now Schopenhauer's words as they float down to us begin to sound less remote, more familiar. Haven't Hanslick and Langer given us the meat of this theory without the scholastic garnish? Even the part about nonhuman nature can be expressed commonsensically: for example, Langer says that the rhythms of the inner life expressed in music may also be those of nature. Schopenhauer's doctrine can be seen as an ingenious but trivial specification, tailoring the harmonic theory of his day to its cosmology. Why not speak clearly, then, in terms of motion or force or unified field theory and forget this stuff about the will?

There are reasons. "Hitherto," Schopenhauer writes, "the concept of *will* has been subsumed under the concept of force; I, on the other hand, do exactly the reverse, and intend every force in nature to be conceived as will." The concept of force we know from outside, from perception; but the concept of will we know from within. "Therefore, if we refer the concept of *force* to that of *will*, we have in fact referred something more unknown to something infinitely better known, indeed to the one thing really known to us immediately and completely; and we have very greatly extended our knowledge." Of course, I am tempted to say that only I have will, while the motions of rocks and rabbits are the result of force. Even the motions of my neighbors seem to be determined by the forces of nature — lust, inertia, gravity, genetics. They seem so *predictable*. The point is, they can say the same about me. "Spinoza says that if a stone projected through the air had consciousness, it would imagine it was flying of its own will. I add merely that the stone would be right."

What difference does all this make to someone who just wants to listen to music, and who tolerates philosophy only if it lets him listen deeper? By means of music, Schopenhauer says, we philosophize without knowing it. The danger in making that philosophy explicit is not that we may do it too well, and so puncture the magic — we are centuries away from that — but that we may get it wrong. A narrow theory can pinch our ears and impoverish our listening. That is what psychologizing, man-obsessed theories of music do, and abstractionist theories like Langer's are only a little better. The first kind of theory ignores nature entirely or mentions her only when some joker writes *Pastorale* at the top of a score, which might make sense if we were dealing with a marginal art like cameo or petit point. The second kind of theory lets music embrace the whole universe, but only around the ankles; that is, at a trivial level of abstraction. All the microcosm and the macrocosm are allowed to have in common is a kind of mobile geometry.

Why are we moved at the sight of a fountain, at the water's yearning rise and dying fall? The answer is in the adjectives, of course; which is not to say that the fountain is just a metaphor. If it is a metaphor, it is the deep kind, not the skimpy kind that gets by on visual similitude alone. The fountain moves us not because it reminds us of how we sometimes feel, but because we know just how it feels. A spray of melody that rises toward the octave, falters before reaching it, and falls to the subdominant moves us in the same way. That phrase is not about fountains and not about human aspirations. It is about the energy more elemental than either that flows through both.

To take such a universal view of music is not exactly revolutionary. In fact, it is fairly reactionary. Pythagoras and Plato connected the harmony of the soul with that of the universe, and this understanding persisted right down to Shakespeare's time. It was then that the Great Chain of Being began to fray as levelers, bastards, and pretenders set degree aside and untuned that string. In Schopenhauer, however, not only has the chain been naturalized, but all its moral luster has been scraped away. We see his pessimism at work, and his Vedic skepticism. The chain is really a snake snapping blindly at its own tail. This is not as pretty a view as Plato's; but from a strictly modern point of view, isn't this the way things are?

Without necessarily drawing his practical consequences, we are drawn to his view of the world. His understanding of music ought to be equally compelling. Not, perhaps, his labored correspondences between the graded Ideas and contemporary musical theory (he goes so far as to root the rule against parallel fifths in the nature of inorganic matter). That might work with Mozart, whose perfection could be said to reflect a momentary equipoise of man and nature, with man securely on top and nature graciously accepting his pathetic fallacy. It won't work with plainchant, Javanese gamelan music, or a Charlie Mingus bass-fiddle solo. But Schopenhauer's central insight is much less culture-bound. He manages to explain how it is that when we listen to music most deeply we seem to trace with one hand the furrows of the mind, with the other the folds of the universe. In other words, music is not just about people. It is bigger than that.

How odd that for hundreds of years Western man should have thought otherwise. But then these were rough centuries, and naturally he was preoccupied with his own affairs. When he paid good money for a concert seat he had no intention of empathizing with vegetables or rocks, still less with the primordial will. He was there to have his own emotions stroked. Or maybe just to put in an appearance, since the concert was a social event. In the concert hall he sat among humans. There were only humans onstage. Nature and its noises were shut out, and there was not even an icon, as in church, to remind him of extra-human zones. Even the instruments were anthropomorphic (the womanly violin family, for example). Music was made by people, for people, so it had to be about people.

In the nineteenth century only a mystic or a hermit could get past this way of thinking, someone like Schopenhauer or Thoreau. "I hear one thrumming a guitar below stairs. . . . I soar or hover with clean skirts over the field of my life." When we hear music, "we put our dormant feelers to the limits of the universe. . . . No particulars survive this expansion; persons do not survive it." It is noteworthy that these and similar meditations are almost always, for Thoreau, set off by music that floats in from a distance or another room. That was how Thoreau took his music when he wasn't playing the flute in a forest clearing. Others might get the same feeling in a church, with the sound of the choir and organ diffusing from above. This rarefied sort of experience has been made available to us as a matter of routine by the phonograph.

The concerto could serve well here as an example. It is a form that seems to speak of the relation between the individual and society. More than etymology connects it to the concert hall and to the problem of how one may act "in concert" with one's fellow men. We have already seen how phonography can change the listener's viewpoint, so that instead of seeing the soloist from the midst of the crowd one sees the crowd through his eyes. But a further possibility is also introduced. The concerto may describe the hero's relationship, not to society, but to nature or the world as a whole. For example, the recording of the Sibelius Violin Concerto by Heifetz and the Chicago Symphony may bring to mind a man walking in northern woods at dusk: a sense of communion without consummation. In concert the very same notes can seem mawkish or clumsy, like a man unused to company. The Beethoven concerto sometimes seems slow and awkward when exposed to the scrutiny of a crowd, while on record (Menuhin with Furtwängler, say) it relaxes, breathing fresh air. Both these concertos failed initially to get a toehold in the concert hall.

Similarly, there are symphonies and overtures and choral works in which we are intended to hear nature even as we stare at sixty or seventy representatives of society. Pastoral music of symphonic size is just one example of what composers may have wanted to do but couldn't until the phonograph came along. They may have wanted to create music without the mediation of interpreters. They may have wanted direct communication with the listener ("from the heart, may it go to the heart"). Their inner visions may have been too personal, or mystical, or nature-mystical to be transmitted in a concert hall, but too richly colored and vast for any medium but the orchestra. Historians connect the symphony orchestra of the nineteenth century with standing armies, nationalisms, and the earth-punishing motions of organized men. Yet Mahler's symphonies, scored for whole regiments, make the motions of the spirit — of one man or of the universe, but certainly not of a group. "Imagine that the Universe begins to sound and sing," Mahler wrote of his Eighth Symphony. "These are not human voices any more, but planets and suns circling." He is not the only composer whose orchestra grew as his vision became more hermetic. One could say that of Bruckner, Ives, Strauss, Berlioz, even Beethoven. It must have been painful for such men to know that their larger works, when they were performed at all, would be confused with such events as the Boston Peace Festival of 1869, which featured an orchestra of a thousand, a chorus of ten thousand, and a hundred firemen banging on anvils.

By the same token, much naively descriptive pastoral music and much program music of the swashbuckling open-air kind may have been conceived in reaction to the close, sentimental air of the concert hall, the drawing room, and the provincial palace. When patrons and subscribers would prate about noble affections, how on earth could one ventilate one's music? How could one show that it did not have the same subject matter as gossip? Maybe by making the flutes simulate a storm. That was not the real subject matter, either, but it was an improvement.

I am thinking of Beethoven, but a century later Debussy faced the same embarrassments. He conceived "a kind of music composed especially for the open air, on broad lines, with bold vocal and instrumental effects, which would sport and skim among the tree-tops in the sunshine and fresh air. Harmonies which would seem out of place in an enclosed concert room would be in their true environment here." It seems to me that the phonograph would have made things easier for these composers, as it has made things easier for their listeners. Debussy, to be sure, had mixed feelings about the Pathé contraption and in this same essay charges that military music among the trees "is like the strident notes of some huge gramophone." But Varèse was to hear the voice of his master Debussy in the new device, recognizing it as the medium of a music "of moving sonic bodies in space," a music equal to the universe.

Here as elsewhere the logical extreme of phonography is electronic music. Stockhausen commented that when one listens to electronic music at home, eyes closed, "the inner eye opens to visions in time and space which overstep what the laws of the physical world around us permit; spatial perspective and the logic of cause and effect in temporal events are both suspended." Cause and effect and spatial perspective are aspects of the phenomenal world, foreign to the will. Stockhausen is here serving Schopenhauer, whether he means to or not. While the human origin of electronic music is a mystery which "there is no point in asking" about, that of ordinary recorded music is a certainty (more or less) which there is no need to think about. In either case you are free to fill your mind with the music itself — or the music with your mind.

When we hear music we expand to fill available space. This is one reason for the Gulliver feeling we get, a feeling of monstrous sensitivity — as though our nerves were stretched across the universe — and vulnerability. (Headphones give this feeling instantly, but in a somewhat different form. While it is hard to say whether my self has expanded or the world has imploded, the violent pri-

EVAN EISENBERG

vacy of the experience makes the sense of implosion stronger. Because the music seems to be coming from inside me, it merges with my direct experience of the will. As a result, the music seems to express my feelings of the moment, even when by its nature it ought to be at odds with them. Another result is that I do not seem to be listening to the music so much as playing it.)

Maybe all art expands the soul. But not all art does it the way music does. For example, architecture should build the soul up, but because our eyes move cautiously across the great spaces we are humbled rather than exalted. The interior of a great cathedral makes us feel small; only when it fills with music does the spirit stretch to its dimensions.

". . . To the man who gives himself up entirely to the impression of a symphony," says Schopenhauer, "it is as if he saw all the possible events of life and of the world passing by within himself." De Quincey, under the influence of opium rather than metaphysics, seems to have felt something similar:

> . . . a chorus, & c., of elaborate harmony, displayed before me, as in a piece of arras work, the whole of my past life — not as if recalled by an act of memory, but as if present and incarnated in the music: no longer painful to dwell upon: but the detail of its incidents removed, or blended in some hazy abstraction; and its passions exalted, spiritualized, and sublimed. All this was to be had for five shillings.

But whether or not one actually "sees" an infinity of images or events, one often has the sense that an hour of music encapsulates a world. A record is a world; even its shape, unchanged from Berliner to the laser disk, suggests this. In rock and roll the spinning disk has other associations, mostly having to do with undirected motion, but there is also the desire to trace a mystic circle around one's own world. "I fled school for the sanctuary of my room," the critic Jim Miller remembers, "where I could summon a world with a choice of singles. That was what rock and roll meant to me."

Every disk is a microcosm, a twelve-inch or four-and-three-quarter-inch world. A shelf of records is a row of possible worlds. Take one out, put it on, and a world unreels, the world one has chosen to live in for the next hour.

How does the record shelf differ from the bookshelf above it? We often think of a book, too, as a world. But a novel, because it refers to specific items of the world's furniture arranged in a conversational grouping, is blessedly partial. It is a room we can escape to from the room we actually live in. It is "a world," but not a whole world, not a version of *the* world. So one can actually read a great novel by Balzac or Jane Austen or Flannery O'Connor as an escape, confident that it will not scrape the tender places of one's daily life. That kind of escape is not so easy with Berlioz, Haydn, or Billie Holiday. (Schopenhauer's explanation of this is different but related: the nonmusical arts let us escape the will by losing ourselves in pure appearance.) Books that try to present a whole world, books of philosophy, and some books of poetry, too often lose their power to touch us. Music alone is at once universal and close to the bone.

Music worthy of the name is greedy, imperious, even when it has lyrics so particular that one could use them to address a letter. It either fits one's mood or contradicts it (or does both); it can no more ignore it than gravity can ignore a stone. When we speak of using music as an escape, we mean we want the gravity of our situation counteracted — not wished away — by the pull of music. We want to reach escape velocity. If it works we are in orbit, circling this world, subject to its deeper laws but seeing it from a higher perspective. Only a handful of books have a comparable reach (no one escapes in a trivial way to Tolstoy or the Vedas or Spinoza).

Suppose I am sitting in a room in no way remarkable, except that the Air from Bach's Third Orchestral Suite is moving through it. I am staring at a patch of rug and the foot of a chair, but absently; what I am really following is the thread of this melody, the walking bass that seems to traverse galaxies at a step. When a record is fitted over the platter, a transparency or slide is fitted over a segment of space and time. The effect is a double exposure. But if the music is worth its salt, it will assert itself as the true reality, and all the lovely furniture of one's room will seem (if one is aware of it at all) a mere picture, a veil of Maya.

Can any other "home entertainment" device pull off this trick — superimpose its own space on the space people live in? Television remains at all times a flat surface, or at best a box in which images dance and wrestle. Books have no relation whatever to the room in which they are read; their space is elsewhere, and we follow them there. Then there is radio, which at times is indistinguishable from the phonograph in this respect; but its real tendency is to conflate my space with other spaces in the world. If the phonograph opens the cramped urban cell into as many worlds as there are records, radio makes the whole world a cozy domestic scene.

In speaking of a double exposure I don't mean that our sense of music must be visual. I mean that it is not just aural; it is the sense of a presence, a reality. We may fill this in with imagined shapes, or we may not. Cavell writes, "Those who miss serious radio will say that, unlike television, it left room for the imagination. That seems to me a wrong praise of imagination, which is ordinarily the laziest, if potentially the most precious, of human faculties. A world of sound is a world of immediate conviction." He is talking about radio drama, but the same goes for music on radio or record. Whether or not imagination's crayon is applied, the reality is there.

An earlier form of this experience is described by Kierkegaard in the first

EVAN EISENBERG

volume of *Either/Or*, where the narrator is obsessed with *Don Giovanni* but would not spend a penny for a ticket. "I stand outside in the corridor; I lean up against the partition which divides me from the auditorium and then the impression is most powerful; it is a world by itself, separated from me; I can see nothing, but I am near enough to hear, and yet so infinitely far away." He does not even want to imagine the Don's appearance, for if one sees him, "one no longer hears him, and in that way he is lost." The Don is not a man but a universal force, "the exuberant joy of life," which animates the entire opera and is "absolutely musical." On a good day, Schopenhauer might hear the will in Don Giovanni.

The effect is not confined to indoor quarters. Thoreau says that music "paints the landscape suddenly as no agriculture, no flowery crop that can be raised." In fact, out of doors it more often paints than opposes what the eye sees. "The murmuring of the breeze," says Debussy, giving his recipe for music *en plein air*, "would be mystically mingled with the rustling of the leaves and the scent of the flowers, since music can unite all of them in a harmony so completely natural that it seems to become one with them. The tall peaceful trees would be like the pipes of a great organ . . ."

Chairs and tables, no less than trees, are objectifications of the will. Even indoors, then, music should at least sometimes paint what we see, deepening its reality instead of contracting it. Schopenhauer says that "we could just as well call the world embodied music as embodied will; this is the reason why music makes every picture, indeed every scene from real life and from the world, at once appear in enhanced significance, and this is, of course, all the greater, the more analogous its melody is to the inner spirit of the phenomenon." Thinking for the moment in terms of analogies of tempo, let us test this. Just as any kind of movement on a screen will seem to synchronize with any music played behind it if there is even the vaguest similarity of tempo, so the music played in one's living room will match whatever goes on there. (John Cage's music and Merce Cunningham's choreography, created independently and then slapped together, are another instance.) But if there is no motion in the room, or the motion is at the far end of the tempo range, then one gets the sense of the visible world as Maya. Out of doors this outcome is possible but less common, since the out-of-doors can seem very nearly as large as music, its motions as graceful and various.

In "The World of the Phonograph," an essay that I read a page of and then put away for two years because it breathed too closely on what I was writing, Paul Rosenfeld tells of a summer spent in a farmhouse where the Orthophonic stood between a screen door and a window looking out on lake, mountain, and sky. Here he discovered the world of the phonograph, "a metaphysical world, very like the physical." In lines as purple as the ghost-poet Holger's he describes how in the chants of the friars of Solesmes he heard "faint opalescent light traveling in streaks across the gray evening clouds"; in the second act of *Tristan*, the womb of the creative earth, "hearth of somber flames"; in the entr'acte of *Khovanshchina* a level near that one but dark as the grave, bearing "the colossal tonnage of the mountains, and with it the world's tragedy." Bach's Toccata and Fugue in D minor had to do with "the angular lightning and the slanting rain," the mechanical play of elemental powers. Brahms was a regal sunset, Mozart a golden, Olympian afternoon, Beethoven "the variegated surface of the earth, a human motion as of a man who strode among the liquid trees, amid fresh winds." The phonograph let Rosenfeld juxtapose works of music with "the natural world that can interpret the experiences they express." Of course, the natural world includes man, and a window open on a city street might give similar insights; indeed, Rosenfeld's imagination was prodded by the human events of "that grave summer of 1931." The concert hall, however, is built to exclude all human events larger than a cough.

"Under the charm of the Dionysian," Nietzsche writes, "nature which has become alienated, hostile, or subjugated, celebrates once more her reconciliation with her lost son, man." But if music might exist without a world, surely it might exist without man. We ought to be modern enough by now to listen to music and hear a world in which the presence of man is contingent, even irrelevant.

Thanks to the atom bomb, we can hear the last movement of Vaughan Williams's Sixth Symphony as a peroration on the absolutely empty field of a future war. (The old composer's rumbling speech, so oddly appended to an early recording, may have been meant by Decca to relieve that emptiness.) But plenty of pre-atomic music can also be heard as nonhuman. Beethoven's outer-space music in the Ninth Symphony — the ascending minor thirds following the words "über Sternen muss er wohnen" — never sounds quite right coming from woodwind players in dinner jackets; it sounds right coming from the blankness of a loudspeaker, preferably one perched on high. But the movement as a whole, to which Nietzsche refers us for a vision of Dionysian ecstasy, remains willfully human. Elsewhere Beethoven, instead of willing away his loneliness, lets it conduct him to icy, untenanted landscapes. The beginning of the Ninth Symphony suggests the creation of the world, an event no human was around to get emotional about. The slow movement of the second quartet in Opus 59 is like a barren planet, unvisited even by the artist who describes it, scattered with ruined porticos and the insteps of statues — or so it seems to me under the influence of the phonograph.

The standard outer-space music of today is electronic, the phonograph finding its own voice. It ranges from video-game blips to the astral extravaganzas of Stockhausen (the first electronic work to be commissioned by a record company, Subotnick's *Silver Apples of the Moon*, falls plunk in the middle of the range). Varèse planned a dramatic work about an astronomer who exchanges signals with Sirius and who, when set upon by the uncomprehending masses, is translated there by *radiation instantanée*. The basis of this story was an American Indian folktale whose hero Varèse connected with the *Übermensch* of Nietzsche.

Let us follow this trail a little farther. Richard Strauss, one of several gray eminences impressed by the young Varèse, wrote his own more direct treatment of Nietzsche's theme. This was not overplayed until Stanley Kubrick used it in *2001: A Space Odyssey*, another story about a man who leaves mankind behind. Immediately the opening fanfare became (like Holst's *The Planets*) a standard audio demonstration piece. The drums and organ could be found in Mouret; what really counted was the sense of galaxies announcing themselves to their chosen one.

Intelligence from another planet is expected to manifest itself in simple geometric shapes. The monolith of *2001* is one such token; and it is easy to feel, as the mighty theme music springs from it, that the disk is another. As it happens, we have chosen the disk as our own envoy to the rest of the sapient universe, such as it may be. At the heart of the spacecraft Voyager II, as it hurries to its appointment unspecified light-years away, is a phonograph with picture instructions that an alien child could understand. On the turntable is a golden record encoded with human music — Bach, Chuck Berry, Balinese gamelan — and, somehow or other, photographs of life on earth. "Billions of years from now," Carl Sagan writes, "our sun will have reduced Earth to a charred cinder. But the Voyager record will still be intact . . . a murmur of an ancient civilization that once flourished . . . on the distant planet Earth."

Officially, the medium was chosen for its simplicity and permanence (a golden record is permanent if you don't play it). Deeper reasons are suggested by the cover art of the book *Murmurs of Earth*, which shows the golden record afloat in space, at home among the other orbs. A record is a world. It is the world scratched by man in a form that may survive him.

R. MURRAY SCHAFER

# Music and the Soundscape

In *The Tuning of the World* I predicted that by the end of the century music and the soundscape would draw together. We have passed the end of the century; there is no need to retract what I said. I meant that the reciprocal influences between what we call music and what we refer to as environmental sound would become so complex that these hitherto distinct genera would begin to syncretize into a new art form. I was speaking of the Western world. In other parts of the world the two types have never been completely distinct, and though they now begin to show signs of separating, I wouldn't care to predict what will happen in places beyond my listening experience.

To understand the momentum for blending today it is first necessary to show how Western music differs from soundmaking elsewhere. In the Western tradition music is an abstract entertainment for the pleasure of the ears alone. The word *abstract* is emphatic. Listeners are not encouraged to associate music with functions or purposes beyond the aesthetic enjoyment it provides. Functional music is relegated to a lower order and music that is made to serve political, mercantile or even religious purposes is always under critical suspicion. Religious music sometimes escapes censure because so many Western composers wrote so much of it; but the conservatories and concert halls where it is taught and performed have been careful to minimize whatever religious messages it may sustain, concentrating on its aesthetic merits.

In order to achieve this purity it was necessary to separate music from the soundscape. The soundscape is a plenum. The music room is a vacuum. Music fills it. Without music in it, it is scarcely a room at all: chairs, a stage, music stands and a podium, these are its scant furnishings. But there is a method in this arrangement. All the chairs face the stage and all the sounds will come from here. This will be the exclusive focus of attention during the concert. No longer are we at the center of the soundscape with sounds reaching us from all directions; now they reach us from one direction only, and to appreciate them we must point our ears, just as we point our eyes when we read. In this quiet space the composer will be able to fashion much more intricate structures than were possible outdoors. The music has a definite beginning and ending.

The audience will arrive before the beginning and remain until after the ending, sitting in rows facing the performers. They have voluntarily surrendered the use of their bodies and their feet and will use only their hands and voices to express their appreciation at the end of the music. In order not to distract from the listening process, the performers also move as inconspicuously as possible and their faces are neutral and expressionless.

Definitely the concert promises psychic rather than somatic satisfaction, and the composer uses the concentration of the audience to arrange his material in a vast architecture of principal and secondary themes, transitions, harmonic centers, modulations, instrumental interplay and dynamic shading — an ideal soundscape of the imagination, elegant, controlled, dissonance-disciplined and invigorating. The economist Jacques Attali claims to find the clue to the political economy of nineteenth-century Europe in the concert of the eighteenth century, dutifully listened to by the bourgeoisie and faithfully transmuted into a harmonious industrial order in which commodities flowed out to fill the world just as tones had filled the music hall.[1]

Sometimes I have thought the traditional sonata form is a model for a colonial empire: first theme (loud), the mother nation; second theme (softer), the supine colony; then follows the rhetorical and occasionally pugilistic exchanges of the development section, the *rapprochement* of the mother and colony in the recapitulation (both now in the home key), and the coda — consolidation of the empire. The classical music of Europe during the era of colonial expansion was a music of departures and conquests, exciting openings and exultant conclusions. That this form of music-making is unusual among world cultures is by now quite well-known. Elsewhere music is effortlessly associated with dance, with physical tasks, with religious rituals and healing ceremonies of all kinds. In those cultures there are many musics, each associated with special activities and celebrations.

In many cultures the word *music* does not exist at all. In Africa, for example, there is no term corresponding to music in Tiv, Yoruba, Igbo, Efik, Birom, Hausa, Idoma, Eggon or the assorted Jarawa dialects; and many other languages have qualifying terms that only partly touch our concept of music.[2] The same is true in other parts of the world: the Inuit have no generic term for music, nor can it be found in most North American Indian languages. Much of the soundmaking in these cultures might better be described as tone magic. There is a special kind of music for healing, another for bringing rain, another to ensure a successful hunt or to defeat one's enemies, etc. Even though they may all use voices and instruments, for the people in these cultures, they are not united and must never be confused. We recall also that the ancient Greeks originally employed the word *mousike* for a whole range of spiritual and intellectual activities before it gradually took on the more restricted meaning we have inherited. Ours is a special concept, nourished in the crucible of European civilization, from which it went out (along with Europeans) to many other parts of the world. What makes it special is its abstraction from daily life, its exclusivity. It has become an activity that requires silence for its proper presentation — containers of silence called music rooms. It exhibits the signs of a cult or a religion and to those outside who have not been initiated into its rituals it must appear strange and abnormal.

The thick walls of European architecture have been a shaping force behind the development of European music from Gregorian chant to serialism. In fact it would be possible to write the entire history of European music in terms of walls, showing not only how the varying resonances of its performance spaces have affected its harmonics, tempi and timbres, but also to show how its social character evolved once it was set apart from everyday life.

The great revolutions in art history are changes of context rather than style. The first big contextual change in Western music occurred when music left the outdoors and entered the cathedral; the second occurred with the appearance of the concert hall and opera house; the broadcasting and recording studio is responsible for the third. Each context produced a plethora of styles but all were governed by the laws of the container in which they were generated. The music of the cathedral is unseen; it rises vapor-like to fill a large resonant space, restricting harmonic and melodic mobility to produce a hazy wash of sound blending with the mystique of Christianity's invisible God. The music of the concert hall and opera house is both seen and heard. Dryer acoustics favor faster-paced music with greater harmonic daring. It is the music of the soloist and the quick-tempered virtuoso. The broadcasting and recording studio introduced the world to schizophonia, or split sound, in which any sonic environment could, by means of loudspeakers, be substituted for any other. It pushed music into new places — in fact, any place — and prepared the way for the coalescence we are now experiencing.

The other great context for music is the original one, the outdoor environment, and this still survives as the one in which much, and perhaps most of the world's music, is produced. It is the context of street music, of the outdoor band or orchestra, of the shepherd with his Pan pipe or of women singing at the village pump. It is the context of tribal music the world over. As such, it is inclusive rather than exclusive and tends to be free rather than purchased. But above all, it blends with whatever other sounds are present. It does not seek walls for protection or an impounded audience for its appreciation.

The perception of sound can most easily be studied from the artifacts and contexts of music. This is not the only way to study the subject, but the history of music, with its cultural variants, provides a repertoire from which deductions can be made about what different eras were expected to hear, and equally

R. MURRAY SCHAFER

what they missed, for in the study of any soundscape what is missed is just as important as what is listened to, perhaps more so. This is the "ground" in the figure-ground relationship, and although such sounds are ignored, they are immediately noticed if they are withdrawn or if attention is directed towards them. Air-conditioning and heating systems are present in this way for modern urban listeners; so is traffic noise. (Recently, listening to a recording of music by the thirteenth-century composer Adam de la Halle, I detected the faint rumbling of traffic, anachronous to Adam's world but evidently inaudible to the recording engineers.)

The medieval schoolmen spoke of God as a presence whose center is every-where and circumference nowhere. It is an acoustic definition of God — as Marshall McLuhan frequently used to point out. It also conforms to listening habits conditioned by plainsong heard in the cathedral, where the singers' voices waft through the space, filling it like incense. Wherever one moves in the cathedral one is always in the middle of the sound. The concert hall, on the other hand, induced focused listening, that is, a rank-ordering of sounds in the same way that perspective painting rank-orders objects, reducing the size of the less important and moving them to the distance. Composers of the nine-teenth century specialized in this dialectic of foreground, middleground and background by means of dynamic shading.

Focused listening contrasts with peripheral listening, in which the ear re-mains open to sounds from any direction or distance, scanning the environ-ment for information from anywhere. It is the perceptual attitude of people who live outdoors or whose jobs involve movement from one place to an-other. The world is always full of sounds. They come from far and near, high and low; they are discrete and continuous, loud and soft, natural, human and technological. They enter and depart in processions as events pass us or we pass by them. This is why the music of the streets has no beginning or end but is all middle. Something is already in progress before our arrival and it suc-ceeds our departure. The dynamics of the sound are a product of its position in space rather than shaping by the performer.

With this in mind we might again consider how certain outdoor environ-ments have been deliberately planned as itineraries through the soundscape. Certainly there are courtly Italian and French gardens laid out in such a way as to encourage the attractive passage past fountains, grottos or aviaries, and the long elegant pathways to the belvedere seem perfect for musical processions. One can scarcely visit those gardens today without imagining the festive enter-tainments that once glorified them. The gardens of Versailles were once the site of lavish operatic and theatrical entertainments during which the pathways and lake were illuminated by thousands of candles in silver candelabra while the fountains played through colored lights. "After listening to the opera or a play by Racine or Molière the king and his court would promenade until dawn or embark in flower-wreathed gondolas on the lake."[3]

On the other side of the world is the seventeenth-century Kiyomizudera (Clear Water Temple) in Kyoto, Japan. I recall walking through the ample garden with the composer Toru Takemitsu, beneath the *butai* platform where the great *gagaku* orchestras once performed. We followed the paths between the blossoms, listening to the birds and imagining how the ancient music must have sounded. Suddenly I realized how cleverly everything had been laid out to facilitate the blending of the loud and soft sounds by means of the winding path.

Years later, when I wrote *Musique pour le parc Lafontaine*, I tried to devise a routine for the musicians within this very large Montreal park that would blend both close and distant sounds for listeners no matter where they happened to be. The piece is itinerant, with the musicians constantly forming and reforming at different locations in the park, sometimes playing in processions, sometimes remaining static in geometrical formations. The work closed by passing a series of phrases from one player to the next along four branches of a cross from the center to the periphery of the park, where another group of instrumentalists slowly moved a repeated motif in a vast circle nearly a kilometer in circumference.

When we move music from one context to another, everything changes since effects intended for one situation must be adapted to another. Listening attitudes also change. The attention of anyone in the open soundscape will constantly be flickering from one point to another; attractions of focus will be rare and unpredictable. This is what radio discovered when it deserted the living room for public spaces; program structures had to be disassembled for casual listening. Music also underwent changes: for instance, the fade-ins and the fade-outs of popular music began to simulate the effect of music passing us by, as in fact it does from the windows of open cars or store fronts.

The influences of the soundscape on music are reciprocated by musical influences on the soundscape. The diatonic tuning of car horns or train whistles are obvious examples. Right now we are witnessing the growth of synthesized tunes played from moving vehicles selling products such as ice cream (North America), propane (Brazil) or used clothes (Italy). The tunes are always well-known and often come from the classical repertoire, but almost all of them contain at least one melodic inaccuracy, due, I suppose, to the tin ear of the engineer who programmed them. In this way the "fake" transmogrifications of well-known melodies are rendered "real" for countless millions of people the world over so that the real tune, if ever heard again, will *sound wrong*; and engineers with no musical ability whatever become musical arrangers of incredible influence. This is how the soundscape of the modern world is being designed, failing more objective or aesthetic values.

R. MURRAY SCHAFER

Where the reciprocity between music and the soundscape is effectively intuited, the interaction can be like that of text and subtext, as when the rhythms of work or the motions of tools inspire the singer, or bird song inspires the flutist. Folk musicians the world over have attested to the effect of environmental sounds on their music, which is often an homage to the *pays age sonore*, as when a fiddle player was said to be able to imitate "the squeak of a gopher . . . crows calling; an anvil on a winter day . . . jack rabbits bouncing off, a goshawk drifting high . . . a flock of geese."[4] And now I am thinking of a visit I made to hear an old peasant woman sing her own folksongs high in the mountains of Argentina. The audition took place in the yard of her farmhouse where we sat on tattered straight-backed chairs while the skins of freshly killed sheep dried on the clothesline, and roosters crowed in perfect unison with her singing, which consisted almost exclusively of leaps of fourths and fifths. She said the inspiration for her songs came while she made *empanadas* in her kitchen; and I don't think she realized how closely they synchronized with the sounds of her yard.

Concert music also often evoked the more populous environment beyond the music room as a kind of nostalgia. Hunting horns or spinning wheels or locomotives found representation here. In fact, the music room often assumes a kind of virtual space that is broader than its enclosure, as when soft sounds seem to fall away to the acoustic horizon or a loud sound seems to push right into the body. The frequency range of the music is another unconscious imitation of the external soundscape. Mozart's music is made up of mid- and high-frequency sounds as was his world, whereas the heavy infrasound of the modern city is reproduced in the guitars of the modern rock group.

Composers have often been explicit about inspirations drawn from the soundscape. A couple of examples will do. Wagner describes how an alphorn invaded *Tristan:*

> This act promises famously; I drew profit from it even from my Riga excursion. At four in the morning we were roused by the Boots with an Alphorn — I jumped up and saw it was raining and returned to bed to try to sleep; but the droll call went droning round my head and out of it arises a very lusty melody which the herdsman now blows to signal Isolde's ship, making a surprising merry and naive effect.[5]

George Gershwin's *Rhapsody in Blue* was inspired by a train journey:

> It was on the train, with its steely rhythms, its rattlety-bang that is so often stimulating to a composer (I frequently hear music in the very heart of noise), that I suddenly heard — even saw on paper — the complete construction of the *Rhapsody* from beginning to end. . . . I heard it as a sort of musical kaleidoscope of America — of our vast melting-pot, of our incomparable

national pep, our blues, our metropolitan madness. By the time I reached Boston, I had the definite plot of the piece, as distinguished from its actual substance.[6]

Europeans will be unfamiliar with the jazz rhythms produced by the short-section unwelded tracks of the American railroad (European rails are welded in long lengths), nor will they know how the three-tone triadic steam whistle could be warped by echoes and doppler shifts to suggest blue notes. But Walt Whitman sensed these variants when in a poem called "To a Locomotive in Winter" he penned a line of shifting *ee*'s: "Thy trills of shrieks by rocks and hills returned."

Another American composer, Morton Feldman, recalled how he gathered all the material he needed for a percussion piece (*The King of Denmark*) while sitting on a beach on Long Island.

> I wrote it in a few hours, just sitting comfortably on the beach. And I can actually conjure up the memory of doing it — that kind of muffled sound of kids in the distance and transistor radios and drifts of conversation from other pockets of inhabitants on blankets, and I remember that it all came into the piece, these kinds of wisps.[7]

And this from Olivier Messiaen:

> In my hours of gloom, when I am suddenly aware of my own futility . . . what is left for me but to seek out the true, lost face of music, somewhere off in the forest, in the fields, in the mountains or on the seashore, among the birds.[8]

I could go on giving examples of this sort from almost every major Western composer to show that they were never indifferent to the sounds around them and frequently sought ways of incorporating these sounds into their work. It is a relatively unexplored chapter in music theory. For years I have tried to draw musicologists' attention to the fact that most of the world's music exists in counterpoise to the soundscape. Ethnomusicologists understand this but it has rarely been acknowledged by those specializing in the history of Western music. To them music is thought to be inspired by music alone: Vivaldi inspiring Bach, Bach inspiring Mozart, Mozart inspiring nearly everybody. The music schools teach of the revolutions of style: Beethoven throwing off Classicism, Debussy rejecting diatonic harmony, Schoenberg embarking on atonality. But these are mere skirmishes compared to the great contextual changes that have shaken the foundations of the art and are shaking it again today.

A few years ago the Viennese music sociologist Kurt Blaukopf began a series of studies in what he called the "non-musical use of music." He sensed an atrophy in the concentration habits of Western listeners as a result of the technical changes brought about by the new media. We all realize the extent to which music is losing its focus. It strikes us at odd times and odd places. Often two or more pieces of music can be heard in a single environment and many other sounds as well. Sometimes while shopping we hear the music of one establishment superimposed over that of another, like an overprinted photograph. Sometimes I have walked in shopping malls late at night and have overheard music playing to no one. And I have imagined a plane crash in which the only survivor will be the recorded music.

It is as if by some law of enantiodromia the Western notion of music is exploding in our faces, breaking out all around us, hemorrhaging into new environments. Certainly the power centers in society are shifting, multiplying, so that the authority once accorded to the concert as the nodal point for musical stimulation has withered. European concert music gradually refined itself into states where even its most devoted listeners were reluctant to follow it (I mean ISCM festivals and the like); but even in its healthiest state it had given rise to a kind of aural hypertrophy in which the ear was not only isolated from the other senses but was even isolated from its more normal habits of functioning.

When I wrote the booklet *The New Soundscape* in 1968 I proclaimed the new orchestra: anything and everything that sounds! I wanted people to begin to think of the soundscape as a macrocosmic composition in which we are all involved, and asked the question whether the orchestration could be improved. Today there are enclaves of acoustic design activity in many countries, but I have been especially intrigued by Japan's contribution, for it seems to combine fresh innovation with a traditional sensitivity to the environment. The Japanese word for music, *ongaku*, simply means the enjoyment of sounds; it is an inclusive rather than an exclusive concept. Thus the Tea Master may make music with his kettle.

> The kettle sings well, for pieces of iron are so arranged in the bottom as to produce a peculiar melody in which one may hear the echoes of a cataract muffled by clouds, of a distant sea breaking among the rocks, a rainstorm sweeping through a bamboo forest, or of the soughing of pines on some faraway hill.[9]

It is just such a kettle that Kawabata describes in his novel *Snow Country*.

> He could make out two pine breezes . . . a near one and a far one. Just beyond the far breeze he heard faintly the tinkling of a bell. He put his ear to the kettle and listened. Far away, where the bell tinkled on, he suddenly saw Komako's feet, tripping in time with the bell.[10]

The synaesthesia suggested by aural illusions is never despised by the Japanese; on the contrary, it is cultivated. In the game known as *Ko wo kiku*, "listening to the incense," each scent is inhaled ceremoniously and then passed to the ear, as if somehow the resolving power of one sense was not enough to extract complete meaning, the experience being additionally complicated by the allusive name given each incense, intended to recall some scene or passage from a romance or legend.

From an active group of soundscape researchers I learned how Japanese gardeners traditionally cultivated the many variations that water produces, not only in their placement of rocks in the beds of streams to modulate the sound, but also in their use of decorative bamboo irrigation pumps (*shishiodoshi*) that tip when filled with water and drop back against stones producing pleasant hollow pitches.

One researcher, Yu Wakao, had devoted himself to the study of water harps — resonating jars, buried under rock basins where the hands were washed before entering the tea house. The jars, which served no purpose, were set so that the spilled water that dropped into them would produce a melodic cascade of hollow pitches from below. The water harps are only found in the oldest gardens; the tradition seems to have been abandoned about two hundred years ago, but the soundscape group hopes to revive it.

These are examples of a consciousness that allows the beauty of sound to expand and permeate the whole of life; it would be futile to debate whether such things were music.

Wondering what made this thinking possible, I came to the conclusion that the traditional Japanese paper house had a good deal to do with it. One can still see such houses in Kyoto and throughout the Japanese countryside, houses with large sliding doors, carefully covered with rice paper. When slid back they open to beautiful enclosed gardens, the light and sounds of which reach in to fill the rudimentary and seemingly famished spaces of the house. Of course, in modern Japan (in Tokyo) such houses are seldom seen. They have been replaced by buildings of glass and concrete smudged with Muzak, for insulation from the natural environment requires cosmetics.

It seems necessary to point out that the rice-paper window is different from the glazed window. Glass resists sound; rice paper invites its penetration. Glazing is a European treatment of wall openings — the result of a primarily visual consciousness; rice paper suggests aural awareness. I am reminded too that in traditional Japanese society young women were taught how to slide open such doors and windows without making unnecessary noise. Prospective mothers-in-law would test them on this refinement. The Western equivalent would be learning to crochet or managing a tea service.

R. MURRAY SCHAFER

It is the absence of walls and doors that allows the Japanese, like many other people around the world, to imagine a music that may impart beauty to the environment without being self-centered or wishing to dominate the entire soundspace. The sound sculptures of Akinoti Matsumoto are typical of this unstrained attitude. A kind of *bricolage*, they are created out of simple materials to be found in any hardware shop. One of these consists of nothing more than a length of plastic fishing line with a hook at one end to attach to the ceiling and a weight at the bottom to hold it taut. Down it slither a large number of small aluminum tubes of varying lengths, drilled at one end and passed through the line. As they descend they shake, touching their neighbors to produce a delicate tintinnabulation.

Another instrument consists of a series of thin metal bars, slowly raised by a small electric motor to fall back in turn on a series of strings tuned to different frequencies. The tempo of the falling bars is very slow so that I was more reminded of the single flowers in vases one often finds in the corners of Japanese homes, or isolated calligraphy scrolls on walls, than anything approaching a music instrument.

The sound environments of Hiroshi Yoshimura have similar intentions. This is what he has to say of Sound Process Design:

> What we are attempting to do, speaking generally, can be called sound design. This includes the adjustment and regulation of sound proper to an environment, along with the composition of music for environments. Possibly for a given environment just one sound would be sufficient. Sound design doesn't mean simply decorating with sound. The creation of non-sound — in other word, silence — would, if possible, be wonderful in a design.
>
> There is no question that our age, in which we are inundated with sound, is unprecedented in history. We need to develop a more caring attitude towards sounds. Presently the amount of sound and music in the environment have clearly exceeded man's capacity to assimilate them, and the audio ecosystem is beginning to fall apart. Background music, which is supposed to create atmosphere, is far too excessive. In our present condition we find that within certain areas and spaces aspects of visual design are well attended to, but sound design is completely ignored. It is necessary to treat sound and music with the same respect that we show for architecture, interior design, food, or the air we breathe.
>
> "Wave Motion" was begun as an environment music series. This music could be said to be an "object" or a kind of sound scenery to be listened to casually [peripherally]. Not being music which excites the listener into another world, it should drift like smoke and become part of the environment

surrounding the listener's activity. . . . This is not music of self expression, not a "completed work of art," rather it is music which changes the character and meaning of space, things and people by overlapping and shifting.[11]

Yoshimura's music exists for spaces. I have heard it in galleries, where it leads nowhere but affects the space it inhabits, changing it in subtly perceptible ways. It is mostly synthesizer music, and this assists its purpose, for the synthesizer is an apparatus of all modern cultures and therefore belongs to none. Most of the background music we know is attached to known instruments and these instruments, as well as playing styles, connect it with specific periods and places: the guitar is Spanish, the accordion is Bohemian, etc. One could listen to the Muzak system in any international hotel or airport and be doused almost exclusively with American tunes played on vintage European instruments. This is how cultural hegemonies are secured, by subliminal advertising.

There is something to be said for the use of innocuous soundmakers in acoustic design, and there is something to be said for indigenous instruments to establish unique character. When a sound object is known and loved it functions more as a sensory anchor, assuring us that we are at home even when other features of the environment are alien or intimidating.

The soundscape designer should know these things. He belongs to no camp; he understands the requirements of the situation, adding to one and subtracting from another. He also knows the value of silence. Through his work, music, environmental sounds and silence are woven together artistically and therapeutically to bring about a new consciousness where art and life touch, merge and are lost in one another.

### Notes

1. Jacques Attali, *Bruits* (Paris, 1977), pp. 93ff.

2. Charles Keil, *Tiv Song* (Chicago and London, 1979), p. 27.

3. Clement Antrobus Harris and Mary Hargrave, *The Earlier French Musicians* (London, 1916), p. 21.

4. W. O. Mitchell, *Who Has Seen the Wind* (Toronto, 1947), p. 189.

5. Letter to Minna, quoted in *The Musical Quarterly*, vol. XXXI, no. 4, October 1945, p. 411.

6. Quote from the Everest Record dust jacket of *Rhapsody in Blue,* William Steinberg conducting the Pittsburgh Symphony Orchestra.

7. "An interview with Morton Feldman," in *Percussive Notes*, vol. 21, no. 6, September 1983, pp. 5–6.

8. Olivier Messiaen, *Le guide de concert,* 3 April 1959. Quoted from John Paynter, *Sound and Structure* (Cambridge, 1992), pp. 42–43.

9. Okakura Kakuzo, *The Book of Tea* (Tokyo, 1956), p. 63.

10. Yasunari Kawabata, *Snow Country* (Tokyo, 1957), p. 155.

11. From a broadsheet, Tokyo, 1983.

R. MURRAY SCHAFER

TSAI CHIH CHUNG

# The Music of the Earth

"Music from the Earth" comes from *Zhuanzi Speaks: The Music of Nature,* a comic book inspired by the earliest portions of the Zhuangzi, a major Taoist text. It was adapted and illustrated by the prolific and tremendously popular Taiwanese cartoonist Tsai Chih Chung, and translated by Brian Bruya. Zhuangzi (369?–286? B.C.), one of the Taoist writers whose existence can be historically verified, believed that listening to the "music of nature" could point us toward a natural way of living that embraces an attitude of spontaneity.

TSAI CHIH CHUNG

TSAI CHIH CHUNG

# II
## Wild Echoes

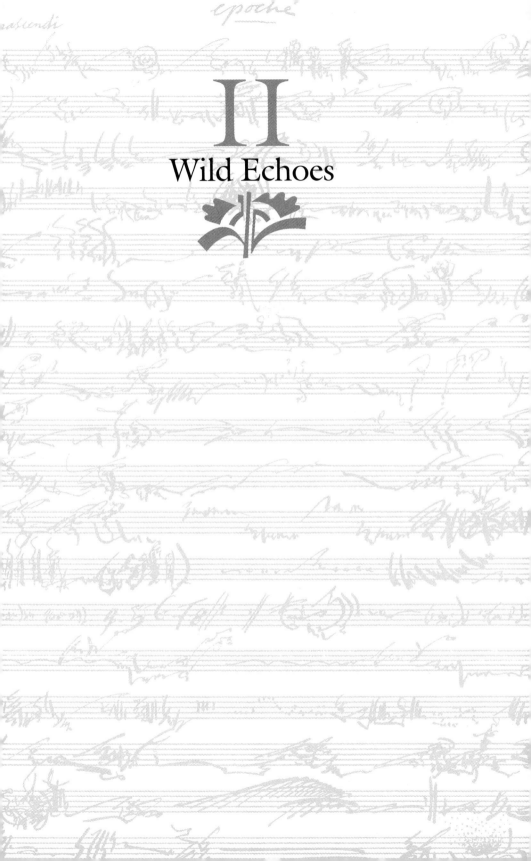

RAFI ZABOR

# From *The Bear Comes Home*

*Rafi Zabor's PEN Faulkner Award–winning novel* The Bear Comes Home *is a most serious book about a bear who plays the saxophone. Fantastical but real, the animal, of course a resident of Bearsville, New York, home to many a famous jazz player, here steps up to the stage with the Art Ensemble of Chicago, one of the greatest and most wide-ranging groups in jazz today.*

In the event, the music had been interesting.

After standing with the band in silence facing east — a nice moment actually, an effective tune-up — things had begun in a rumor of gongs and birdcalls, and the Bear had stayed out of it, a few stray notes excepted. Standing at his bass, Malachi Favors began muttering into a bullhorn, Lester was breathing hoarsely in and out of his horn, and something in these gathering strands of music caught on his fur and before he knew it he was involved in a converse of whispers with Roscoe Mitchell on the other alto while Joseph Jarman roamed the gong-world behind him, occasionally punctuating the groundswell with a bicycle horn. Now, the Bear had never considered himself a flat-out free atonal player — he hoped he sounded like himself, though it was pretty obvious he came out of Bird, Ornette and Jackie McLean — but as he and Roscoe tangled further and drums and bass came up under them like some thickening storm and Jarman raised a rattle of bells and chimes before the rising wind, in a matter of minutes the Bear was involved in successive tumults of freeblow with Roscoe's pretty much atonal alto, and the band's whole sound rose up in a wave. When the crescendo subsided, the rest of the night was blown clear of obstruction, and the Bear went into it happily and without much worry. The audience, which applauded pretty much on schedule after each of the music's episodes, didn't bother him either.

There was a long sort-of blues, the rhythm section solid, Malachi Favors' bass huge and warm without, the Bear noticed in some surprise, the benefit of amplification. The Bear had some fun with Bowie, trading choruses, then drifting into some less marked-out call and response. There was a long percussion jam in which he crossed the stage, grabbed a mallet and whomped away at a big bass drum, and then someone called Jarman's impossibly uptempo Coltrane tribute, "Ohnedaruth," and all the horn players blew their brains out in succession. Bowie played last, pulled out his pistol at the end of his outing and emptied his clip of blanks into the lights.

So far so good, thought the Bear as he squeezed tight on the reed and blew out a skirl of multiphonics, but then Bowie, looking as if he'd gone mad for all the scientific sobriety of his labcoat, reached into his pocket, loaded another clip into the automatic and fired another brace of blanks into the avid, crowded tables of the nightclub yelling, "Bang bang bang motherfuckers," and a busload of tourists at a row of tables near the front — some tour director must have sent them to see the Art Ensemble by mistake or for laughs — who had been only mildly alarmed at the first shots and the presence of what seemed to be an actual bear onstage now went into blind panic, flinging chairs aside and bolting through the tightly packed crowd for the exit. Their panic spread through the club, no one sure what had happened or what had not, and it pretty much cleared the house. The band retired backstage laughing, Jarman threatening to kill Lester Bowie twice, and the Bear stood there onstage looking through pistol smoke.

He heard Jones calling from the club's front door, but he also saw a lone figure seated at a table, and the Bear's jaw dropped in deference: it was Ornette Coleman: the master: he made me.

The Bear stepped down from the stage through the remaining gunsmoke and walked to Ornette's table. Ornette was wearing a black silk suit and he seemed untroubled by the gunshots and the emptying of the club. He smiled up at the Bear. "That was interesting," Ornette said in a faraway, gentle voice, "but what I wonder, even though you play a thousand times better than I ever could, was how come you play so much like a human person. What I would like to know is do you transpose from bear to human and if so why you do it, because if I played with you what I'd like is for you to play bear without transposing and I could play like me even if I don't know if that says man and then we could see what the total added up to if no one did the adding. You know?"

Even though he felt the hemispheres of his brain crossing, the Bear was sure Ornette was right. Why *did* he transpose? Why was he so weak as to want to assimilate? "You're right," he told Ornette redundantly.

"You see," Ornette told him, "I think you play quadripedally, so what would a quadripedal tone be if you didn't transpose it to two-footed music. That would be the really interesting thing. By the way," he said, "I wouldn't worry about the audience leaving. They used to walk out on me all the time."

"Bear," he heard Jones calling, "there's a mob out on the street and I think I hear a siren."

"Let's play sometime," Ornette suggested.

"Maybe we could leave together," said the Bear.

"No that's all right," Ornette told him. "I'd like to hear the rest of the set." He gestured up at the empty stage.

29 November 1995  GHOST TRANCE MUSIC

Live transmission; hand movements of Gregor Kitzis and Anthony Braxton
improvising on violin, toy violin and blaster / Knitting Factory, new york city /

Myn O'H—

## Sax Can Moo . . .

# SAX CAN MOO...

**SAX CAN** MOO MEOW SQUEAK **SPEAK**

GROWL SQUAWK                                    MOAN
                        BARK HONK PURR BLEAT WHINNY

**GROAN** RASP ROAR BRAY HOWL sHOUT QUACK COUGH

NEIGH CHIRP GAG GRUNT LAUGH BURP...............

...HISS KISS WHINE SIGH HOOT PEEP PIPE POP SHAKE ZAP HUSH

SCREA

CHEER FEAR TAP WOO CROAK CROW COO SNiP SN AP SLAP

WHISTLE CACKLE CLUCK CLACK CLICK WHEEZE WHOOSH RASP HACK CROON DROO

SPUTTER UTTER MUTTER FLUTTER TWITTer TITTe

SLAVER WHiSPER WHEEDLE SLURP SUCK HACK      YOCK YAK SN

SLATHER DANCE SING WHIMPER PICK PECK SNEEZE TEASE      F R E

SCRAPE SMACK WHACK GLISS GLIDE SNEER SMEAR LEER

P BAP siP BUZZ PANT SNORE FART GULP SHRIEK YODEL

UCKLE CHORTLE GURGLE GIGGLE WHIRR BARK CAW HICCUP WAIL STUTTER

HUDDer CHATTer SHATTer SOB

IGGER PEAL QUAKE YAWN WOOF YOWL CHEEP SNORT FIZZLE SNIFFLE DRONE

 E

# From *Piano Pieces*

To play the piano is to consort with nature. Every mollusk, galaxy, vapor, or viper, as well the sweet incense of love's distraction, is within the hands and grasp of the pianist. The result may be a mess or a blessing, but too often resembles a de facto hand-me-down, a vestigial imitation, a weary if wily synthetic.

Sound is the ether which sustains and infuses the universe. But not the one isolated sound, always groupings and multiples of sound. A single sound is but a vanity, a betrayal of communion and community. The presumed beauty of a single tone is rather like Helen without Troy: a narcotic without dreams. Before the invention of ecology there was merely consort: a calculus of variegated sonorities in a four-dimensional phase, a topological dance choreographed by Balanchine but in sound.

When the shepherd sings, the earth moans, the wind murmurs, the aspen trembles. Each refrain is but a response to a chorale audible only to Schumann's elect, to the better and silent portion of human character. When Artur Schnabel said that he played the rests, if not the notes, better than other pianists, he was acknowledging that subliminal choir only silence can reveal.

Cantabile is the cartilage connecting any two sounds, whether made by bone or braying. It is the silken fiber which binds two grains, two islands, two exiles. It is the urge to fathom, to accept, to exonerate the alien gasps of mistrust, the lonely pleas, the harsh deeds, the frigid icons. It is the necklace and DNA of the chain of being. It is, according to Beethoven, the most important thing in piano playing.

By itself even the sweetest tuned tone is an aberration. Beautiful tone, the adornment of our profession, is ultimately a narcissistic void. There are only tones, tones to be gathered like berries or shells, and to be strung together after scrupulous investigation of the chemistry of shells and berries and of their mating habits. And how do shells and berries mate? Listen to the left hand in recordings by Rachmaninoff, to the network of responsiveness it authors and its relationship to the melody.

A tone is beautiful only in context. Or as Edward Steichen pointed out, in the first stage of photography one is interested exclusively in the foreground tree. In the next stage, the surrounding shrubs and grasses become the focal point. Then finally we turn back to the tree, but within the dynamic of reciprocal planes. The conductor Charles Munch once said that the reason God gave us two ears was so that what goes in one may go out the other. God also gave us two hands. What one reports, the other retorts.

Each hand has two parts, in dire and direct opposition. Thus the thumb works against the fingers, creating two prongs which form a flexing claw to explore the spectrum of sound. But most pianists play with one hand, all quarters falling into an amorphous and garbled blend of sound, whether smooth or coarse. A minority play with two hands, approximating the zones of high and low. A few elect to play with four hands, the thumbs like horns and violas. The effect can be like spinning objects in curved space, near and far, the fixed poles of illusion and reality dissembled, disarmed, and disarming.

John Constable observed that the art of reading nature is no less "acquired" than the art of reading hieroglyphics. To grasp and delineate the relationship between melody and bass is no less elusive. One may speculate that the topic of free will versus predestination should be thoroughly researched (or splendidly intuited) before melody and bass, the surrogates for fantasy and fate, can be properly matched. Therefore, the logical starting point for the education of a pianist might well be the study of Greek tragedy.

The idea of technique is consistently misunderstood. People think that piano technique is a matter of double thirds, fast octaves, and such specialized tricks, analogous to the current debasement of figure skating into nothing more than a series of triple axels and toe loops separated by long intervals of coasting and prayer. Technique, like poetry, is but handmaiden to the music, and should be entirely at the service of the imagination. Without imagination there is no technique, only facility. Catching a sound, like catching a fish, is a function not of physical prowess but of the hand's sensitivity in gauging the currents and resistance of the musical flow.

The hand must be supple. As the Navajo tradition advises, we should move through space with the lightness of a hummingbird. But as the athletes counsel, our actions, our motions must begin with the larger muscles of the torso, with the legs and the back. The balance and buoyancy which can derive only from the back's support is a necessary precondition to the flexibility of the hand. The hand may caress only because the back sustains. The resulting lightness of hand expresses itself through the reciprocal oscillation of thumb and fingers, which may vibrate as rapidly as the wings of a bird or as slowly as the arms of a Balinese dancer.

To know the piano is to know the universe. To master the piano is to master the universe. The spectrum of piano sound acts as a prism through which all musical and nonmusical sounds may be filtered. The grunts of sheep, the braying of mules, the popping of champagne corks, the sighs of unrequited love, not to mention the full lexicon of sounds available to all other instruments — including whistles, scrapes, bleatings, caresses, thuds, hoots, plus sweet and sour pluckings — fall within the sovereignty of this most bare and dissembling chameleon.

Ontogeny recapitulates phylogeny. The human organism embraces the history of its evolutionary ancestors. The human hand echoes the manifold talents of animal limbs, from slithering to rending. Every gesture of our hand at the piano is indebted to the memory and model of some animal's magical properties of motion and locomotion. When our playing is dead, dry, dehydrated, dogmatic, or dormant, it is often because we have forgotten our ancestors.

The hand is structured; the hand is fluid. Both paradigms are true, and both co-exist; but they must be individually addressed before their ultimate integration.

The sequence of development typically proceeds as follows: (1) the child's hand is initially resilient, spongy, amorphous; (2) some degree of structure and conformation is imposed, if only by way of analogy to patterns of meter and mode; (3) after the hand has developed an "appropriate" position capable of clarifying and controlling the notes, the demands of expression and virtuosity require some loosening of the outer mold. Nevertheless, while flexibility is vital, it should not subvert a basic concept of profile and organization.

As in every athletic activity, there is a continuous dynamic embracing both static and moving components. The contemporary love affair with viscous fluidity, activated against the demonic pariah of tension, is no less exaggerated than an earlier model of the hand so rigid that it could support a dime on its back while in motion.

Tension: the great bugaboo, bit, and gulag of enlightened folk. On the other side, for rejecting loose indulgence and all its languorous dissipations, there is the law-and-order constabulary (but now in eclipse). In the middle is the poor piano student, set adrift by the current apostles of free ride, free fall, free lunch, all blessed with a shot of Zen.

There are certain things, however, to keep in mind. Zen serendipity, legitimately admired, is yet based upon a highly structured regimen which does not

RUSSELL SHERMAN

allow for random choice (or nonchoice) until all aspects and all possible solutions to a problem have been exhausted. Moral: when one knows the notes, the rhythms, the passages, and the memory inside out under strict control procedures, only then is freedom eminently desirable.

Piano playing, however uniquely invested with a multitude of human and superhuman implications, is still but another variety of muscular exertion. A careful analysis of other (and in the physical sense no less complicated) athletic activities illustrates, as in Zeno's paradox, a character of motion which is both continuous and incremental — proceeding from station to station. Without locating the stations, the motion deteriorates to anarchy, however attractively choreographed.

To paraphrase Mendelssohn's cogent dictum, when compared to chronically ambiguous words, music is a far more precise agent for articulating shades of meaning. Any musician worth his salt must believe this, must believe that only music can describe the delicate interplay between subject and object which unlocks reality. And if the color of the leaves which we may impute to a phrase in Schubert may seem to vary from day to day, from performer to performer, so it varies in "reality," according to transient patterns of light, chemistry, and the moods of the observer.

For some, the leaves may compound into characteristics of bark or moss. For others, into clouds or cherrystone clams. But the essential quality remains, and is of a character which is neither subject nor object but rather the product of the eye and of recognition fully concentrated. Nor is this quality derived from (or perjured by) the vagaries of temperament alone; instead its author is the process of mind projecting identity and worth onto putatively neutral objects (but with distinct properties).

The shortage of fantasy in modern performance and criticism is a function of limited attention to the artifacts of man and nature. As disposable merchandise becomes our daily provender, Rilke's observation that his generation would be the last to know "things" becomes ever more poignant.

Of all the charming conceits propounded by the defenders of the good and the musical, the most innocuous, yet perhaps noxious, is the ideal of the "natural." As though nature were a compound of Plato and PlaySkool, orderly mannequins agreeably deployed with set palm trees rippling in the background. However, if the "natural" were truly a derivative of nature, then musical performance would be quite different. It would express the turbulent, the menacing, and a beauty as voluptuous and volatile as in the poetry of Gerard Manley Hopkins. The better part of what is called natural is the effortless: physical and musical friction ameliorated by elegant coordination. The worse part is an accommodating flow which ceases to be either statement or substance, but is merely spin.

Emerson wrote a poem that speaks poignantly to the issues of beauty and truth, the elevated and the commonplace, the noble and the dark sides. It is titled simply "Music."

> Let me go where'er I will
> I hear a sky-born music still:
> It sounds from all things old,
> It sounds from all things young,
> From all that's fair, from all that's foul,
> Peals out a cheerful song.
>
> It is not only in the rose,
> It is not only in the bird,
> Not only where the rainbow glows,
> Nor in the song of woman heard,
> But in the darkest, meanest things
> There alway, alway something sings.
>
> 'Tis not in the high stars alone,
> Nor in the cup of budding flowers,
> Nor in the redbreast's mellow tone,
> Nor in the bow that smiles in showers,
> But in the mud and scum of things
> There alway, alway something sings.

Plainness, darkness, roots, salamanders, stones, moss, grains have their music too. Not sounds of celestial beauty; nor the indulgent, plastic mimicries of love, the light and heavy metal of futile abandon. More like the sounds of serious contemporary music, where Orpheus meets the Druids, where star, soil, and turbulent sea mingle in some witchcraft of cubism redeemed, a kind of "concord" sonata in which concord and discord are resolved by their faith in things as they are, as they were, as they were meant to be. It would be nice if people really listened to this music — and faced the facts. Above all, the facts of growing: its steady, stately, carefully grained tempo.

Mud and scum are not exclusive to nature alone, but are also virulent members of the soul brigade. Their tones can be harsh and furious, but more often they speak in grey monotones of despair, alienation, and emptiness. "A flat calm, great mirror of my despair," writes Baudelaire, supreme investigator of anomie and morbid addiction. Nor can one be surprised any longer by the inevitable symbiosis connecting alienation to its vengeful counterpart, violent wrath.

RUSSELL SHERMAN

In his exquisite and gripping study of the poetic process, *The Bow and the Lyre*, Octavio Paz outlines his therapy for resisting modern man's accelerating flight from the Garden of Eden into a world made pallid and plastic by technological glut. The remedy is poetry, of course, poetry as fact and as metaphor to repair the augmenting gulf between man and his surroundings, man and his being. There are two necessary steps: first, a profound contemplation of nature until we are in tune with its rhythms, can hear and articulate them, can overcome our instinctive fear of alien forces; and then, an essential recovery of that nothingness which precedes being, that state of benign uncertainty which is the original but corrupted source for the bastardized progeny which currently afflict us: futility, anxiety, boredom.

Therefore, to study what Nietzsche calls "the incomparable vivacity of life," and to fashion statements and artifacts of appreciation; to accept bravely the condition of nothingness as the inalterable premise of existence; and to construct a being which can incorporate such tenuous roots and beginnings: these are the facts and their appropriate responses, according to Paz.

What has all this to do with musical performance and piano playing?

In response to the indifference and inaccessibility of the natural world, Paz offers a delectable, penetrating haiku from the pen of the Japanese poet Buson.

> before the white chrysanthemums
> the scissors hesitate
> for an instant

The commentary of Paz follows:

> That instant reveals the unity of being. All is still and all is in motion. Death is not a thing apart: it is, in an expressible way, life. The revelation of our nothingness leads us to the creation of being. Thrown into nothing, man creates himself in the face of it.
>
> The poetic experience is a revelation of our original condition. And that revelation is always resolved into a creation: the creation of ourselves. The revelation does not uncover something external, which was there, alien, but rather the act of uncovering involves the creation of that which is to be uncovered: our own being.

When we play music we describe and echo the tableau of natural forms, their shapes and arrangements, as uncovered by the composer's imagination, which yet must be filtered through our own. There is no other way. And in acknowledging this tableau, this revelation, we must "hesitate," we must doubt, as the composer doubted, for no valid creation can issue unscarred by doubt, by that vast flux of wonder which precedes the construction of being.

When we play, this gentle, uneasy, fluctuating, nameless, stark condition of wonder infiltrates the tone and diction of every tone; without it no fake bluster of certitude, no glib assurance of set formulas can compensate or cover up the existential void. This doubt, born in fear and trembling, is not a liability; it is a sign of a contemplative wisdom which is unafraid to admit fear into its poetic construct, and which is the indispensable prelude to conviction and faith.

Eloquence and grace, vitality and charm, faithfulness and vision: the game of life, the life of music.

JARON LANIER

# Music, Nature, and Computers
## A Showdown

*The Joy of Ugliness*

Whenever we hear the manipulative sedation of Muzak or witness the visual horror of franchise logos that surround us like wildflowers, we should be grateful. These are high expressions of the side of human nature that is able to stand apart from nature. Ugliness is the apparatus of our ability to have object relations with nature. We are unique among creatures in this respect, and it is only this asset that allows us to open our senses to the beauty of nature.

This is the reason I suspect computers will ultimately be considered the best news ever for the ecology movement. People are able to make worse art with computers than without them, which is plain to see and hear. How does computer technology accomplish this feat? To understand this feature of our most revered and metaphor-friendly artifact, we must examine how computers work.

*Efficient Ugliness Machines*

Before computers came along, musicians genuinely loved their instruments. Yet my experience has shown that the artists and musicians who do the best work with digital technology hate their tools. Even after forty years of playing an acoustic instrument, a musician will find there is still more to be learned. Mastery does not reduce the mystery. The acoustic instrument is still in part a piece of infinite nature, ever yielding, but never fully conquered.

Digital technology, in contrast, can't make a sound unless it is programmed, and programs can't exist without freezing a theory into fact. A note in a computer that is used to make music is no longer an interpretation, an instruction, or a model. It's a real thing — or, more precisely, a mandatory thing — that was once someone's idea of what a musician should do. (MIDI [musical interface digital interface] provides one example of this reduction.) This is the exact origin of the bland or nerdy feeling that permeates computer art. We are listening to and repeating our own ideas as they were fixed in programs, instead of confronting mysterious nature. In this way, computers seduce in the most devastating manner by appealing to our narcissism. As an example of their power, I would point out that musical notes didn't even really exist before computers. They used to be nothing but interpretations of what musicians did.

## Much Ado about Nothing

We live in the information age, but information doesn't exist. Or, as I put it in the mantra I've used to keep myself from getting confused about this for many years, "Information is alienated experience." Computation can be perceived as happening all around us if we care to look.

I grew up near the west Texas town of El Paso, which is bisected by a mountain that I would frequently visit as a kid. At night, the city was a panorama of traffic patterns, and I noticed that there were a few natural oscillators and other circuits present in the city's streets. So I started designing fantasy cities that implemented various algorithms and came up with a midwest-style town that accomplished a rudimentary Fourier analysis of waves of traffic that came in on the freeway.

Now imagine aliens in their flying saucer approaching a city coursing with cars, and ask yourself, "Aren't they going to be even stranger than I was as a kid?" I mean, they might discover that schools of fish in the ocean are actually calculating large prime numbers by their motions. After all, no computer is perfect — they don't last forever, and they often crash. Even if they don't crash, they have bugs, which means they don't do exactly what we intend for them to do. Why should an alien find what we think is the computer more readily than other candidates that are also performing unintentional computation?

There was a wonderful feature in *Scientific American* some years ago on simple homemade machines that calculate classic problems in computer science, one of which was a string contraption that worked out network traversal problems. Shortly after it was published, I noticed a woman wearing a woven skirt that looked a lot like this contraption, and I couldn't help but wonder if she was inadvertently performing calculations as she flounced by.

These musings are significant because they bring that mysterious thing called "meaning" back into the picture after computers and information tried to banish it. How do we recognize our own computers, ever? This seems to me to be a profoundly important question. How is it that we are not aliens to ourselves?

## Computers Rehabilitated as Conduits

There's an obvious question the reader must be asking at this point in the essay: If you dismiss computers so severely, why bother working with them? To answer this question, I propose a reconsideration of childhood.

For all our lucid memories, for all the work of the Piagets of the world, we have to admit we started as different sorts of creatures than we have become, and we cannot be certain of what children experience.

With that caveat in mind, consider the proposition that small children experience a drastic contrast between their internal experience of themselves and what they're able to share with other people. The internal experience is one of infinite freedom of imagination and optimism coupled, naturally, with an awkward self-centeredness. A child starts out as lord of the universe. Imagination becomes experience without resistance (through the means of fantasy) and is thereby rewarded and propelled. As children get older, they discover something that can only be described as God's greatest infliction of indignity on children: the shocking truth that the only world in which other people reliably exist, particularly parents, and the only world in which sustaining things like food exist, is this physical world. What a disastrous demotion! This is one of the two great limitations that people must adjust to; the other is mortality.

The reason that children in particular get excited about computers, networks, and especially virtual reality is that information technology suggests a new way through this fundamental dilemma. The shared, simulated worlds enabled by the computer are the first ones that are both fluid, like imagination, and objectively shared like the real world.

The computer can be used as a link between imaginations — a conduit that makes fantasies, if not real, then at least objective. Understand this, and you understand the wondrous, ecstatic side of computer culture.

Every once in a long while, technology serves us in its sweetest role, as the bearer of surprising good news about human nature. Most recently, this happened with the World Wide Web, proof that people are capable of happy, productive, massive anarchy. The Web wasn't needed, but was simply wished for. We brought it into being without money, planning, advertising, authority, or any other form of social coercion. For the first time in history, so far as I can tell, millions of people from all over the world suddenly cooperated in peace to build something beautiful.

Let's take a moment to note that long before the Web, another technological phenomenon reflected our better side even more dramatically. In most historical eras, and in most cultures, musical instruments have been among the most advanced technological devices produced, often edging ahead of weapons in sophistication. So, think about this: We have put as high a priority on making gizmos that make new sounds as we have on finding ways to kill each other.

Now imagine musical instruments and the Internet merging. Imagine user interfaces that allow people to blow, dance, and sing whole worlds into existence for each other. I believe this will happen.

Maybe we will be lucky and witness this taking place in our lifetimes. Or maybe our children will. The art form of the next century is being born right now: a fusion of the great arts of the twentieth century — jazz, cinema, and programming. It will not be packaged, or packageable. It will be a spontaneous shared dreaming through the Net. We will nurture each other through it and find our meaning in it. But we will have to be careful not to be seduced by technology itself.

### The Real Reason This Matters

The purpose of most technology has been to protect people from nature. Now we've gotten so powerful that our own behavior threatens us more than nature does. Our fears, jealousies, and paranoias have been amplified by weapons of mass destruction and hyperconsumption to the point that we might destroy ourselves completely. Yet we don't give up the quest for more technology, because we've fallen in love with it. It has become our talisman. The future of technology, and the survival of our race, depends on shifting the foundation myths of technology away from the seeking of power and toward the ultimate adventure of bridging the interpersonal gap. Music must not be seduced by technology but must seduce technology. If there was doubt about the mission of art in the twentieth century, there can be no such doubt in the twenty-first: The purpose of art is to distract us away from mass suicide.

DAVID DUNN

# Nature, Sound Art, and the Sacred

*In the sound of these foxes, if they were foxes, there was nearly as much joy, and less grief.*
*There was the frightening joy of hearing the world talk to itself, and the grief of incommunicability.*
*In that grief I am now as then, with the small yet absolute comfort of knowing that communication*
*of such a thing is not only beyond possibility but irrelevant to it.*

In the conclusion to his book *Let Us Now Praise Famous Men*, James Agee describes the depth of meaning and intelligence conveyed through the late night calls of two foxes. In his nine-page description of these calls he invokes archaic sentiments and a profound contradiction that humans must always have felt. We hear in the world talking to itself a sense of otherness that simultaneously mirrors our deepest sense of belonging. Agee compares the quality of laughter in these fox calls to the genius of Mozart "at its angriest, cleanest, most masculine fire." Somehow we have always intuited that music is part of our reflection to and from the nonhuman world. We hear the alien quality of the nonhuman in our music and the humanity of music in nature. The following discussion is an attempt to wrestle with the "grief of incommunicability" that arises through our attempts to both hear and talk to the world.

## ASSUMPTIONS

Each of us is constructed as a miraculous community of systems that function together to form the coherent totality of a living thing capable of sensing the external world. Because that coherence is finite, there are real limits to what we can sense. The sound we hear is only a fraction of all the vibrating going on in our universe. What we do hear is the result of a dance between the world and how we are made. In a real sense, we organize our reality out of this dance. Since this is true for all living things, and since each thing is made differently, each form of life hears a slightly different multiverse. Each species of insect, frog, bird, and mammal listens to a distinct reality that arises from the constraints of how it is constructed.

When we look at the world, our sense of vision emphasizes the distinct boundaries between phenomena. The forward focus of vision concentrates on the edges of objects or on the details of color to help us define and separate contours in space. We usually see things as one window frame of visual stimuli jumping to the next. In contrast, the sounds that things make are often not as distinct, and the experience of listening is often one of perceiving the *inseparability* of phenomena. While we often see something as distinct in its environment, we *hear* how it relates to other things. Think about the sound of ocean surf or the rush of wind in trees.

I do not mean to imply that our hearing is somehow less discriminating than our vision. Actually, the number of nerve fibers that connect our ears to the brain is greater than the number that connects the eyes. Our ears are better at discriminating certain kinds of complex phenomena, and we can often hear relationships between things that our eyes require external instrumentation to recognize. Take, for example, the ease and exactness of matching two frequencies when tuning, which musicians take for granted; in the visual domain, such precision requires sophisticated tools. Mathematics in Western culture was born from our sense of sound and not vision; Pythagoras heard the ratios of the monochord vibrating that became arithmetic. Since then, philosophers from Plato to Adorno have discussed the sacred properties and special responsibilities of music to society.

I wonder if music might be our way of mapping reality through metaphors of sound as a parallel to the visually dominant metaphors of speech and written symbols. I think that most musicians can relate to the idea that music is not just something we do to amuse ourselves. It is a different way of thinking about the world, a way to remind ourselves of a prior wholeness when the mind of the forest was not something out there, separate in the world, but something of which we were an intrinsic part. Perhaps music is a conservation strategy for keeping something alive that we now need to make more conscious, a way of making sense of the world from which we might refashion our relationship to nonhuman living systems.

We have yet to articulate fully the importance of music and the immense cognitive and social terrain that it addresses. The fact that we have yet to discover a human society without it says something very profound. Recent discoveries about the ability of music making to alter the hard-wiring of brain development say even more. I have a gut intuition that music, as this vast terrain of human activity and inheritance of our species, will provide us with clues to our future survival, and that is a responsibility worth pursuing.

Most of us listen to recorded sounds in the form of music or broadcast media. Seldom is this done with direct concentration. As distinct from their former role in traditional societies as a primary social integrating mechanism, most forms of music are now used merely as a means of distraction. The merchandising of music has become what Jacques Attali has called a "disguise for the monologue of power. Never before have musicians tried so hard to communicate with their audience, and never before has that communication been so deceiving. Music now seems hardly more than a somewhat clumsy excuse for the self-glorification of musicians and the growth of a new industrial sector."

Music as a discipline has generally failed to transcend the constraints of its status as entertainment. Gregory Bateson has discussed an essential distinction between art and entertainment: Whereas entertainment is the food of depression, being easy to engage but lacking long-term interest, art requires discipline to engage but leaves one richer in the end. In this time of ecological crisis, we need to embrace every tool we have to remind us of the sacred. Not only can aural and musical metaphors provide us with a means to describe the world in ways that remind us of our physical connection to the environment, but the physical act of using our aural sense, in contrast to entertainment, can become a means to practice and engender integrative behavior.

Attentive listening to the sounds around us is one of the most venerable forms of meditative practice. It has been used to concentrate awareness on where and what we are and to quiet the incessant chatter of the mind. What we hear from other forms of life and the environment they reside in is information that is unique and essential about patterns of relationship in context. It is an experiential basis from which we can shape an understanding of what Bateson has called the sacred: "the integrated fabric of mind that envelops us." The attempt to expand our ears toward a greater receptivity to our aural environment has been the major focus of some of the twentieth century's most important musicians. Edgard Varèse, Pierre Schaeffer, and John Cage sought to expand the resources of music beyond the vocabulary of pitch and harmony that had previously defined it. Through the "musical" manipulation of the noises of everyday life, they achieved an understanding of the meaning of these sounds as aesthetic phenomena, opportunities for a deepened awareness of the world we live in. Perhaps because of their contribution to art, we now can understand the need to extend these ideas farther. The sounds of living things are not just a resource for manipulation; they are evidence of mind in nature and are patterns of communication with which we share a common bond and meaning.

When Cage expressed that the emancipation of music required the use of all sounds as a resource for composition, he unfortunately was also establishing a precedent for the exploitation of "sound" as a decontextualized commodity that could be defined and manipulated by a set of cultural codes called music. The result of this ideological stance has been to set in motion a tautological game: The expansion of "music" becomes synonymous with an additive process of simply commandeering new phenomena into its cultural framework.

DAVID DUNN

Parallel to this process has been the asking of a supposedly profound question: Are these sound-making activities music? Underneath the surface triviality of this question is the disturbing assumption that attaining the mere status of music itself forms a meaningful discourse.

The complex of activities that have formed the emergence of environmental music and sound art as artistic genre is in part a response to this dilemma. Such activities share a general impulse not only to differentiate themselves from traditional musical activities, but also to ask a different question: What is the meaning of these sound-making activities if they are not traditional music and not intended to be? My answer to this question is in part the explicit content of my sound art work, to recontextualize the perception of sound as it pertains to a necessary epistemological shift in the human relationship to our physical environment. My belief is that there is an important role for the evolution of an art form that can address the phenomenon of sound as a prime integrating factor in the understanding of our place within the biosphere's fabric of mind.

As the ecology movement has repeatedly articulated, the traditional epistemological dichotomies between humans and nature are no longer tenable. We must instead develop a participatory relationship between humanity and the greater environmental complexity of the biosphere that is mutually life-enhancing.

The political implications are that issues of freedom and dignity must now include the *total fabric of life* within which we reside, and new modes of experience that can help recover those aspects of human integrity rooted in a sense of connectedness with the nonhuman world must be explored. These demands not only require a heightened awareness of the role of art and the artist, but of the very metaphors we use to organize reality. Francisco Varela has pointed out that visually based spatiotemporal metaphors are the worst for describing the denseness of interpenetration of phenomena that give rise to the world. When we predominantly speak of the world in topological terms we impose a fixed time-space relationship on the rich dance of living things. We constrain our understanding of the true interdependence of life. Music as a language is one of our best means for thinking about the fabric of mind that resides everywhere. Sound as a vibrant plenum reminds us of the profound physical interconnectedness that is our true environment.

MY WORK

Over the past twenty-five years, most of my creative work connected with the relationship of sound and nature can be described as fitting into two fairly separate categories. In the first category are environmental performance works intended for outdoor performance. The second category consists of tape compositions derived from environmental sounds that are a hybrid between electroacoustic composition and soundscape recording. What follows are descriptions of representative works from each of these two categories.

### Category 1: Environmental Performance Works

Through these compositions it has been my goal to deconstruct the materials and attributes of music as a means to explore and demonstrate the emergent intelligence of nonhuman living systems. As distinct from John Cage who wanted to decontextualize sounds so as to "allow them to be themselves," I have focused on the recontextualization of the sounds of nature as evidence of purposeful-minded systems. The song of a bird is not just grist for compositional manipulation; it is a code of signification not only between members of that particular species, but also for the extended fabric of mind that forms the biohabitat within which that species resides. Whereas Cage wanted to abstract these sounds, I'm interested in regarding these as conscious living systems with which I'm interacting. These sounds are the evidence of sentient beings and complex-minded systems. Many of my compositions have consisted of establishing an interactive process through which a collaborative dialogue emerges that is inclusive of this larger pattern of mind.

The resulting projects not only are descriptive of their environmental context, but also generate a linguistic structure intrinsic to the observer-observed relationship. They are an expression of the composite mind immanent in a particular connective instance. I refer to much of my work as "environmental language" to distinguish it from the more general "environmental music." The issue is not how one can bring out latent musical qualities in nature, but rather, what is necessary to stipulate an intrinsic sonic structure emergent from a specific interaction with nonhuman systems. My process has been to set up an interaction with the environment using sound as the vehicle or medium through which the interaction unfolds. Because I cannot know what the outcome of these interactions will be, I am often gaining information from an experimental situation that can't be arrived at otherwise. Although such a process is similar to what *experimental* refers to in the scientific sense, I am only making a claim for experimentation within the domain of an experiential exploration of sound and consciousness from a transdisciplinary perspective. Through combinations of analog, digital, and traditional sound-generating devices, I have designed real-time performance interactions in wilderness spaces where the resulting events reflect a larger system of mind inclusive of myself and these other living systems. Two of these works are described.

*Mimus Polyglottos* was an experiment in interspecies communication that Ric Cupples and I initiated in 1976. Both of us were fascinated by the mimicry of mockingbirds. Ric had been photographing them in their urban milieu, usually on top of one of their favorite perches, television aerials. I was living at one end of Florida Canyon, with the famous San Diego Zoo at the other end. Some nights I would be awakened by the inexplicable sounds of monkeys and tropical birds from my backyard. It took me awhile to figure out that the sounds didn't come from zoo escapees, but from the mockingbirds who traveled up and down the canyon.

Ric and I spent several months researching the literature on mockingbirds and recording them in the city. Our idea was to formulate an audio stimulus that would engage the birds but also challenge their ability to mimic. At first we did a variety of experiments in locating the birds by playing back recordings of one bird to another. This allowed us to acquire essential knowledge of proper mockingbird etiquette: how to approach the birds and what sort of proximity to maintain. The final stimulus tape was made out of frequency-modulated square waves, a notoriously problematic waveform for audio systems. We made the tape with the mockingbird frequency range in mind and ratios of sound to silence that were characteristic of their song. The tape was first played without warning to a single bird at approximately three in the morning. The bird's response was typical of the reactions we got from several different mockingbirds. It initially reacted with enthusiasm, trying to match various parameters of the electronic sound: pitch, rhythm, and timbre. At a certain point it appeared to withdraw but slowly began to build its confidence until it was interacting with an extraordinary range of accommodation to the stimulus sounds.

The result of this experiment is one of my favorite examples of the unexpected ability of humans and animals to be aware of each other and to engage creatively. I'm also fascinated by the fact that this occurs through something generally regarded as artificial. Whereas humans often reject aspects of technology as something evil compared to the rest of nature, the bird does not. To my ears, the mockingbird is just as fascinated by the sound made by these dancing electrons as by another bird. Of course, I've also heard them imitate washing machines and Volkswagen motors so there's no accounting for taste even among mockingbirds.

II

*Entrainments 2* was composed for and performed in a specific wilderness site. Three performers prerecorded stream-of-consciousness descriptions and observations of the surrounding environment from three mountain peaks in the Cuyamaca Mountains of California. These recordings were subsequently mixed with static drones derived from an astrological chart for the time and location of the performance. Playback of these sounds occurred from portable cassette recorders with self-amplified loudspeakers and sufficient amplitude to be audible from the center of the performance configuration. In the center of the space was placed a computer programmed to sample and immediately output periodic sound blocks through a central loudspeaker. The input signal to the computer was from a parabolic microphone. A performer carried this microphone while walking slowly around the perimeter of a large central circle. This performer also recorded the overall performance with binaural microphones. Three other performers carried portable, self-amplified oscillators while walking slowly around the perimeter of three outer circles. The performance took place at Azalea Glen, Cuyamaca State Park, California, on May 19, 1985.

While *Entrainments 2* intentionally borrows metaphors from a variety of archaic philosophical traditions (feng shui, geomancy), it can most readily be understood as an attempt to be in contact with the "spirit of a place." More precisely, this spirit can be defined through a cybernetic definition of mind that serves as a heuristic hypothesis. An important scientific concept of the late twentieth century has been the idea of emergent properties: Through a complex process, patterns may arise that appear to transcend their generative agents. In the case of this composition, mind can be understood to reside in all of the pathways of interaction that arise from the system of sound making that we specified and in which we participated. Experientially this was most noticeable in the relationship to time that the prerecorded voices evidenced. Observations made days before the performance coincided exactly with real-time events occurring during the performance. The resulting time and memory compression was experienced as if, on their prior visits, the speaking voices had described events that would happen in the future, and then those events did take place.

These descriptions illustrate a transition that my work has pursued over the past two decades: a progressive expansion of context, moving from interactions with a single member of another species toward interactions with complex environments. In a very direct way I have tried to expand the sense of "mindedness" that I'm working with. My idea of environmental language is an experiential, dynamic process that explores whatever tools and metaphors are available toward a greater understanding of the profound interconnections between sound, language, and the environment. It is my contention that the exploration of these linkages suggests an essential role for the evolution of sound

DAVID DUNN

art and music: the creation of human actions that reinforce the inclusiveness of the larger systemic mentality resident in the interactions of environment and consciousness.

### Category 2: Hybrid Soundscape Compositions

There are many parallels in sound collecting to other means by which we document and "bind time" in order to study, intensify experience, or cherish the past. The similarity of recorded sound to photography has been considered, but "phonography" has yet to be taken seriously as a discipline beyond its commercial or scientific applications. Its status as an artistic genre is still quite tentative despite appropriate efforts in this direction. Although the best known and most serious work in this area has been the soundscape recording movement initiated by R. Murray Schafer and his colleagues at the World Soundscape Project and later the World Forum for Acoustic Ecology, the audio documentation of "natural" acoustic environments has become a commercial success story. Several recordists market their recordings as purist audio documentation of pristine natural environments with particular appeal to the armchair environmental movement. Personally, I find something perverse about many of these recordings, as if an audio description of a place could ever be something other than a human invention. Sometimes the sounds are intrinsically beautiful but are too often marketed as if their mere existence were somehow doing the environment a big favor. I can certainly understand arguments for the preservation of actual biohabitats — but not as recorded sonic objects. The premise appears to be that these recordings will somehow sensitize the listener to a greater appreciation of the natural world, when in fact they are more often perpetuating a nineteenth-century vision of nature and, at best, merely documenting a state of affairs that will soon disappear.

There were two experiences in particular that charged my cynicism about soundscape work and the aesthetic role of phonography. Several years ago, I was hired to do audio field recordings for a new aquarium project. Because the focus of the exhibition was on two of the major watersheds of North America, the Mississippi and Tennessee river basins, my job (along with a colleague) was to gather sound from each biohabitat, which would later be mixed and correlated to the aquarium exhibits as canned audio playback. We were to provide the raw source materials that would later be used to conjure a sonic portrait of these places. This meant that we were to travel to the remaining sites of virgin hardwood forest in the Smokey Mountains of Tennessee and to the cypress swamps of the Atchafalaya Basin of Louisiana and document the acoustic environments. Both of these expeditions turned out to be extraordinarily difficult because these environments were, for our purposes at least, nonexistent. What remained were small vestiges of these once grand habitats — so small, in fact, that there was simply no unique acoustic identity left to capture. We spent weeks in each location, waiting out the long periods of incessant automobile, plane, and boat traffic to capture enough snippets of wildlife sounds to enable phony mixes to construct convincing audio portraits of places that do not actually exist.

While doing sound recordings in an African game park for a zoo project, I traveled to remote watering hole habitats. The fantasy I had nurtured for weeks about my impending African safari experience was instantly shattered when I set up my equipment. As I put on my headphones, I immediately heard the sound of a kerosene-driven pump used to bring water up from the aquifer to the watering hole. This, I was later told, was the rule and not the exception. These pumps are a common feature in many game parks because of the artificial boundaries imposed on wildlife by humans. Without them, much of the wildlife would perish without access to water. At first their presence profoundly disturbed my wild safari fantasy, but I later understood that Africa is no different from the rest of the earth's fast transition of wilderness into global park. The important thing to understand is not only how humanity has radically altered the biosphere, but also the depth of the responsibility we now carry for its survival.

I came away from both of these situations feeling that my involvement supported something duplicitous. My job was to pretend that I was not present in the situation in order to create a false representation of the reality and then foist this upon a naive public. It would have been a classic example of confusing the map for the territory, except that the map wasn't even in the right ballpark. Such fakery is even more reprehensible because it lures people into the belief that these places still fulfill their romantic expectations, and it gives the illusion that all is well when it is not.

As an alternative position, I have preferred to apply a compositional aesthetic to the creation of soundscape works. I am interested in evolving an intrinsic relationship to a subject rather than inventing or fantasizing a musical event. This is the idea of composition as a strategy for expanding the boundary of what is reality itself. If I want to transcend the limiting conditions that my current state of knowledge imposes on me, to invent or improvise something from that condition will obviously not suffice. I will merely reiterate the previously known conditions. By paying close attention to the reality of what actually is, there arises the opportunity to participate in the emergence of something that is mutually created between the subject and myself. I have then danced toward a definition of the reality that I am participating in, rather than from a preconceived one that is probably no longer relevant. Given this philosophical stance, it is obvious that I will be very "present" in the editing process,

DAVID DUNN

but this does not mean that I wish to impose myself or some fantasy on the materials. Instead, I seek to invoke patterns of relationship intrinsic to the materials themselves. Discussion of two such works follows.

### The Lion in Which the Spirits of the Royal Ancestors Make Their Home

The title of this work derives from the Shona phrase *Mhondoro Dzemidzimu*, which I ran across in David Lan's book *Guns and Rain: Guerrillas and Spirit Mediums in Zimbabwe*. Lan is a writer and social anthropologist who was born in South Africa. His book is a brilliantly written account of the role that traditional spirit mediums played in Zimbabwe's war for independence. He details the facts concerning the profound significance of an anticolonial war fought with the guidance of the Shona royal ancestors communicating through these spirit mediums. The title specifically refers to one of the traditional beliefs of Shona religion that I took as emblematic of African religious beliefs in general.

The concept for the disc originated after the fact. I went to Zimbabwe partially as a tourist and partially on assignment (as described earlier) for a friend whose sound design firm specializes in audio installations for large public institutions. We needed to gather some sounds from African watering hole habitats for a couple of projects then under development. The concept of how to "compose" the overall piece came a few years later in response to a request from the Australian Broadcasting Commission for an extended radio piece. The unifying premise arose from the realization that none of these sounds were "pure" in the sense of simple naturalistic representations of the African environment or traditional culture. All of the sounds I recorded were clearly problematic and contradictory. They were recordings of the current reality of social and environmental change and not representations of a fantasy Africa that no longer exists. In that sense it was the reality of Zimbabwe that led me to the piece and not a preconceived idea.

My foremost interest was in composing an articulation of those patterns of the sacred that emerge or persist within (and despite) the contradictions and conundrums of rapid cultural change. Although these sounds can be heard as further evidence of an environment, nation, and world undergoing mutation and threat of annihilation, they can also be heard as evidence for processes of dynamic adaptation in which the tribal and wilderness voices speak not only as something under siege, but also as phenomena capable of survival in a way that may inform our collective survival here on earth.

For example, in one of the recording cuts we hear a human habitation wedged between the African wilderness and a two-lane paved highway that serves as a major trucking route. The length of this cut is just about the average time between passing vehicles. In the foreground are various nocturnal insects.

In the distance are frogs and the village ambience itself: voices, drums, and a braying donkey. This recording reinforces one of the most powerful impressions I had of the relationship between African culture and environment: an overwhelming sense of the persistence of spirit as an intrinsic component of the African ecology. For many African people, the sounds of animals are not merely the calls of separate organisms. They are the voice of a spirit form resident in that individual but also present in all the members of its species. That spirit is like a persistent and collective intelligence that defies geographic separation. This concept not only is present in the beliefs of the traditional religious practices, but appears as an essential trait of domestic life. It can even be understood to include the influence of the dead (both human and animal) as a resonance from the past that informs all aspects of daily life and is essential to the vitality and interaction of all living things.

### Chaos and the Emergent Mind of the Pond

We usually associate the intelligence of life forms with how big they are or with their proximity to us on the evolutionary tree. The tiny size and alien quality of insects and spiders presents us with a challenge. How could they possess anything but the most rudimentary of mental functions, tiny automatons without thought or feeling? The amazing sophistication of social insects belies this assumption. Ant societies are particularly impressive, and the observed behavior of bee colonies has taken on mythic proportions. We know that bees communicate a large range of information about the details of their environment through dance (along with sound and smell). Although this "waggle dance" is regarded as the only insect "language" yet known, there are clues that others await discovery. One candidate is a water beetle of the genus *Berosus*. These little critters appear to have a vocabulary of faint sounds that they emit underwater for purposes of warning and mating.

This work was composed entirely from underwater sound recordings made in vernal pools in North America and Africa. My intent was to articulate the amazing complexity and apparent intelligence that these sounds signified. After a couple of years of listening to these small ponds and marshes, I came to understand a pattern to their underwater sound making.

The one consistent factor is how beautiful and complex these miniature sounds are. I have finally reconciled myself to the gut feeling that these sounds are an emergent property of the pond: something that speaks as a collective voice for a mind that is beyond my grasp. I know that this is not a scientific way of thinking, but I can't help myself. Now when I see a pond, I think of the water's surface as a membrane enclosing something deep in thought. Even for someone who has had a lot of experience listening to animal sounds, the feeling that these pond sounds are some sort of alien language is irresistible.

DAVID DUNN

The philosopher Ludwig Wittgenstein once said, "If a lion could talk, we could not understand him." He meant that the schism between human culture and the lion's world is so great that a mere linguistic code cannot bridge the gap. What I like about this statement is how it respects the otherness of the animal world and recognizes how codes of communication, like these insect sounds, arise from the unique organization of living things.

Science has begun to probe deeply into the possibility that our assumptions about animal intelligence and communication have been too simplistic. For centuries, much of humanity has claimed superiority over the nonhuman world, and our older models of evolution have guaranteed this view. The justification for this argument was often based on an assumption that because animals do not possess language, they are simply organic machines to be ruthlessly exploited. New evidence suggests that thinking does not require language in human terms and that each form of life may have its own way of being self-aware. Life and cognition might be considered synonymous even at the cellular level.

We can embrace the alien for its right to exist without destroying it or demanding that it either serve us or exhibit human traits. Along with humans, other forms of life exist as co-conspirators in a mystery of which we have only a small glimpse. Perhaps the most important feature of their being alien is that they are part of a puzzle through which we can truly know what we are.

DAVID JAMES DUNCAN

# My One Conversation with Collin Walcott

*For Glen Moore, Ralph Towner, and Paul McCandless*

In the mid-1980s, during a severe August drought, I stopped by to gab with my neighbor, Jon (who pronounces it "Yawn"), and happened to arrive at his house just as his Baldwin upright piano (Yawn called it his "Ax") was heading out the door into the local piano-tuner's van. As I grabbed a corner and helped lift, I learned that a jazz quartet called Oregon was going to be playing an out-door concert the following night, and that Yawn's Ax was headed off to serve as one of the two "concert grands" the band had requested. When I learned that a free tuning went with the loan, I said, "Hey!"—and a short time later the piano-tuner's van was jouncing up my mud-rut driveway, destined to make my moth-eaten, hymn-beaten, five-owner Jansen upright Oregon's second "concert grand."

In defense of these pianos I should explain that we lived, geographically, on a decidedly rural portion of the Oregon coast, which implies that, culturally, we lived in what the national jargon would term a vacuum. On Forest Service maps we were a green thumbprint with a few blue veins (the creeks) running through us. On highway maps we were nothing at all—solid color without symbols or words. But there, nevertheless, we were, smack in the middle of Downtown Vacuum, our various oddball houses sprouting like Cubist mush-rooms from the abandoned dairy pastures, clearcuts and river valleys. And somehow or other these internationally renowned musicians had found us and decided, despite our pianos, to play some music.

The place Oregon played was called Cascade Head—a twelve-hundred-foot "mountain" whose eastern end is actually a ridge buried in the Coast Range, and whose western end is actually a cape amputated by the Pacific into a ser-rated series of basalt cliffs and inaccessible coves. The concert took place at a little arts center named Sitka (after the local spruce trees), in a grassy outdoor alder-and-spruce-ringed bowl.

Because it was necessary to park at the bottom of the Head and hike a steep half-mile to reach this bowl, the arriving faces had that benign quality faces get when the psychic umbilicus connecting humans to cars is severed. And they grew more benign when, in a building behind the concert bowl, they discovered a local restauranteur catering wine and imported beer, and the baker from the co-op serving up delectable carbos. Meanwhile the local ocean was serving up a low summer fog that crept eastward through the trees like a spectator with no ticket. The fog cooled things fast, but with most of the rest of North America smoggy or humid and pushing 100 degrees that day, I heard no complainers. We sat on green grass in gray light, those who'd brought blankets sharing with those who hadn't. The band was on time, and already warming up.

For a while I bustled around the crowd like a demented father, pointing out my enstaged and honored piano to everybody I knew. My friends mostly gawked at it, then winced, so my pride soon grew containable. I sat, and began to check out the band.

Though I'd heard many, maybe all, of their recordings, I'd never seen Oregon in person. I eyed Glen Moore first, since he was the guy standing closest to my Jansen. He was wearing bright red pointy-toed genie slippers and even brighter maroon pants, but to judge by his smile he'd done it on purpose. Instead of plucking, tuning or even touching his stand-up bass, he just goofed around with a friend's baby daughter, zooming her low over the stage, *mmrowwing* her round and round the spotlights. His bass, at least, looked ready for action: it sported a snarling gargoyle head and appeared to be at least a thousand years old.

Ralph Towner stood with his back to us, adjusting the valves or something on a Prophet 5 synthesizer, tuning six- and twelve-string guitars, blowing warm air through a flügelhorn, playing deft warm-up scales on Yawn's Ax. (I noticed Yawn not ten feet away, chest puffed, eyes glistening, pointing out his shining Ax to other concert-goers. But Yawn had an excuse: the Ax really is a nice piano.) When Towner finished the Prophet 5's valve job and showed his face, he looked a little as if he'd been working swingshift at United Grocers. But half an hour or so into the concert his fatigue, or whatever it was, had vanished, and I realized the United Grocers' look must have been merely the prefix appearance of a man whose body has become hopelessly addicted to the making of music.

Paul McCandless, in contrast to Moore and Towner, looked alert and fiery from the start, even in dirty, unlaced tennis shoes. His name and face brought to mind some indomitable, straitlaced, nineteenth-century Scottish missionary who'd set out to convert the heathen world to God knows what, but by a stroke of luck had instead been converted himself, to unlaced heathen horn-playing.

Then there was the percussionist, Collin Walcott — a man whose name had me expecting a contemporary of Dickens, Trollope, or Thackeray, but who instead sat buddha-style in the middle of things, his long bald head shining, his face solemn and focused, his manner comfortably, contradictorily Oriental. He had a synthesized drum set just to his north — the first I'd ever seen — its heads and cymbals full-sized in sound, but no bigger than tea saucers. He had five different tablas to his south, a sitar to his east and a bewildering semicircle of rattles, chimes, clackers, bells, whistles, finger-drums, triangles and unnameable noisemakers to his west. He was the first Western "jazz" percussionist I'd ever seen sit flat on the floor like an East Indian. And after a night of watching him play in that position, the thought of the standard drummer perched on a steel stool, convulsively whacking with both feet at a high hat and drum, seemed a trifle inane.

The concert began in a cool gray dusk. Sunset consisted of a few minutes during which the fog and white alderbark turned golden. Then it grew dark, the cool turned decidedly cold, and we listeners began to need the music not only as a source of pleasure but as a source of heat. A little later the no-see-'ums came out in clouds, convening mostly beneath the spotlights, so that the band needed their music to transcend the fact that they were being devoured alive. A little after that the baby girl Moore had taken on the preconcert zoom got tired and needed the music to calm her to sleep. A heater, an insect antidote, a lullaby: Oregon's music served many purposes that night. But what it did last it did best. What it did last — so it seemed to me — was bring on its own annihilation. But we'll cross, or stumble into, that chasm when we come to it.

There is something uncanny about live music, about watching living, breathing musicians as their music is being born. For all its technical perfection, a recording is just what it says it is: an accurate but lifeless replica of a living event. It leaves out the flickering hands, bending bodies, skilled, exerted breathing; the sharp, almost desperate inhalations by the horn players; the screek of the pick against the wound strings of the guitar; the nods, fleet smiles, deft understandings flickering back and forth between performers. These visual nuances are satisfying in themselves, but also guide a live listener toward the intent of every silence and sound. And there is a cumulative effect to the best live music. One piece sheds light on another, like stories in a strong collection, till your ears begin to master a lexicon. And when song after song reaches climax after climax, energy is not only generated, it's congealed, distilled, intensified, like sunlight passing through a magnifying glass. The sounds burn clear through the mind and hit you somewhere deeper. That, at least, is the alchemy concert-goers hope for. What can't be described, of course, is what a band does to put a listener in this state. We call it *music*, but so what? *Music* is just a word for something we love largely because it consists of things that

DAVID JAMES DUNCAN

words can't express. Likewise, the heart is just a word for something in us that music sometimes touches. But once these two somethings, heart and music, do touch, there is only one of them.

Music is the food whose peculiarity it is to enter us through the ears. Music is an inexpressible from outside us touching an inexpressible within, causing the frenetic persona that normally wedges itself between outside and inside, creating twoness, to vanish. Gospel musicians used to shout out certain words when they felt inexpressibles touching, maybe *hallelujah*, or *amen*, which literally means simply, "It is so." These were magic words once, both of them. Then people learned to shout them when they weren't feeling anything in particular, and the words took revenge by becoming hokey as hell. They still are hokey. But during Oregon's performance that night I longed for the presence of such a word: beery shouts and clapping seemed far from sufficient to acknowledge the beauty of what we were receiving.

Maybe two hours into the concert Oregon played a Towner composition called "The Rapids" that had inexpressibles touching all over the mountain-side. It is so. In fact it is, or was, so much so that just as the music was fading, a green brilliance flashed through the fog, and just as we began applauding there was a polite peal of thunder. Everybody laughed. Like a shouted *hallelujah*, genuine "thunderous applause" at a genuine Oregon concert on the Oregon coast seemed hokey. But it happened. And right afterward, when I sniffed the air, I sensed more about to happen. Something electric was going on. Something meteorologically electric. It hadn't rained in two months, and the satellite picture in the paper that morning had shown a North Pacific cloudless clear to Japan. But as a Caucasian I am part-Asian, as a part-Asian I'm part Hindu, and when my Hindu part sniffed the air and saw more faint green flashes, it began to suspect that the fog was now much more than fog, and that Indra, the Rainmaker, was hiding in it, drawn by the music, listening closely.

We found out later that there had been a lone backpacker up on Cascade Head that night. Knowing nothing of the upcoming concert, this young man had toiled up a swale to a point maybe a quarter-mile beyond and five hundred feet above our little declivity in the spruce and alder grove, pitched his tent in open meadow, cooked his dinner on a tiny propane stove and leaned back against the ridge to study the stars — when astonishing sounds began to pour up out of the fog. He had no idea who or even where the musicians were. But the long swale's acoustics, he said, were great. And because he was perched above the fogline, he was aware of things we never suspected down in our bowl. He saw, for instance, the way the Head jutted out into the Pacific, its entire seaward face crumbling, thanks to old storm batterings. He saw that the general source of the music was not — as it seemed to us — a cozy, sheltered glade, but a tenuous, fogbound fold in that same battered, seaward face. And he saw the moment when, far out in the ocean, gigantic whorls of vapor began to rise up off the fogbank, drift inland and upward toward the summit of the Head and gather there, darkening, congealing, intensifying, till they became a towering, blue-black entity that bore no relation to vapor. This thunderhead, he said, formed above the sea off our solitary headland like a listener created by the music itself. And when it moved in to listen more closely, when thunderhead met Cascade Head and they too began trying to become one thing, the entire sky above our niche began to spark and rumble. It is so.

The band began a song called "Taos" — a composition as indescribable as any piece of music. To get a handle on what happened next, I'll describe something that isn't music, which this music was something like. Let's say that "Taos" is a wordless narrative describing a seven-minute-long natural event. Say it takes place in uninhabited desert, perhaps somewhere (as the name suggests) outside Taos, New Mexico. Say it takes place, like our concert, late in the evening. The sun is just vanishing. The sky is cloudless. Things are cooling after a day of sweltering heat. The shadows, once long and black, turn blue, then gray as the sun vanishes, then grow indistinct . . .

The music begins, like everything on this planet, with the water: Walcott's tablas dripping a steady, assonant stream of drops, Moore's bass *tok-tok-tok*ing in high, percussive overtones, Towner's Prophet also pouring out something percussive, quiet and wet. It sounds as though there is a seep, a tiny spring, hidden in the scorched rocks and warm shadows. And when McCandless kindles a little tin whistle we realize there's a bird, too — some solitary, nameless desert bird the music brings so near to life that we feel its heartbeat. The bird drinks at the seep, then seems to go wandering, and the mood is so benign, the chords so simple, that you think the song is about almost nothing — a little divertimento. But then the overtones end, the bass gropes deeper, the tablas give way to an insistent, staccato cymbal beat, the bird keeps flitting along, and though there is no increase in volume and no dissonance — nothing diminished or augmented or even minor to warn you — there comes a moment when you realize that the day has ended, the desert nights are cold and the little bird's flitting is in deadly earnest. What is it looking for? Or who? Moore's bass stays deep, the volume low, the mode insistently simple, almost heraldic, as in a medieval chant. The whole band joins in a chord that seems to believe in but can't quite find resolution. The tin bird cries out in panic now. Then the cymbals crash, the mouth of an immense desert cave comes into view and the bass erupts — two astounding, tympanic tones rising from the depths of the cavern. The bird's cries grow frantic. And finally it comes: resolution, the same tremendous bass notes, but doubled, booming out in fours now, and the flickering cymbals are the wingbeats of the little bird, the piercing tin whis-

DAVID JAMES DUNCAN

tle its joy, and the synthesizer the answering voices of its thousand sisters and brothers, bursting from the cave's mouth in a cloud. Again and again the four tremendous bass notes. Again and again the ecstatic birds, swirling round their lost brother in a cloud that finally vanishes, with a beautiful echo, back into the cavern . . .

There is the description, the handle. Here is what happened as the music was played:

The very first time Moore's bass groped deep, all around us, all over the Head, the thunder joined in — the pitch, the timing and tone, the volume of the peal all so perfectly wedded to the music that some of us couldn't take it in. The acid-retreads among us gaped reverentially at the bass's gargoyle head. The scientists peered up into the trees, trying to make out the gargantuan hidden speakers that would let them chalk it up to the marvels of technology. But the next time the bass dove for the cavern notes, the thunder was there again: a perfectly pitched, perfectly played crescendo. This time no one missed it. Towner turned an incredulous face toward his compadres. McCandless, mouth full of whistle, bulged his eyes and nodded. Moore threw back his head and laughed. Walcott just played on. Brilliant green flashes shot through the cloud. And to the end of the song the guest musician, the thunderhead, played its part to perfection. Call it weather, call it coincidence, call it Khizr or Indra or anything you choose, we heard it as pure music, it came from all over that mountain, and it turned us inside out. Then the music became visible: just as the desert birds began swirling back into their cave a real wind swirled down upon us, the real trees began to churn and the early dying leaves from a thousand alders whirled round us like birds. The song ended, the air filled with ozone, and our bodies remained so full of the sense of listening that the music in us refused to die. *It is so.* We cheered ourselves hoarse, applauded till our hands stung like hail. Then Moore, sensing too late the impending downpour, said, "If you'd like to hear us again, you can catch us in October — in Greece."

Like the auntie who gives you the same dang pair of socks each Christmas, the god Indra, when pleased, can think of just one gift. Cascade Head gets a hundred inches of rain per annum, the stage had no roof and we wanted more concert, so a greater godly gift, under the circumstances, seemed like no rain at all. But gods will be gods, and when musicians please one they must accept the consequences, though their instruments, amps and bare heads be exposed to the sky.

Trying to dispel some of the energy they'd brought down upon us, Oregon set out on a courageous but ill-advised coda — a contemplative little piece, with Walcott on sitar and Towner on guitar. Thunder smashed it into meaningless fragments. Wind blew the shards away. The first few drops fell, enormous and warm. Then came the downpour, the cold gusts, the crowd's insane, frenetic cheering. The stage was a puddle in seconds. Spotlights started exploding. An alert technician doused everything electric but the lights. Most of the audience fled, whooping and shouting, but a score or so of us altruists and piano-owners ran down to the stage, hoping to help.

It was a deluge, a real Ark-launcher. Everyone was soaked through in seconds. A couple of tall guys jumped up, grabbed the whipping canvas canopy, pulled it over the stage and lashed it, but the wind drove the rain straight in under it. Water ran down the amplifiers, drenched the instruments, stung our faces, and despite our incurable elation we could see that, for the musicians, it was a disaster. Walcott cased up his sitar first, Towner his guitars. A stagehand packed up the Prophet 5. Moore — with admirable carelessness — tossed a tarp over his priceless gargoyle and turned to help McCandless, the two of them popping woodwinds into cases quick as bagboys sacking grocks. My friend Yawn was a marvelous sight, staggering round under the bank of exploding spotlights like King Lear in Act Five, roaring, *"My Ax! O God! My Ax!"* till a bunch of brawny volunteers muscled it into the piano-tuner's van. I checked my own piano: its top was off and nowhere to be seen; a microphone was dangling down inside; a soggy blanket had been draped over the treble clef, but I could hear rain dripping like coffee through a filter, thumping the soundboard, soaking the felts. Moore hadn't played a note on it. I was going to need that free tuning. I didn't care. I stretched the sopping blanket down over the bass clef — just to keep the damage symmetrical — and wandered over toward Walcott.

He was hunched in the midst of his forty or fifty instruments, piling, covering and desperately packing them away. Out on the lawn a few Zorbas were still dancing and screaming, and a woman in a sopped T-shirt, bouncing in braless stereo, shrieked, *"The ultimate Oregon concert!"* It came out sounding like a faked hallelujah. In the face of the real storm, even works of would-be ecstasy felt wordy. Walcott looked miserable. A lot of his life was splayed out in the rain. There would be warping and water damage. I asked if there was anything I could do. He looked up and, in a tone incongruously calm, dry and New Yawkish for a man so wet and Oriental, said, "Yeah. Make it stop."

I nodded, then solemnly set about doing a pseudo-Hopi anti-rain chant as I hopped in a puddle on one foot.

Walcott seemed marginally amused at best.

But a minute or so later, the rain stopped.

That was my one conversation with Collin Walcott. And there won't be another. The following December, right after we'd all failed to "catch them in Greece," he was killed in a car wreck en route to a concert in East Germany. It

DAVID JAMES DUNCAN

is written that "the Believing Mind is the Buddha-nature." And I believe. But when I think of Walcott sitting cross-legged amid his instruments like a serious child surrounded by toys he lived only to give away, I feel nothing but loss. Yes, the Believer's Mind is the Buddha-nature. But in disguise. And what a disguise! In the face of a real storm, even buddhistic words feel wordy. Yet my instruments, my toys, are words. And when I learned that this wonderful maker of music was gone, I was moved to make some sentences in an attempt, however hopeless, to give as Collin Walcott had given.

The clouds, that August night, dispersed shortly after the music ended. And in bright sunlight the following morning, that solitary backpacker came down off the Head, looking for some sign of the marvels he'd witnessed. He found an old cedar stage covered with fresh-fallen alder leaves. He found, in the grass, the fast-fading imprints of a few hundred human bottoms. No native tribe ever left a cleaner camp. And after the grandeur he'd witnessed, this cleanliness confused the backpacker. How much had he heard? How much had he dreamed? Would anything he'd heard remain free of dream later?

Spotting the Sitka caretaker, he rushed over and cried, "Last night! That *music*! Who *were* those guys?"

But when he was told, "A band called Oregon," he just shook his head and laughed. Laughed, then failed, as I have, to tell how for one long song, one sweet seven minutes, he'd watched them play, like an instrument, an entire headland and sky.

MICHAEL ONDAATJE

# From *Coming through Slaughter*

*Poet Michael Ondaatje wrote the novel* Coming through Slaughter *in aphorisms and detached fragments about the near-legendary "founder" of jazz, Buddy Bolden, who is said to have lost his mind playing a single long note. Here is the moment where the music consumes him and his nature changes:*

March is slowing to a stop and as it floats down slow to a thump I take off and wail long notes jerking the squawk into the end of them to form a new beat, have to trust them all as I close my eyes, know the others are silent, throw the notes off the walls of people, the iron lines, so pure and sure bringing the howl down to the floor and letting in the light and the girl is alone now mirroring my throat in her lonely tired dance, the street silent but for us her tired breath I can hear for she's near me as I go round and round in the center of the Liberty-Iberville connect. Then silent. For something's fallen in my body and I can't hear the music as I play it. The notes more often now. She hitting each note with her body before it is even out so I know what I do through her. God this is what I wanted to play for, if no one else I always guessed there would be this, this mirror somewhere, she closer to me now and her eyes over mine tough and young and come from god knows where. Never seen her before but testing me taunting me to make it past her, old hero, old ego tested against one as cold and pure as himself, this tall bitch breasts jumping loose under the light shirt she wears that's wet from energy and me fixing them with the aimed horn tracing up to the throat. Half dead, can't take more, hardly hit the squawks anymore but when I do my body flicks at them as if I'm the dancer till the music is out there. *Roar.* It comes back now, so I can hear only in waves now and then, god the heat in the air, she is sliding round and round her thin hands snake up through her hair and do their own dance and she is seven foot tall with them and I aim at them to bring them down to my body and the music gets caught in her hair, this is what I wanted, always, loss of privacy in the play-ing, leaving the stage, the rectangle of band on the street, this hearer who can throw me in the direction and the speed she wishes like an angry shadow. Fluff and groan in my throat, roll of a bad throat as we begin to slow. Tired. She still covers my eyes with hers and sees it slow and allows the slowness for me her breasts black under the wet light shirt, sound and pain in my heart sure as death. All my body moves to my throat and I speed again and she speeds tired again, a river of sweat to her waist her head and hair back bending back to me, all the desire in me is cramp and hard, cocaine on my cock, eternal, for my heart is at my throat hitting slow pure notes into the shimmy dance of victory, hair toss victory, a local strut, eyes meeting sweat down her chin arms out in final exercise pain, take on the last long squawk and letting it cough and climb to spear her all those watching like a javelin through the brain and down into the stomach, feel the blood that is real move up bringing fresh energy in its suitcase, it comes up flooding past my heart in a mad parade, it is coming through my teeth, it is into the cornet, god can't stop god can't stop it can't stop the air the red force coming up can't remove it from my mouth, no intake gasp, so deep blooming it up god I can't choke it the music still pouring in a roughness I've never hit, watch it *listen* it *listen* it, can't see I CAN'T SEE. Air floating through the blood to the girl red hitting the blind spot I can feel others turning, the silence of the crowd, can't see

*Willy Cornish catching him as he fell outward, covering him, seeing the red on the white shirt thinking it is torn and the red undershirt is showing and then lifting the horn sees the blood spill out from it as he finally lifts the metal from the hard kiss of the mouth.*

What I wanted.

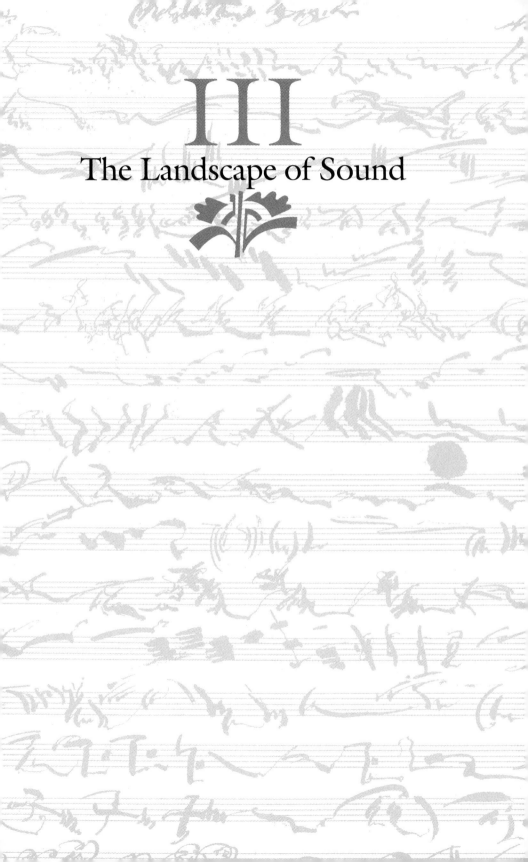

# III

# The Landscape of Sound

# From *Rubicon Beach*

*Steve Erickson's novel* Rubicon Beach *begins in Los Angeles in a post-earthquake near future, a city of canals where the earth itself makes music and radios are forbidden. Paroled convict Cale tries to make sense of the situation.*

I kept asking people where the sound came from and finally someone explained, The sea, the sound was the sea, seeping in under the city and forming subterranean wells and rivers. The rivers made a sound that came up through the empty buildings, and the echoes of the buildings made a music that came out into the streets. One day you'd see a building standing upright and the next day it was entirely collapsed, the earth caved in around it, the music turning into a hiss from out of the rubble. In Chinatown they called the shops along the water the Weeping Storefronts; at night you could hear them gurgling and howling in the dark all the way from the library tower. I went there one night after checking out an isolated hardware store for a radio. The clerk asked if I was a cop. I'm no cop, I said. He thought about it a moment and looked me over and then said, No radios here. I'm a lawabiding citizen, he said. He said, You new around here or what? and I said, Sort of, and he said, Check out Chinatown, bub, but watch it. I went to two merchants in Chinatown before the third led me into a back room and asked for the fifth time if I was a cop and sold me a transistor radio. He wrapped it in paper and had me put it in my coat pocket and let me out the back door. By now I knew there was something wrong. But I had the radio and didn't notice anyone following me for a change, so after walking briskly along the wharf toward home I decided maybe I wasn't in such a hurry.

Staring into the sun from the harbor, I saw before the shadowmansions of the lagoon something like a black mountain rising from the water, alive with insects; not until it blocked out the sun entirely could I tell it was a boat. Its dark wood hull was blotched with oil and slime, and a cloud of soot hovered over the deck. The deck was swarming with voices, Asian and Spanish and Portuguese and German, to the dull percussion of the tide and the sobbing of the storefronts at my back. The vessel glided past the first dock where I had originally disembarked and then headed into the canal gate, its engines cut and the whole hulk of the thing slipping along soundlessly. The silence of it snuffed the yammering of the people. Just a lot of faces, old Chinese women in scarves and bareheaded Latinos and their wives and here and there a child, all watching from the edge of the boat — or so I thought. When they got right next to me about thirty feet away I saw, in the fast groan of the last sun and the few nagging lights of Chinatown, the nullified blaze of all their dead eyes; every one of them was blind. A towering wooden crate of blind people drifting the waterways of East L.A. I turned around and took my radio home.

At the library I closed the doors and slid the bolt without checking for squatters first. If there were squatters tonight, room and board was on me. I read at my desk awhile and went to bed. Not long after turning out the light there was a dull thud in the distance, so quiet I might not have noticed but for the way the tower shook. It lasted only a few seconds but I lay there half an hour gripping the sides of the bed so hard I could have broken my hands. Then I got up and took a shot of brandy and got back in bed and read some more and tried to fall asleep. There was the sound of sirens and shouting. Finally the music put me out — the city music, not my radio — and I noticed it was different music, the sound of the buildings in the distance had changed. The last thing I thought of was all those blind people watching me across the water.

CLAUDE SCHRYER

# The Sharawadji Effect

A defining moment in my life came in 1993 while driving alone, from Ottawa to Montreal, in a dense snowstorm. I was listening to the radio, and the composition that was playing literally "lifted" my spirit into another level of perception. The work carried me *into* listening. I don't recall what this particular piece was about, but I clearly remember and cherish the sensation it has left me. Ever since, I have been trying to touch and possibly create such a listening experience by means of electroacoustic soundscape composition.

I still wonder what touched me that night. Was it the radio or was it the storm that caught my ear? Was it the combination of the two? Or perhaps it was the combination of three elements: the listening space, the radio broadcast, and me?

Industrialization and new technologies have transformed our sound environment. New sounds have appeared, have transformed our concept of hearing, and have modified our aesthetic criteria in a decisive fashion. These aesthetic criteria have evolved to such an extent that we now willingly accept "noise" as music, but we also recognize that "music" can be noise.

We hear differently today because we are increasingly listening to the world through the prosthetic loudspeaker, and our values of good and bad sounds are blurred by the seemingly endless offerings of new technologies, combined with a generally poor public education in acoustic perception.

Considering the phenomenon that Canadian scientist Ursula Franklin has described as "cultural conformity," in which "the technology of an activity defines the activity itself and in so doing, excludes the emergence of alternatives,"[1] might the technology of sound production be defining the aesthetic of the sound? Are we choking under the pressure of electronic technology, incapable of controlling or directing it?

Perhaps in response to these concerns, the notion of ecology and social responsibility of technological artists has emerged recently in the domain of electroacoustics. Artists from diverse disciplines are exploring and employing the soundscape in their work. Their interesting and timely reflections on problems of acoustic ecology are expanding the debate and nourishing discussions on the quality and organization of the soundscape in urban and natural environments and how our listening process has changed.

I believe that artists, and electroacoustic artists in particular, can become a conduit for our collective memory and help us better understand the breadth of our acoustic environment, which we rarely actually hear in everyday life. They can propose new associations, acoustic games, and poetic metaphors, can challenge our perceptions of reality and pose fundamental questions about the co-existence of electronic technology in an environmentally aware and responsible way.

For example, in 1992, the FM network of Société Radio-Canada (the Canadian French-language national broadcasting service) produced a special project called *Droit de cité*. The idea was to commission sound artists to transform Montreal soundscapes into musical performance pieces, which were broadcast live, without warning, during regular broadcasts. As a result, sound artists were able to shake the fundamental listening conventions of the average classical music listener. That same year, I and other sound artists created the Bicycle Orchestra, an electroacoustic band on wheels made of recycled bicycle and electronics parts, which performed in the streets and parks of Montreal. Our intention was to create a performance instrument that could demonstrate, in an amusing and inventive way, some basic principles of ecological thinking through the combination of street performance and electroacoustics.

But for me the most interesting and effective way to address the ecology/technology paradigm is through electroacoustic soundscape composition. Since 1989, I have been in the process of developing a theory and a practice of electroacoustic soundscape composition that attempts to address some of these issues.

It is my journey *into* the soundscape through the medium of electroacoustics that I want to discuss here, and my quest to discover the "unexplainable beauty," or Sharawadji Effect, in the music of the acoustic environment.

A term coined by seventeenth-century European travelers who had visited China, the Sharawadji Effect has been described by Jean-François Augoyard and Henry Torgue as an aesthetic effect that "comes about as a surprise and will carry you elsewhere, beyond strict representation — out of context":

> In this brutal confusion, the senses get lost. A beautiful Sharawadji plays with the rules of composition, manipulates them and awakens a feeling of pleasure through perceptual confusion. . . . Whether in a dreamlike or anxious state, we are sometimes completely deaf to the environment. However while on a walk or on a journey, our spirit can combine availability, atten-

CLAUDE SCHRYER

tion, perspicacity and therefore become receptive to new things, including sonic fantasy. . . . Sharawadji sounds, as such, belong to everyday life or to known musical registers. They only become Sharawadji by decontextualisa-tion, by a rupture of the senses.[2]

Although, according to Augoyard and Torgue, the scrambling of the rules of sound that can result from the unpredictability and diversity of soundscapes in an urban context might be more likely to elicit a Sharawadji Effect, the sonic richness of nature is equally capable of creating such an experience:

The growling of thunder or the furore of a volcano, which illustrate the sublime in nature according to Kant, can generate fear, but also pleasure for one who feels safe. Nonetheless, if power and sound intensity contribute to the loss of references, it is the quieter sounds which trouble the spirit and lift it to cosmic proportions. . . . When, in the country, all sound activities of animals are suspended at the same time for a few seconds, thus produc-ing a violent rupture, it is by silence that can be born the Sharawadji Effect.[3]

Searching for the Sharawadji Effect is essentially a state of awareness, in which one tends an open ear in the hopes of experiencing the sublime beauty of a given sound in an unexpected context.

Electroacoustic soundscape composition is analogous to photography. But in-stead of using a camera I use a microphone to capture sound images that can be manipulated in the studio and subsequently represented as a reflection of reality in a new context and/or as an abstract artistic creation. The sound-scape composer records the acoustic environment as both the subject and con-tent of a composition, teetering on the border between representation and abstraction.

Unlike the musique concrète aesthetic of "reduced listening" (écoute ré-duite), where sounds are appreciated independently of their source for their abstract musical value as a "sound object" (objet sonore), electroacoustic sound-scape composition has everything to do with context. So while for the mu-sique concrète composer an objet sonore is one sound source among others, for the soundscape composer it is a complex web of information in context. Thus the social and spiritual context of a soundscape can be used as a compositional element on par with the traditional musical elements of pitch, melody, har-mony, and timbre. The composer draws upon the conscious and subconscious sonic memories of the listener and uses these as an anchor for navigating in and around dimensions of sound that have the potential to communicate otherwise intangible emotions.

For example, if one were to record a train, the musique concrète composer might want to slow down the sound of the train so as to exploit the interesting polyrhythms, or play the sound backwards to manipulate the rich rumbling texture. The soundscape composer might apply the same procedures to the sound, but her attitude toward the sound might also reflect a concern for its origin and context: What kind of train was it? Where was it going? Were people speaking on that train, and if so what language? What were the ambient sounds surrounding the train? The soundscape composer might want to have the sound recorded from a variety of locations and at various times of day, with each recording analyzed for its musical and anecdotal potential.

Montreal-based acousmatic composer Francis Dhomont has considered the sometimes uncomfortable cohabitation of electroacoustics and ecology:

> One important aspect of sound ecology is, of course, that it should not be too . . . sonic. But what should one make of the torrents of decibels spewed out by our loudspeakers, with ever more powerful lows, ultra-lows, mids, highs and ultra-sonics? . . . Like you, I consecrate kilometres of polyester to preserve the songs of cicadas, frogs, streams and nightingales, to avoid losing them forever. . . . Will they compensate for the disappearance of real life?[4]

I agree that we tend to exploit electronic technologies at the expense, or at the very least, in ignorance of the environment. The challenge is to find ways to combine ethical uses of electronic technologies with the principles of sustainable development. In this sense, inspired by Dhomont, I have developed two parallel activities in my sound practice: one as an electroacoustic soundscape composer who takes advantage of technological developments and the other as an acoustic ecology activist who strives to reconcile technology and ecology.

French composer Luc Ferrari reminds us that "one has to learn to recognize sounds on top of each other, in relation to each other, that is to say, in layers, and this can be learned by the sensitivity that we develop and by awareness." Luc Ferrari's work is concerned with the sensitivity and sensuality of listening. He is passionate about the sounds he records and invites us to learn how to listen to the world, one layer at a time. His electroacoustic soundscape masterpiece "Presque rien #1" (1970) is an evocative portrait of everyday activities in a small fishing village. Very little happens in this piece, but every sound is of vital importance.

Composer and acoustic ecology activist Hildegard Westerkamp has found some common ground between electroacoustics and her ecological and musical convictions. She underscores the value of electroacoustic technology in soundscape composition as a practical tool for expression and for listening: "The sound studio allows for immediate interaction with sound, an intimacy, a conversation, like a slow motion improv. In a sound studio one can be a musi-

CLAUDE SCHRYER

cian and composer at the same time." But while these technologies have allowed unprecedented freedom to create with and about the acoustic environment, she cautions us about some of the drawbacks of studio work:

> It can distract endlessly from the content of what we want to say; it can demand an inordinate amount of attention to technical detail and it can also distract our audiences from really hearing our work. But no matter how much technology we put between our composing selves and our final composition, between ourselves and our audiences, it is still ears and bodies and psyches that perceive our pieces.[5]

Ultimately, the electroacoustic medium can serve as an acoustic mirror of society and help us learn to better listen: to ourselves and to the world around us. Since 1989, I have progressively detached myself from the instrumental concert music tradition and have allowed myself to *touch* sonic matter through electroacoustics. My reaction has not been so much a Glenn Gould–like renunciation of the concert hall but rather a natural extension of my desire to create a "contemporary" music — not just a music of our time, but a music created from and with our time.

In response to the growing world ecological crisis, I have felt a need to become involved in the environmental movement, at both political and artistic levels. Since I had musical training, I chose a path that combined the ecology of sound with music and concerned myself with the *sonic* and *musical* quality of our environment. Following in the tracks of composers such as R. Murray Schafer, Hildegard Westerkamp, and Barry Truax, and others involved with the World Soundscape Project in Vancouver, I adopted the notion that artists can help design a more imaginative and balanced soundscape.

My artistic practice involves a five-step process of listening, recording, analyzing, transforming, and orchestrating recorded soundscapes into electroacoustic portraits, and the most important elements of this process are listening and recording.

Sometimes I use poetic figures to explain my work: I use the wind as a verb, water as a noun, the beep of a truck as an adjective, and silence as a comma. I want to conjugate noise in the future and in the past. I want to bring the listener *inside* a story, space, experience, or sensation, with or without words, with or without transformation, and also with or without music.

For me, recording soundscapes is a kind of performance in which I play the microphone as a musical instrument. An essential part of my composing process occurs during field recording. Apart from the DAT-machine recording of two-dimensional stereo sound on tape, a parallel recording process takes place that I call "emotional recording": the recording of sensations and vibrations from the space by the body and the spirit. These emotions can subsequently be called upon to guide the inner structure and spiritual map of the composition.

I try to record sounds that upon repeated hearing *resonate* in me, cleansing me and shaking me up. I listen for sounds that evoke the fragility of our environment and that demonstrate the importance of awareness, listening, and silence. When I record, I meditate on and analyze the space. What are its microscopic and macroscopic components? What is my rapport and my emotional relationship with the space? How can I capture and transmit the multiple dimensions of a space by means of a microphone and loudspeakers? It is important that I be aware of the limitations of my recording equipment and plan how to frame my recordings in terms of my specific needs. As a result, the recording is unique for each project — the movement of the microphone, the choice of perspective, the background, the levels, the presence or absence of breath, the stereophonic angle.

These recordings are then edited into sections and combined based on their musical potential. I try different combinations until I find a satisfying "alchemy" between the elements and then mix them, layer upon layer. For instance, in the "Transportation" movement of my 1996 soundscape composition *El medio ambiante acustico de Mexico*, I used five transportation sounds to create a poetic portrait about movement and the musicality of transportation sounds. The piece begins with a recording of a moving wagon in the Mexico City subway, with its characteristic low-filtered rhythm of rubber wheels on a cement floor and the polyphony of the passengers' voices. This is cross-faded with the rhythmic metallic pulsation of a diesel train, then a creaking truck driving up a mountain with boys whispering in the background, a dense urban traffic jam with the drones of car engines and horns, and ending with the panting of out-of-breath mountain climbers.

The Sharawadji Effect was already present in these recordings. The editing and mixing process simply brought them to life.

Although I've made a number of electroacoustic soundscape compositions since my snowstorm trip in 1993, I still have not been able to re-create the sensation I experienced then. Nor have I been able to create an electroacoustic composition that can compare with the inexplicable beauty I sometimes hear in the acoustic environment.

I'm not sure it is possible.

But the search for the Sharawadji Effect, be it "the sensation of plenitude sometimes created by the contemplation of a complex soundscape" or "by decontextualisation, by a rupture of the senses," or "aggressive sounds, of technological or industrial origin, that suggest to certain ears a beautiful and trouble-

CLAUDE SCHRYER

some strangeness," or "the quieter sounds which trouble the spirit and lift it to cosmic proportions," is at the heart of my compositional process, and guides not only my way of making music but also my way of life.[6]

Swedish musicologist Ola Stockfelt said (in the spirit of John Cage) that "the listener and only the listener is the composer of the music."[7] To which I would add, as R. Murray Schafer has suggested, that the listener is not only the composer of the music but one of the performers as well.

## Notes

1. Ursula Franklin, "The Tuning of the World" conference proceedings, Banff Centre for the Arts, 1993.

2. Jean-François Augoyard and Henry Torgue, "Sharawadji" (assisted by Martine Leroux) in *Listening to the Acoustic Environment: Repertory of Sound Effects* (Paris: Editions Parentheses, 1995), pp. 126–32.

3. Ibid.

4. Francis Dhomont, "To Our Fellow Electroacousticians to Come (Maybe)," *Musicworks* 55 (1993), p. 31.

5. Hildegard Westerkamp, "Sounding Out Genders: Women Sound Artists/Composers Talk about Gender and Technology," at ISEA Panel Presentation, Montreal, 1995.

6. Augoyard and Torgue, 126–32.

7. Ola Stockfelt, "Cars, Buildings, and Soundscapes," in *Soundscapes: Essays on Vroom and Moo* (Tampere, Finland: Department of Folk Tradition, Institute of Rhythmic Music, Tampere University, 1994), pp. 19–38.

# Sonic Images

*Our normal waking consciousness, rational consciousness as we call it, is but one special type of consciousness, whilst all about it, parted from it by the filmiest of screens, there lie potential forms of consciousness entirely different.*
William James in *Varieties of Religious Experience*

*"How can I stop talking to myself?"*
*"First of all you must use your ears to take some of the burden from your eyes. We have been using our eyes to judge the world since the time we were born. We talk to others and to ourselves mainly about what we see. A warrior is aware of that and listens to the world; he listens to the sounds of the world."*
Don Juan to Carlos Castaneda in *Journey to Ixtlan*

1. Can you find the quiet place in your mind where there are no thoughts, no words, and no images?

2. Can you remain in this quiet mindplace by listening to all the sounds you can possibly hear, including the most distant sounds beyond the space you now occupy?

3. Do you ever notice how your ears adjust inside when you move from one size space to another? Or from indoors to out of doors or vice versa?

4. Who is very familiar to you? Could you recognize this person only by the sound of her or his footsteps?

5. What is your favorite sound? Can you reproduce it in your mind? Would you communicate to someone else what your favorite sound is?

6. Have you heard a sound lately which you could not identify? What were the circumstances? How did you feel?

7. What do you sound like when you walk?

8. What sound is most familiar to you? Can you describe it without referring to the source? What is its effect upon you?

9. Imagine the sound of a bird call. What kind of bird is it? When did you last hear it? What does it sound like? Can you imitate it?

10. What is the most silent period you have ever experienced? Was it only a moment or very long? What was its effect on you?

11. Can you imagine an animal sound? What kind of animal is it? What are its habits? What is it doing? Could you imitate the sound of that animal?

12. What is the most peculiar auditory sensation you have ever experienced?

13. Can you imagine a plant or tree? What kind of plant or tree is it? Where is it located? What sound comes to mind?

14. What is the most complex sound you ever experienced? What were the circumstances and how did you feel?

15. Can you imagine or remember some emotional experience? What nonverbal sound is associated with this experience?

16. Can you imagine the distance between any two sounds you are now hearing?

17. Can you imagine that you are in a very quiet, comfortable place, with plenty of time, with nothing bothering you? Can you imagine that you are in tune with your surroundings, and in the distance, beautiful sound is moving closer to you? What is that sound? What happens to you?

Sonic Images was presented in September 1972 at California State University, Los Angeles, at the invitation of Madeleine Hamblein, director of the Los Angeles Chapter of Experiments in Art and Technology, during a conference for Architects and Designers called *Shelter for Mankind*.

PAULINE OLIVEROS

# The Poetics of Environmental Sound

"The Poetics of Environmental Sound" consists of a listening exercise and quotations from about 150 different responses to the exercise. The quotations are arranged as if the sounds and emotional qualities effect a collaborative musical composition.

It was first assigned to students at the University of California at San Diego as part of a liberal arts course known as The Nature of Music. This course encourages students to develop musical perception through group improvisation, graphic notation and tape composition.

Theory students of Alvin Lucier at Brandeis University and Allen Strange at Indiana University also participated.

> *"I Heard A Boy Singing*
> *Long Long Ago.*
> *He Rode With The Reins Loose*
> *And Let The Horse Go."*
> Robert Duncan

Listen to the environment for 15 minutes or a longer but predetermined time length.
Use a timer, clock or any adequate method to define this time length.
Describe in detail the sounds you hear (heard) and how you feel (felt) about them.
Include internal as well as external sounds.
You are part of the environment.
Explore the limits of audibility:
(highest, lowest, loudest, softest, simplest, most complex, nearest, most distant, longest, shortest sound)

*"But Never Silence"*

"One thing I noticed right away was the absence of silence. There is always some kind of sound in the air."

"And between the thumps in the silences that grow longer, I am reminded that there is no silence."

"You'd never guess that so much sound could come out of a library which should be so quiet."

"It was like an orchestra with no rests, no silence anywhere."

"One instance I particularly remember came after a long period of intense silence."

"If it weren't for these breaks in the monotony, this constant sound would become as a silence."

"I desire silence but there is none."

*"I have just been in concert: the continuing concert of environmental sounds. I can hear it still."*

"I sit quietly with my alarm clock, close my eyes and open my ears. At this point, the curtain rises and the performance begins. My very surroundings seem to come alive, each sound revealing the personality of its creator. There are several sounds which become fixed in my ear like some 'basso ostinato': the continuous whirring of factory machinery in the distance and the hollow sound of plopping water in a nearby fountain. This background of sound is interrupted by the piercing motif of a bird. A sudden breath of air sweeps across the deck. The pages of my book respond with quick snapping sounds. The door at the entrance squeaks and moans on the same pitch like an old rocking chair, then closes with a thud. I can hear the drapery from an opened window rustling against the coarse plastered walls, while the drawing cord syncopates against the windowpane."

"Cars smack the air and tires slap the road giving off that highway sound, a low hiss that has no beginning or end, just a peak. The drone is established and only the sharp, high-pitched chirps and tweets of the birds persist in breaking the undertone."

*"Only a couple of minutes have passed and things are getting really involved already."*

"And then there were sounds that crept up on me, coming out of the drone, sharing the stage with or stealing it from the fountain, and then blending themselves unnoticed back into the drone. Obviously these were sounds without clearly-defined boundaries. A minor example of this type of sound is of a bus on a nearby road. The sound reached a level of only slight prominence and then disappeared leaving the listener unsure of the veracity of its very existence. But the sound of a jet-fighter traversing the breadth of the campus was quite a different matter; first there was the drone, then the jet, and then the jet was all I knew. It did not, however, dominate, so to speak, the sound of the fountain.

PAULINE OLIVEROS

Actually, for the time that it was at its maximum, it adopted the fountain, so that the splashing seemed to be just another sound of the jet. And then the jet left while the ever-present splashing and droning continued."

"Every once in a while a bad apple would pass that would break the pattern; a poorly tuned car, or one that was going too fast would seem out of place."

"At the moment these background sounds are being heard, they are linked together by other irregular and random sounds."

"Another car door slams and as if cued by a conductor, a buzz saw starts in a neighbor's yard. The intensity of the sound is so great now that I feel it rather than hear it. It stopped! The radio, the buzz saw, and the wind. Now I can hear a spider spinning its web while an innocent fly buzzes around my head."

"Funny, there are more sounds now than when the record player was on. Now I hear a symphony of a different sort."

"I was amazed that I could hear myself blink. It is about the softest sound I ever heard."

*"Five minutes have passed — only five minutes! Such a complex of varied sounds in such a short time. Well, onward — the sounds aren't waiting for me but are going on."*

"At times I was tense waiting for some noises and then they would come in a large group and I would have difficulty remembering all the sounds."

"It seems that a person hears what he wants to and anything else just doesn't exist."

"Distant voices enter . . . first a solo: a male-female duet . . . and then a whole choir. There are never words, only sonorities."

"One of my favorite sounds is the surge of my own heart when my ear is pressed against my pillow. Even as a youngster of five or six, I would listen to this pulse and try to speed it up or slow it down. I would fill the inner part of the beat with my own imaginary sounds. I used to hold balloons against my ear and chew apples or just listen."

"Everything is watery and the sound of someone's voice rides into my ears on rivulets."

"One of the dryers is providing an undercurrent of 'La Cucaracha' or something similarly Spanish in light clicky sounds: Chick Chicka Chick Chick, Chick Chicka Chick Chick . . . then a more relentless Chicka, Chicka, Chicka,

Chicka. The Chicka is joined (and nearly drowned out) by a more dynamic washer in the rinsing cycle, slowly going Swish Swash, Swish Swash."

"It's amazing the way the different sounds seem to build up to a climax and then diminish as in a musical composition."

"It all sounded very rhythmical and as if it had purposely been put together in a certain way. After this I began to notice groups of sounds at a time. A door slammed and then a turnstile clicked; at almost the same time another door closed. Then an airplane created a loud-textured noise and a pile of books smashed down this time. I noticed one girl go up the stairs in very even steps and then a boy skipped up. Whispering began, the chair squeaked, the turnstile clinked and steps getting louder."

*"Sounds are very complex now. It is all but impossible to get them down; there seem to be a thousand things going on at once. Twelve minutes have passed."*

"Even when I was listening I missed some sounds. The explanation being that part of the sounds are filtered by the mind from consciousness . . . even when one is paying attention. I did find that soft sounds were lost easier than loud sounds. This is probably because soft sounds tend to lull one while strong and loud sounds which are associated with unpleasant experiences attract one's attention."

"One curious thing I have noted is that the very building I am in has a noise of its own. Perhaps it is caused by the heating system. Wherever I go I can hear a soft hum of noise which seems to come from the ceilings and walls. Usually this noise is covered up by more demanding and raucous sounds, but now in a period of relative quiet, I can peel back the layers of other sounds and listen to this very unobtrusive hum. A shot! What sounded like a gunshot just occurred beneath my window. I'm not sure it was a gunshot (I've never actually heard a real live gunshot), but it sounded like what one would expect from a gun. Perhaps it was a balloon or a cap pistol. Whatever it was, it was loud and short. There was no echo or diminuendo. It immediately grasped my attention, and for a brief second, I could hear no other noise except that."

*"I also noticed that my disposition was affected by the type of sounds I heard."*

"The climax came when the roar of a motorcycle was met with a very unexpected bang of an object dropped in a nearby room. My nerves jumped as I settled back to the rustling leaves."

"Just outside my window and a couple of floors down hisses some exhaust outlet. It hisses so quietly I can barely hear it unless I lean far out the window.

PAULINE OLIVEROS

Also through this same outlet emanate clearly but weakly, from the seeming subterranean depths of underground garages, the screeches of cornering tires and the growl of automobile exhausts. Loosing the reins on my imagination, I might describe this last sound like the enraged sounds of a modern-day mechanical dragon. Combining the wind sounds and the automobile sounds late at night, a tableau forms that could send the sanest of men into eerie fits of terror. The wind whistles gently; leaves skitter and scrape across cement; tires screech in such a succession that it would seem that humans could not be driving. In addition, sea gulls' occasional caws intermittently intrude. The high bushes wave back and forth directly across from my window as if there was a human soul imprisoned, silently crying for release. Next door to my apartment building are little tarpaper shacks. At late hours black cats patter about like shades of times long ago. The inhabitants of these tarpaper shacks meanwhile make silent shapes on windowshades, while the tarpaper shacks creak and groan as if they too contained an embodied spirit. Also at this hour small birds flutter as if the air was losing its fabric and could no longer support them."

"Nearing the end of the fifteen minutes, almost as if it were planned, a girl sitting in the distance let out with a steam kettle, 'shhh' in an effort to restore 'silence' to the library."

*"Sounds keep coming and going."*

"The fifteen minutes seemed to go like a flash, especially toward the end."

"After listening to life, I feel I can appreciate it a little more. It is a shame a lot of other people do not take the time to do the same."

"It is a fascinating experience to become aware of all the sound companions one may discover in a once-believed quiet place."

"It seems to me that the whole world of sound is given a form like that of a concert piece."

"Sounds have a way of reminding you of something, and I guess most of the time people don't even realize that it was a sound that caused them to think about something because then they get tied up *thinking*, and not really *hearing* any more."

"After a time the 'earlids' began to close. That is, all sounds assumed a drone quality — the first sign of approaching sleep. Arousing myself somewhat, I noticed that the sounds were displaying an organization — the organization of living things. Each was an instrument within the orchestra. Each was made with its own unique sounds. I was very much entertained, and a smile came to my face. Hunger was getting the best of me. Knowing I could return at most any time, I left my reserved seat within the 'auditorium.'"

"At the end of the concert, I began to feel quite amazed with my surroundings. To think how utterly fantastic the work I just heard was, left me somewhat spellbound. Everything seemed to fall into place. Even though the tones heard may not have been intelligible as those of a manufactured musical instrument, the work certainly seemed to have a structure to it. I have a feeling that Webster really didn't know how much he was covering with his dictionary definition."

"Opening my eyes, I know the piece is over and the normalcy of the situation is astounding. It seems artificial to see dryers and people and carts, and the minute I begin seriously considering them with my eyes, the sounds fly right away."

"I thus depart with a new, an unusual experience: I have heard a composition from the 'Sounds of Silence.'"

# BRIAN ENO

# Ambient Music

In 1978 I released the first record which described itself as Ambient Music, a name I invented to describe an emerging musical style.

It happened like this. In the early seventies, more and more people were changing the way they were listening to music. Records and radio had been around long enough for some of the novelty to wear off, and people were wanting to make quite particular and sophisticated choices about what they played in their homes and workplaces, what kind of sonic mood they surrounded themselves with.

The manifestation of this shift was a movement away from the assumptions that still dominated record making at the time — that people had short attention spans and wanted a lot of action and variety, clear rhythms and song structures and, most of all, voices. To the contrary, I was noticing that my friends and I were making and exchanging long cassettes of music chosen for its stillness, homogeneity, lack of surprises and, most of all, lack of variety. We wanted to use music in a different way — as part of the ambience of our lives — and we wanted it to be continuous, a surrounding.

At the same time there were other signs on the horizon. Because of the development of recording technology, a whole host of compositional possibilities that were quite new to music came into existence. Most of these had to do with two closely related new areas — the development of the texture of sound itself as a focus for compositional attention, and the ability to create with electronics virtual acoustic spaces (acoustic spaces that don't exist in nature).

When you walk into a recording studio, you see thousands of knobs and controls. Nearly all of these are different ways of doing the same job: they allow you to do things to sounds, to make them fatter or thinner or shinier or rougher or harder or smoother or punchier or more liquid or any one of a thousand other things. So a recording composer may spend a great deal of her compositional energy effectively inventing new sounds or combinations of sounds. Of course, this was already well known by the mid sixties: psychedelia expanded not only minds but recording technologies as well. But there was still an assumption that playing with sound itself was a "merely" technical job

— something engineers and producers did — as opposed to the serious creative work of writing songs and playing instruments. With Ambient Music, I wanted to suggest that this activity was actually one of the distinguishing characteristics of new music, and could in fact become the main focus of compositional attention.

Studios have also offered composers virtual spaces. Traditional recording put a mike in front of an instrument in a nice sounding space and recorded the result. What you heard was the instrument and its reverberation in that space. By the forties, people were getting a little more ambitious, and starting to invent technologies that could supplement these natural spaces — echo chambers, tape delay systems, etc. A lot of this work was done for radio — to be able to "locate" characters in different virtual spaces in radio dramas — but it was popular music which really opened the subject up. Elvis and Buddy and Eddy and all the others sang with weird tape repeats on their voices — unlike anything you'd ever hear in nature. Phil Spector and Joe Meek invented their own "sound" — by using combinations of overdubbing, homemade echo units, resonant spaces like staircases and liftshafts, changing tape speeds and so on, they were able to make "normal" instruments sound completely new. And all this was before synthesizers and dub reggae . . .

By the early seventies, when I started making records, it was clear that this was where a lot of the action was going to be. It interested me because it suggested moving the process of making music much closer to the process of painting (which I thought I knew something about). New sound-shaping and space-making devices appeared on the market weekly (and still do), synthesizers made their clumsy but crucial debut, and people like me just sat at home night after night fiddling around with all this stuff, amazed at what was now possible, immersed in the new sonic worlds we could create.

And immersion was really the point: we were making music to swim in, to float in, to get lost inside.

This became clear to me when I was confined to bed, immobilized by an accident in early 1975. My friend Judy Nylon had visited, and brought with her a record of 17th-century harp music. I asked her to put it on as she left, which she did, but it wasn't until she'd gone that I realized that the hi-fi was much too quiet and one of the speakers had given up anyway. It was raining hard outside, and I could hardly hear the music above the rain — just the loudest notes, like little crystals, sonic icebergs rising out of the storm. I couldn't get up and change it, so I just lay there waiting for my next visitor to come and sort it out, and gradually I was seduced by this listening experience. I realized that this was what I wanted music to be — a place, a feeling, an all-around tint to my sonic environment.

BRIAN ENO

After that, in April or May of that year, I made *Discreet Music*, which I suppose was really my first Ambient record (though the stuff I'd done with the great guitarist Robert Fripp before that gets pretty close). This was a 31–minute piece (the longest I could get on a record at the time) which was modal, evenly textured, calm and sonically warm. At the time, it was not a record that received a very warm welcome, and I probably would have hesitated to release it without the encouragement of my friend Peter Schmidt, the painter. (In fact, it's often been painters and writers — people who use music while they work and want to make for themselves a conducive environment — who've first enjoyed and encouraged this work.)

In late 1977 I was waiting for a plane in Cologne airport. It was early on a sunny, clear morning, the place was nearly empty, and the space of the building (designed, I believe, by the father of one of the founders of Kraftwerk) was very attractive. I started to wonder what kind of music would sound good in a building like that. I thought, "It has to be interruptible (because there'll be announcements), it has to work outside the frequencies at which people speak, and at different speeds from speech patterns (so as not to confuse communication), and it has to be able to accommodate all the noises that airports produce. And, most importantly for me, it has to have something to do with where you are and what you're there for — flying, floating and, secretly, flirting with death." I thought, "I want to make a kind of music that prepares you for dying — that doesn't get all bright and cheerful and pretend you're not a little apprehensive, but which makes you say to yourself, 'Actually, it's not that big a deal if I die.'"

Thus was born the first Ambient record — *Music for Airports* — which I released on my own label (called Ambient Records, of course). The inner sleeve of that release carried my manifesto:

Ambient Music
The concept of music designed specifically as a background feature in the environment was pioneered by Muzak Inc. in the fifties, and has since come to be known generically by the term Muzak. The connotations that this term carries are those particularly associated with the kind of material that Muzak Inc. produces — familiar tunes arranged and orchestrated in a light weight and derivative manner. Understandably, this has led most discerning listeners (and most composers) to dismiss entirely the concept of environmental music as an idea worthy of attention.

Over the past three years, I have become interested in the use of music as ambience, and have come to believe that it is possible to produce material that can be used thus without being in any way compromised. To create a distinction between my own experiments in this area and the products of the various purveyors of canned music, I have begun using the term Ambient Music.

An ambience is defined as an atmosphere, or a surrounding influence: a tint. My intention is to produce original pieces ostensibly (but not exclusively) for particular times and situations with a view to building up a small but versatile catalogue of environmental music suited to a wide variety of moods and atmospheres.

Whereas the extant canned-music companies proceed from the basis of regularizing environments by blanketing their acoustic and atmospheric idiosyncrasies, Ambient Music is intended to enhance these. Whereas conventional background music is produced by stripping away all sense of doubt and uncertainty (and thus all genuine interest) from the music, Ambient Music retains these qualities. And whereas their intention is to "brighten" the environment by adding stimulus to it (thus supposedly alleviating the tedium of routine tasks and levelling out the natural ups and downs of the body rhythms), Ambient Music is intended to induce calm and a space to think.

Ambient Music must be able to accommodate many levels of listening attention without enforcing one in particular; it must be as ignorable as it is interesting.

*September 1978*

Like a lot of the stuff I was doing at the time, this was regarded by many English music critics as a kind of arty joke, and they had a lot of fun with it. I'm therefore pleased that the idea has stuck around so long and keeps sprouting off in all sorts of directions: it comes back round to me like Chinese Whispers — unrecognizable but intriguing. Those early seeds (there were only four releases on the original Ambient Records label: *On Land* and *Music for Airports* by me, *The Plateaux of Mirror* by Harold Budd, and *Day of Radiance* by Laraaji) have contributed to a rich forest of music.

BRIAN ENO

# Speaking from Inside the Soundscape

I am speaking to you primarily as a composer who chooses to compose with the sounds of the environment. But I am also speaking as someone who once emigrated from one culture to another, someone who is concerned about the health of the soundscape, someone who is still learning to listen and remains astonished and fascinated by the complexities of listening. Astonished, because the process of listening is always full of new experiences and surprises. Fascinated, because sound and listening are intimately connected with the passing of time and therefore with how time is spent, how life is lived. The soundscape voices the passing of time and reaches into every moment of our personal and professional lives. It reaches right into *this* place and *this* moment of time, becoming a lived soundscape for all of us in this room.

---

TAPE:[1]  *listen    lislisten    listen    lislisten*
          *listen listen listen listen    listen listen listen listen*
          *listen    lislisten    listen    lislisten*

---

We are inside the act of listening. We are here to listen to the listening.

---

TAPE:[2]  Sound of footsteps. Then they stop. Then voice: *"Today is the 6th of December. I'm on Hollyburn Mountain. It's a very sparkling, cold, sunny day. It's very still up here. I hardly dare to talk for fear of covering all the little sounds that are happening around me here. I am standing on a trail that goes through the forest. . . .* Tape fades

---

Together we are creating a quality of listening and soundmaking in this sonic space, the quality of time passing.

TAPE:[3] City ambience. Then voice over ambience: *"The city is roaring tonight*————*It's quite a clear evening*—————*I hear a muddle of sound*—————*That's the city*—————*A large undefined sound*————*anonymous sound of the city*——*from anonymous sources."* Train horn sounds in mid-distance (———  ——— – ———long long short long: signal for train crossings). Children's voices screeching a block away. *"Thank God for the kids and for those signals, train horns*——*"* Trainhorn sound. *"*——*that give a definition to this place, that give it a name."* Ambience fades.

I have been asked to speak *about* the musical, artistic aspects of the soundscape. The more I thought about this, the more I realized that I cannot speak about anything involving the soundscape if I want to stay true to an ecological consciousness that positions itself inside the soundscape, as part of and participant in the soundscape, not as outsider, observer, or commentator.

TAPE:[4] Footsteps on snow fade in under live talk

So, my speaking today will be an attempt to speak from inside the soundscape, more specifically from inside *this* soundscape, from inside remembered soundscapes, from inside my experience and knowledge of soundscape, from inside the musical, artistic aspects of the soundscape.

TAPE continues: Footsteps continue. Stop. Then voice: *"Nobody has been here*——*since the last snowfall*—————*Listen to the icicles."* Icicle sounds, then tape fades.

As infants, we truly did exist inside the soundscape. We listened and we made sounds from inside that place. We were, in fact, incapable of stepping outside of it.

TAPE:[5] Waves crashing. Then voice: *"A sound, to me, is very much about time. Time passing. The quality of time passing. How it passes. And if we listen to that, we are very much inside the sound, very much inside the soundscape."* Wave ambience fades.

By listening we got an impression of the world into which we were born,

HILDEGARD WESTERKAMP

and with soundmaking we expressed our needs, desires, and emotions. As babies, listening was for us an active process of learning, one way of receiving vital information about our surroundings and about the people who were closest to us. And whatever we heard and listened to became material for vocal imitation, for first attempts to articulate, express, and make sounds.

Listening and soundmaking (input and output, impression and expression) were ongoing activities, like breathing, happening simultaneously, always in relation to each other, in a feedback process. The relationship between the acoustic information we received as babies and what we expressed vocally was balanced. And in this balance between listening and soundmaking, we never questioned how our time passed. It simply passed by virtue of our being active inside each moment.

TAPE:[6] Rain/wave ambience. Then a mix of voice speaking words and phrases: *"Delicate balance————carved——carved out of ordinary time— voices, birds, crickets, child, wind—sounds in the wilderness, echo————echo in the wilderness————voices—carved out of time—child, wind—echo in the wilderness—changing, exploring, for listening————voices, birds, crickets, child, wind————the pleasure of——listening."* Ambience fades

The pleasure of listening. And the pleasure of soundmaking.

TAPE:[7] Baby's voice inside a watery, composed soundscape.

Depending on the social and cultural environment in which we grew up, this open and energetic approach to life got shaped — expanded or curtailed to a greater or lesser degree — as we grew into our particular surroundings. As they are growing up and developing their distinct voices, children are frequently told to be quiet and to listen to what adults, their parents and teachers, have to say. In this kind of situation they become reluctant listeners, and they rarely have a chance to express, to make sounds, to use their own voices.

TAPE:[8] Breathing sounds and heartbeat composed with other sounds.

All creative process is based on the desire to re-create a state of wholeness, a type of "oceanic state." As grown people, reaching such a state of wholeness must become a conscious task. In fact, it may have to be developed into a skill, a discipline, a meditation. The refusal to place ourselves apart from the whole or to speak *about* the soundscape, but instead to place our speaking and sounding squarely into its center, transforms our ways of speaking, our ways of listening.

---

TAPE:[9] Flowing water, waves crashing. Then voice: *"Water wind——wind waves——wonder——sound——listen sound, water——crickets birds——birds crickets desert——sound desert wind desert——crispness——liquid crispness rain rain liquid-rain liquid water—wind—wind sound—wind sound forest——body forest body breath——breathing voice breathing crispness breathing crispness rain——rain rhythm rain wind rhythm wind rhythm breath rhythm—voice tiny sounds tiny sounds silence quiet crispness quiet cricket liquid crispness cricket brids quiet liquidity tiny sounds tiny sounds spirit rain spirit rain spirit forest spirit spirit"* Rain ambience fades.

---

Gregory Bateson wrote: "The problem of how to transmit our ecological reasoning to those whom we wish to influence in what seems to us to be an ecologically 'good' direction is itself an ecological problem. We are not outside the ecology for which we plan — we are always and inevitably a part of it."[10] Mark Riegner has described "genuine ecological consciousness" as " . . . an awareness that does not just think about ecological relationships but cognitively experiences the activity of relating."[11] And Thoreau asked: "Where are the words that speak for nature, that still have earth clinging to their roots?"[12]

We might ask: Where are the words that speak for soundscape, that still have some truth ringing from the heart?

The problem of sound overload and excessive noise forces us to find those words and to position ourselves inside the soundscape, in fact, inside of any aural experience.

---

TAPE:[13] Sound of electric organ playing Christmas songs, then voice over music: *"This is live Muzak——an electric organ and two fashionably dressed women, smiling, laughing, playing, alternating in playing the music ——————smoothly sliding from one song to another."* Muzak fades.

---

In the spirit of "genuine ecological consciousness" we must place ourselves inside even this soundscape — not to be consumed by it, but to receive it with open, alert ears. And in the act of being inside such a moment and such a place we become action, we create. My physical presence produced the spontaneous words you heard. What I called "live Muzak" I would also call a form of music-as-environment (or functional music). In this case, the music produced the mood in the mall and also demonstrated a product — the electric organ or keyboard. In my opinion, this is the opposite of what soundscape composers are trying to do.

Music-as-environment, itself always a commodity, determines the tone of commodity exchange. Through its very "tone" it tries to conceal its relationship to money and power, its function as mediator of human relations and its function as "moodsetter." Without it — so its producers might like us to think — we may not be able to interact, may not feel safe. It engulfs us acoustically, shuts out the problems of the outside world, and makes the consumer environment sound as if "that's where the action is." It has established itself as a cultural system, a "place" in the world, the "womb" of twentieth-century urban living. Because urban life revolves around making and spending money, and because such a focus sets up a particularly stressful lifestyle, it is music-as-environment that seems to offer a bearable pace. But it is a false womb, of course. It can only exist inside the world of money.[14]

It is the type of music that no one really listens to, not only because stress blocks us from really listening, but because it is designed not to be listened to. It is deliberately designed to place us inside the soundscape without our noticing that we are inside it, that we have been sucked into its profit-seeking agenda. The aim of strategic marketing design of sonic space is to put the consumer in a passive, non-listening position.

It is high time that we, as soundscape composers, acoustic ecologists, and soundscape designers, implement our own listening skills and sound-design knowledge, and speak back to the forces that have assumed the authority to silence us, to place us as passive receivers.

One very effective way of bucking that acoustic marketing strategy and its placement of the listener is to record, to highlight, to reveal and expose it and broadcast it back into the soundscape, ideally over the radio waves. At one point, many of us — composers, audio artists, sound recordists — decided to spring into action, using audio technology to do exactly that, not only to document a soundscape, to preserve disappearing sounds, to record nature sounds, but to analyze both social and musical meanings and actively to speak back to that which we find unacceptable.

---

TAPE:[15] *Ave Maria*, store ambience, sound of cash register. Then voice: *"We're at Eaton's. A few days before Christmas. This is the men's clothing department. Two loudspeakers are placed close to the cash register."* Rustling of bags—————————*"The music invokes the image and atmosphere of a cathedral, and thereby the memory of religious celebration.*—————————*It creates a holy atmosphere around the cash register, makes it an altar."* Man asks recordist: *"Just* wondering what you are doing." Recordist answers, "Oh, I'm just recording the music." Sound of cash register——*"It is as if one is involved in a holy act while paying for the goodies."* Music fades.

---

The microphone is a seductive tool: it can offer a fresh ear to both recordist and listener; it can give us access to a foreign place as well as open our ears to the all-too-familiar; or it can provide a way to capture and speak back to the unbearable.

At the point when the ear becomes disconnected from direct contact with the soundscape and suddenly hears the way the microphone "hears" and the headphones transmit, at that point the recordist wakes up to a new reality of the soundscape. The sounds are highlighted and the ears are alerted precisely because the sounds are on a recording.

Not only are the sounds highlighted, but the entire experience *feels* to the recordist as if he or she is more intensely *inside* the soundscape, because the sound is closer to the ear and usually amplified. Paradoxically, though, the recordist is separated from the original direct aural contact with the soundscape, especially from the spatial dimensions of closeness and distance, from the ability to locate the sound accurately.

In that contradiction lies the seduction of the microphone: it feels like access, like closer contact, but it is in fact a separation, a schizophonic situation. Soundscape recordists exist in their own sound bubbles and hear their surroundings differently from others who are in the same place. They are like foreigners or outsiders, whether the place is their home or unfamiliar territory.

The microphone collects all sounds indiscriminately. It does not select or isolate them. This is similar to how ears behave when we are in foreign surroundings: initially our ears and psyches are incapable of selecting and making sense of what they hear. All sounds stream in unfiltered. Our ears are naked and open, much like those of the newborn, and can only become selective once we have begun to recognize and understand the sounds of the place.

In that state of nakedness, the newborn's ear, the untrained ear in a foreign place, or the technological ear — the microphone — are all equally powerful awareness-raising tools.

When the recordist is in a foreign country he or she is located in a sound bubble *within* another sound bubble — doubly separated and at the same time doubly exposed, naked by virtue of hearing through a microphone or headphones and with a stranger's ears.

---

TAPE:[16] A mix of conversations with sellers in the streets of New Delhi: *"Hallo hallo hallo hallo. Where're you from? Canada. What is this? This is a*

*microphone. You speak? A microphone. This is a microphone. This is a micro-*
*phone. Why you. . . ? So, I'm recording the birds, what you're saying, our conver-*
*sation. . . . Where're you from? . . . Us talking. Do you want to say your name*
*more clearly? What's your name? My name Mulcha. Hallo hallo, what's your*
*name? My name Chedalla. What's this, Madam? It's a microphone. Micro-*
*phone. So, I'm recording. Yeah? Yes. Good good. Where're you from? Canada.*
*French or English? No, from Vancouver. Canada. Where're you from? Canada.*
*Are you from Delhi? Uuuhm Khajurao. — Canada. French or English. En-*
*glish. Where're you from? I'm from Khaj. From where? Madhja Pradesh. UP*
*—— Canada Toronto Montreal Vancouver—Vancouver——What's your job?*
*Pardon me? What's your job? —What's my job! Yeah. —Hallo hallo, what's your*
*name? Ram Anjur Ram Anjur. Your name is Anis—yes—Anis Amud? What*
*is your name? Rhadu Rhadu? And what is your name? Sanje. And Lathu. How*
*old are you? Me? Twelve. My name Mulcha. Mulcha. Yeah. And your name?*
*My name Chedalla. Where're you from? Canada.* Tape fades.

If acoustic ecology is the center from which we choose to function, we must always ask ourselves where we are situated — from the moment of the first listening, the first recording, to the last building block in any project. It is all too
easy to get carried away into the world of sound experimentation, electroacoustic music, by our sound-materials, and forget the connection to the central focus of ecological thinking.

How do we avoid the very real danger of simply creating yet another product, one more CD with yet more amazing sounds? Let's be clear that when we
hear animal sounds from, say, the Amazon on a CD, we are listening to sounds
that have been frozen into a repetitive medium and format and have been imported into our soundscape. They have become, at best, interesting aural information for us — a story, a type of text from another place. In the worst case,
they have become an imported product, a sound without any real meaning
beyond the "wow" experience, or, like "new age Muzak," an excuse for further
non-listening, or perhaps just another object on our shelves. We must ask ourselves, when we compose a piece or produce a CD, whether we are bringing
our listeners closer to a place or situation, or whether we are deluding ourselves and inadvertently participating in the place's extinction.

Environmental sound is a type of language, a text. And the technology
through which we transmit the sounds has its own language, its own process.
If we truly want to reveal meanings with recorded environmental sound and
draw the listener inside these meanings, then we must transmit precise information and demystify processes obscured by technology. When we have done
something as simple as condensing the duration of a dawn chorus in order to

fit it into a predetermined time frame on a CD, let's *say* so and explain *how* we have accomplished that. Let's *name* the voices of the place. Let's mention the weather, for example, or the season, the landscape, the social and natural context. At the very least we need to draw attention to the inherent confusion regarding time and place when we work with recorded environmental sound.

---

TAPE:[17] Camel sounds audible underneath and between spoken sentences. *"At this moment it's November 28, 1992. I'm riding on a camel in the desert near Jaisalmer in Rajasthan, India. Yet at this moment it's June 22, 1993. I'm riding on the airwaves together with my camel. On 102.7 FM, Vancouver Co-operative Radio, CFRO. This is* Wireless Graffiti, *live from the Vancouver East Cultural Centre. My name is Hildegard Westerkamp and this is "From the India Sound Journal."*

Desert ambience fades out, then fades up again.

*"Camelvoice November 1992, here in Vancouver, June '93 at the Vancouver East Cultural Centre on Co-op Radio, riding the airwaves, disembodied from the sand, the heat, its voice. Where is the camel at this moment? Where is it eating? Who is riding it, recording its voice, photographing its body? Where is it now, reproduced many times all over this ... uhm ... global village? Is it still the same camel chewing and digesting loudly in the village of Sam, Rajasthan?"* Tape fades.

---

Let's be honest and clarify the context. And, rather than fooling the listener with our use of technology, let's invite the listener into the place of our creative process and our imagination.

---

TAPE:[18] Urban rumble, then voice: *" ... and I can't hear the barnacles in all their tinyness. It seems too much effort to filter the city out.*

Urban rumble, low frequencies slowly get filtered out.

*Luckily we have bandpass filters and equalizers. We can just go into the studio and get rid of the city, pretend it's not there. Pretend we are somewhere far away.*

A dense texture of high-frequency sounds.

*These are the tiny, the intimate voices of nature, of bodies, of dreams, of the imagination.*

High-frequency sounds fade out.

---

Each recorded work — whether a sound document, nature recording, or a soundscape composition — itself becomes an entirely new soundscape experience, heard in a new context and a new location. For the recordist/composer, it is lifted out of a remembered and lived time and a more or less familiar place into the entirely new, often unknown place and time of its reproduction. For the listener, it has been lifted out of unknown, unlived time in a foreign or perhaps remembered place into a living moment in a more or less familiar place.

How can we possibly achieve resonance between our — the recordist/composer's — experience and that of the listener? How can we bridge these different localities of experience?

These are questions we will hopefully continue to pose in our creative minds. They can only be tackled inside each individual soundscape production or project. Ideally, if we have managed to strike a chord in our listeners, the listening experience will re-emerge as valuable memory and information at a later point, or it will encourage listeners to visit, hear, and experience firsthand the source place and context of which the work speaks.

Then we will have come full circle. The work will have created the naked, open ear in the listener, a curious ear that has moved him or her into action, into *inter*action with the soundscape.

Our many recording activities and the sophisticated equipment and techniques used cannot re-create the healthy balance of listening and soundmaking experienced by the young baby. But the "naked ear" of the microphone can arouse an attentiveness in our listening, which will have a direct influence on how we speak with environmental sounds through our compositions and productions. A new balance between recording/listening and composing/soundmaking can be achieved. It may demand cultural detours, but it belongs to this and the next century.

Relearning to hear and decipher the soundscape like a new language; treading carefully with curiosity and openness, aware that as recordists we remain outsiders; always attempting to engender a naked, open ear; these may be the ways for the composer to continue who wants to speak from inside the soundscape and at the same time transmit a genuine ecological consciousness.

---

TAPE:[19] Water sounds, birds, frogs, processed rain drops.

---

# Notes

Except for the excerpts from "Voices of a Place" (notes 5, 6, and 9), all tape excerpts are from compositions, film soundtracks, or radio programs by the author. As well, the spoken voice in the tape excerpts, except for the baby's voice in "Moments of Laughter" (note 7), is that of the author.

1. *This Borrowed Land* (National Film Board of Canada, 1984), Bonnie Kreps, director.

2. "Soundwalking: Silent Night," Vancouver Co-operative Radio, Winter 1978/79.

3. "Soundwalking: Trainhorn Vancouver," Vancouver Co-operative Radio, Winter 1978/79.

4. "Soundwalking: Silent Night," Vancouver Co-operative Radio, Winter 1978/79.

5. "Voices of a Place," by Sylvi MacCormac, Vancouver, 1998.

6. "Voices of a Place," by Sylvi MacCormac, Vancouver, 1998.

7. "Moments of Laughter," 1988. Baby's voice: Sonja Ruebsaat at six weeks of age.

8. "Breathing Room," 1990.

9. "Voices of a Place," by Sylvi MacCormac, Vancouver, 1998.

10. Gregory Bateson, *Steps to an Ecology of Mind* (New York: Ballantine Books, 1972), p. 504.

11. Mark Riegner, "Goethean Science: Toward a Heightened Empathy of Nature," *Environmental and Architectural Phenomenology Newsletter*, 9/1 (1998): 10.

12. Quoted in Max Oelschlaeger, "Earth Talk: Conservation and the Ecology of Language," in David Rothenberg, ed., *Wild Ideas* (Minneapolis: University of Minnesota Press, 1995), p. 47.

13. "Soundwalking: Silent Night," Vancouver Co-operative Radio, Winter 1978/79.

14. Hildegard Westerkamp, "Listening and Soundmaking: A Study of Music-as-Environment," Simon Fraser University, M.A. thesis, 1988, p. 35.

15. "Cool Drool," 1983.

16. "Soundscape Delhi," a work in progress, 1998.

17. Two excerpts from "Camelvoice," performed at the Vancouver East Cultural Centre, June 22, 1993.

18. "Kits Beach Soundwalk," 1989.

19. "Talking Rain," 1997.

DOUGLAS QUIN

# Toothwalkers

### Arrival at Twin Hills

The plane climbed and whined away toward the fish cannery for the next leg of the Togiak run out of Dillingham, Alaska, and we were left with our gear on the runway at Twin Hills. A ship and scattered flotilla of small craft were marooned in the marshy tundra and tidal swamp that stretches from Twin Hills to Togiak. A group of girls raced by on a four-wheeled all-terrain vehicle, squealing and giggling as they spun and churned up dirt. The eldest of the three was no more than ten — a Yup'ik smile stuffed into a purple and pink parka. From a rise in the opposite direction an old woman came motoring along on her four-wheeler laden with dry goods from the cannery store at Togiak Fisheries. Her engine sputtered as she dipped into town: a hamlet of homes, satellite dishes, antennae, propane tanks, and vehicles in various degrees of service in the shadow of the Twin Hills. Most of the houses rested on blocks and low scaffolding, periodically adjusted to accommodate the yaw and spasm of the frozen ground.

The beach was an igneous black and ashy sand that deepened to a turbid pitch in the water. Bear tracks meandered along the beach and through town along with those of people, dogs, and caribou. Two caribou, one sporting a worn blue halter, wandered amid the houses, foraging on tufts of grass. They noted our movements with a feral edge and went on grazing. An outboard motor shop overflowed with propellers and parts. Rigs dangled, dismembered on sawhorses; motor oil colored the mud with fluorescent streaks.

Everywhere, debris sank into the earth around homes: household appliances, cars, snowmobiles, and cast-iron shapes whose purpose was a russet enigma. The immediacy of survival and seasonal opportunity has inured most to the unsightliness of this refuse. To the unaccustomed eye of someone from the Lower Forty-Eight, the detritus speaks of abandoned aspirations and surrender to the exigencies of difficult circumstance. A new stainless steel and molded plastic conveyor belt unit for the fish cannery lay in a cocoon of shrink-wrapping next to a ship's anchor sloughing oxide layers of purple and red.

A mackerel sky spawned from the west and clouds streaked orange fanned

above Togiak as the six of us arranged and rearranged our bags and got acquainted. Ken Whitten and his wife, Mary Zalar, had traveled from Fairbanks. He is a caribou specialist with the Alaska Department of Fish and Game — tall, whitehaired with a neatly trimmed beard, and somewhat taciturn. She has reddish hair, freckles, and a gregarious disposition. Margie Campbell, a recently widowed bush nurse out of Dillingham, had come with Wendy Couch and Vi Norbo. Vi was born and raised in Alaska and had seen it change from frontier to statehood, and you could tell Wendy had done a lot of camping and trekking over the years. These women, all in their mid-sixties, were out to have an adventure.

What brought us together was a common excitement: to witness the spectacle of thousands of walruses hauled out on an island scarcely the size of Central Park. We were waiting for Don Winkelman, our host and boat pilot, who would come to pick us up sometime in the afternoon when he returned from Round Island, part of the Walrus Islands State Game Sanctuary in Bristol Bay. Every backpack bulged with photographic equipment, except for mine, which was stuffed with microphones and recording equipment. Much of my interest for this trip centered on the acoustic ecology of *Odobenus rosmarus divergens*. I had come to record the sounds of Pacific walruses on this island sanctuary. My purpose was to listen, to gather material for use in musical compositions, and to assist with collecting baseline data on acoustic disturbance and walrus behavior for the Alaska Department of Fish and Game.

Our anticipation was fueled by walrus imaginings — literary, graphic, fanciful, and scientific. For me, the mythic presence of these creatures was informed in childhood by storybook images. When I heard John Lennon's enigmatic evocation in "I Am the Walrus" at the age of eleven, the walrus became indelibly associated with music. The Beatles brought me back to Lewis Carroll's fable of "The Walrus and the Carpenter" in *Through the Looking Glass*:

> "The time has come," the Walrus said,
> "To talk of many things:
> Of shoes — and ships — and sealing wax —
> Of cabbages — and kings —
> And why the sea is boiling hot —
> And whether pigs have wings."[1]

Before the trip, I read European exploration journals, studies in scientific periodicals, and Yup'ik and Inupiak hunting stories, but it was the earliest impressions in the capricious corridor of memory that were most enduring. In all, it was a vaguely surreal, yet vivid, preamble to the experience I was about to have.

## Natural Histories

In the Anchorage Museum of History and Art, there is an eighteenth-century etching from James Cook's account of his expedition to discover a northwest passage. The image by John Webber, called *Sea Horses*, depicts walruses being attacked by men in a boat firing muskets at close range. The compressed and symmetrical composition of animals, men, and limited geographic features, such as ice, reveals a controlled theatrical space. The walruses are grouped to the left, formalized with pronounced necks. Their eyes have been slightly enlarged and curiously reoriented to the front of the head — a disquieting anthropocentric suggestion. In reality, the eyes of a walrus are diminutive and on the side of the head. The ship's crew is on the right, a compositional mass of seated and standing figures firing in unison. The work is somewhat reminiscent of Goya's *Executions of the Third of May*.

A description of walruses and an accompanying print from nearly two hundred years earlier are found in Gerrit de Veer's account of Willem Barents's northern voyages. By Barents's reckoning, off the north coast of Novaya Zemlya on July 6, 1594, he had reached 77°55'.

> There was a lot of wood which the sea had borne, *Walrusschen*, or sea cows, which are sea monsters of terrible power, larger than beef cattle, and have rougher hide than sea dogs [seals], with short, thick fur. Their muzzle resembles that of a lion. They almost always stay on the ice, and we have diffi-

DOUGLAS QUIN

culty killing them, on account that the deathblow is effective only to the side of the head. They have four feet and no ears.

They produce but one or two young and when met by fishermen on the ice, they shove their young in front of them into the water, taking them between their forelegs, like arms, they dive with them and feed repeatedly; and when they want to revenge themselves and attack the boats, or defend themselves, they again cast off their young, and go at the boat in an extreme rage. On either side of their muzzle, they have two teeth, about two feet long, which are as valued as elephants' teeth, particularly in Moscow and Tartary, and in other places where they are used, because they are no less white, no less hard, no less smooth than ivory. The fur of their beards is like little quills, similar to those of a porcupine.[2]

A hunting scene by Levinus Hulsius (Lieven Hulst) reproduced in the 1598 German book is titled *Ineffective Attempt to Kill These Sea Monsters We Call "Sea Cows."* A shore party, armed with pikes and axes, sets upon hauled out walruses. To the left of the composition, in the middle ground, a polar bear lies prostrate, tethered to a stake on a floating iceberg. A small boat, filled with men, moves in the pack ice. A seaman leans to attack another swimming bear with an ax. Two ships are anchored in the distance. The walruses in this woodcut are streamlined: represented as somewhat smaller than in life. Their facial features are codified and resemble dogs, with a canine muzzle, small ears (in spite of the author's account), and slight tusks. The curvature of the tusks has been diminished and stylized into something of a caricature, with the result that they fit awkwardly, like a saber-tooth prosthesis. The fore flippers have been interpreted as the front limbs of a dog with paws.

Both illustrations rationalize the walrus either in terms of known animals or the fantastic realm of monsters. The central hunting action affirms control and domination over nature in the face of supernatural dread. The image of plentiful supply, no doubt, also made convincing advertisement to expedition patrons and commercial prospects who would seek to exploit the ivory tusks.

In science, the walrus cannot be easily classified. The Latin term comes from Linnaeus in 1758: *Odobenus rosmarus*, or "tooth-walking sea horse." The etymology of the word *walrus*, in English, is obscure and confused, derived from the Old Norse *rosinhvalr* and possibly *hrosshvalr*. These terms mean "horse-whale," which, duly noted in the *Oxford English Dictionary*, is "zoologically improbable."[3] The Vikings hunted walruses for ivory, and written accounts of the hunt come down from the ninth century. Linnaean taxonomy has given us two, and possibly three, subspecies: *Odobenus rosmarus divergens* (Pacific walrus) and *Odobenus rosmarus rosmarus* (Atlantic walrus), with Russian researchers recognizing *Odobenus rosmarus laptevi* (an isolated population from the Laptev Sea). To people of the Bering Sea, two types of walruses exist: those animals that yield to the hunt and those that do not.[4] One system of classification is based on morphology and physical attribute; the other involves a disposition toward the hunt that looks to spiritual distinction.

North of Round Island, into the Bering Strait, lies Ugiuvuk (named King Island by James Cook in 1778). For the Inupiak King Islanders, in whose traditions and culture the walrus has figured prominently, toothwalkers were at once a communal prize and a powerful social metaphor. The animal was never hunted by men alone and on foot, unlike seals and polar bears. The timing of walrus migration is such that they could only be successfully hunted at the vernal breakup of the sea ice, and then only by groups of men in boats, in a practice called *angunniaqtuat*. The crew of a *umiak*, or skinboat, represented the central political unit of organization in Inupiak life. In this cohesive fraternity, whoever succeeded in hunting was accorded social status and economic reward. In this way, the walrus bestowed solidarity, and its skin was a valued commodity and trophy.

The distribution of a walrus kill involved a different protocol and attendant celebratory rites. The *umiak* captain received one half of the animal.[5] The skins were used to make the roofing and walls of houses as well as the hulls of boats. Walrus hide rope was diversely used and offered as a gift at dances. *Kauk*, or aged walrus skin, was viewed as having a mystically protective quality — allowing one class of the animal to elude hunters. *Kauk* is identified with social solidarity. It was presented to visitors and eaten on special occasions. Likewise, the liver, nose, and flippers were considered delicacies. The intestines of the walrus were sewn by women into durable, waterproof parkas. Walrus tusks are still valued for carving, as is the *baculum*, or penis bone. The latter was worked by Inuit carvers in rendering storytelling sticks; these are said to have been used by women as they traced stories in the snow.

In material, mimesis, and metaphor, the walrus was also important to musical consciousness and communion. Inuit communities in Greenland once fashioned drumheads from the sacs that lie along the pharynx of the animal — the primary anatomical function of which is a resonant chamber for a walrus's distinctive belling or gonging sounds. Walrus vocalizations also inspired the musical voices of hunters. In one particularly striking example, the King Island Dancers perform an invitational dance, with a walruslike "chugging" forming a rhythmic component of the chorus. In the following children's song, aspects of which recall "Goldilocks and the Three Bears," a traveler says:

> I went to Diomede. They gave me some *kauk* to eat.
> It was too tough.
> So I went to Wales. They gave me some *kauk*.

DOUGLAS QUIN

It was too soft.
So I went to King Island. They gave me some *kauk*.
It was just right. So I ate lots.[6]

The moral of the story? "A King Islander feels at home only in his own village."[7]

### The Trip to Round Island

In the morning, with our gear loaded and a clear weather report from Round Island, we stowed our things and launched. Gulls squabbled and formed a haphazard assembly line in the water chasing scraps of fish waste from the processing plant. We hugged the shore and picked our way along a drifting labyrinth of gill nets. Faded fluorescent buoys lolled in the waves, and the salmon were running with the tide. Don cleared the inlet. The swell was gentle and we plowed into Bristol Bay. Summit and Crooked Islands emerged and disappeared into fog not yet burned off.

We had not been traveling long when the drone of the motor dropped to a moan. Don slowed down to look at a bear: a floater. It had been dead for several days, and the smell floating on the surface mixed with the salt air and diesel fumes of our idling engine to conjure a dull, rancid stench. The big male had been shot and his front claws torn out. He bobbed and turned in the water on his back, stiff with rigor mortis, arms outstretched and penis erect. A length of cord wound across his torso, binding a forearm to the neck. His fur was black and brown with a golden honey color along the belly. I watched him disappear, his wounded paws reaching up from the foam.

As we moved farther into the bay, Round Island appeared off the starboard bow, sweating a heavy dew through scattered clouds. Walruses could gradually be seen as a pinkish orange band at the shoreline, still a few miles distant.

### Coming on Island

When our boat arrived at Round Island, we were greeted by a departing Australian film crew that had spent three days shooting the sanctuary amid inclement weather. Parakeet auklets squawked while shuffling their ranks on the rocks. Their brightly colored beaks and big red feet animated the island's rocky cove, along with pigeon guillemots whose feet are even more colorful. Kelp and a variety of briny oozes covered the many rocks, which made for tricky footing. We formed a chain up the rock face and passed along packs, boxes, tents, cameras, and lenses. Once established in our tents, we convened for orientation with Kiana Koenen, the Alaska Department of Fish and Game sanctuary manager, and Paul Arné, a wildlife biologist and summer volunteer. After a few basic rules were outlined, I set out to one end of the island as my fellow travelers spread out in the other direction.

## Round Island

A central thoroughfare and a branching array of cul-de-sac trails terminating at overlooks skirt one side of the island; the other side is inaccessible except by sea. At the lower reaches, up from the cliffs, grasses are often waist-high and thick, arcing into the tracks, concealing rocks and mud. It is a twilight world traveled by red foxes, birds, and insects. Within the steep, scree-strewn ascent to a plateau, the slopes undulate into sound corridors. Grasses thin into patches of tundra bog, ground cover, and mosses. Boat Cove and the beaches are scalloped out of the island, leaving a succession of parabolic aspects to face the sea. The wind can roar and howl through these hollows, and in still moments the most delicate details of sound can be discerned, each with its own particular reverberant quality as rock surfaces reflect echoes in countless ways.

Main Beach is an isolated reach of pebbles and rock at the base of a precipitous peninsula. It is here that the greatest number of walruses congregate — sometimes numbering in the thousands. This is the *ugli*, or the place where walruses haul out. Thigmotropic ripples through the herd played out in small dramas; sleep was disturbed, and basking positions renegotiated. Some of the younger males lost precious ground and fell into the water from hard-won positions at the periphery. Dominant male tusk displays were resolved with occasional sparring lunges and often with the infliction of deep wounds.[8] From a distance, more than two thousand walruses assumed a singular, continuous motion — slowly undulating against the sea and shore. I settled in to listen. Snorts, snores, whistles, and wheezes formed a continuum. Flatulence, roars, discrete vocalizations, and teeth clacking punctuated the scene along with passing birds.

## On the Water

I had hoped to be able to travel out on the water to record with my hydrophone, but boat travel was allowed only if the following conditions were met: a favorable point in the tide cycle, calm seas, clear skies, and a fair weather report. Add to this the presence, or absence, of animals, and the odds seemed staggering. In the two weeks I was there, I had only one opportunity to venture offshore. The previous days had brought unpredictable seas and some dramatic tides. The beaches were deserted, and the walrus population had been largely absent. Presumably, they had gone farther out in the bay, foraging for food. As my last day "on island" wore on, a diffuse haze burned off. By evening, the water was like glass, and a high tide chortled in the recesses around Boat Cove. Walruses, who had abandoned the beach, were returning by the hundreds. Paul and I donned our Mustang survival suits and lowered the *Achilles* from its nested mooring high in the rocks. We motored out beyond Flat Rock in the direction of Main Beach.

From my experience of recording beluga whales, I used a tactic of approach that seemed to work well. This involved setting a course to a point where the current would carry the boat into the animals — drift-netting for sound — without using the engine. The hydrophone was lowered fifty feet; Paul and I listened through headphones to an incredibly raucous chorus. From a gonging or belling sound, which is produced by the dynamic action of pharyngeal pouches, to whistles, voiced exhalations, grunting and roaring, and an impressive clacking of teeth, walruses are extremely gregarious and communicative creatures. Snapping shrimp and other benthic animals could be heard as a rustling of gentle noise. Through sound, the unseen world took on tangible dimension.

The walruses came in twos or alone, and sometimes in small pods. One old bull pulled up alongside the boat within a few feet of the bow. He was large and a pallid, whitish color. To tolerate the cold, walruses divert blood from their outer surface to their core. This sometimes gives them a ghostly pallor. When hauled out in the sun, they flush red, pink, and ocher with vasodilation. The walruses kept arriving in great numbers, streaming to the haul-out at Main Beach. For several hours, we drifted and listened. Seaweed and shoals of seabird feathers floated by, as did islands of foam and flotsam. As the tide turned, we made our way back to Boat Cove.

The sky was slate-blue with feathered, fringed clouds and dissipating cirrus strokes. Crevette creases folded into the setting sun; an occidual easing flushed amber, green, then gray on the walk back to camp. The solstice had passed and it was getting darker sooner. Above me, a liquid yellow light gathered, splitting the sea, looming, floating above an oblique gathering of silent stones. Exhausted, I lay down, suspended in the sounds of an evening sortie of kittiwakes passing above my tent. Their approach in pairs was announced by a hocketing alliteration which moved in and out of phase, a chorus of shifting phrases. Walrus blows sounded from the promenade. A bellow came across the water from Flat Rock; my thoughts and sensations became unglued within the sound — a hypnagogic hallucination. Walruses adjusted themselves by rolling on the rocks. I could hear their hollow grinding and knocking on the beach. All the experiences of the week began to merge, combining sounds from the cliffs to the beaches and into the water. Cormorants cooed and muttered. Pigeon guillemots and parakeet auklets whinnied and whistled.

## Notes

1. Lewis Carroll, "The Walrus and the Carpenter," *Through the Looking Glass* [1871] (Cleveland: Forum, 1965), p. 235.

2. Gerrit de Veer, *Prisoniers des glaces: les expeditions de Willem Barants (1594–1597)* (Paris: Editions Chandeigne/Unesco, 1996), p. 44. Translation by the author.

3. *The Compact Edition of the Oxford English Dictionary* s.v. "walrus."

4. Most of the information about King Island walrus hunting comes from discussions with King Islanders Gabriel Muktoyuk and Deanna Kingston and from the following article: Sergei Bogojavlensky and Robert Fuller, "Polar Bears, Walrus Hides and Social Solidarity," *Alaska Journal*, 3/2 (1973): 66–76.

5. From the introduction by Ursula Ellanna (Utamana), *Ugiuvangmiut Quliapyiut: King Island Tales* (Fairbanks: Alaska Native Language Center/University of Alaska Press, 1988), pp. 3–6.

6. Reprinted in Bogojavlensky and Fuller, "Polar Bears, Walrus, Hide," p. 73.

7. Ibid.

8. For scientific information about walrus ethology and ecology, see F. H. Fay, "Ecology and Biology of the Pacific Walrus, *Odobenus Rosmarus Divergens Illiger*," *North American Fauna* (1982): 279; E. H. Miller, "Walrus Ethology I: The Social Role of Tusks and Applications of Multidimensional Scaling," *Canadian Journal of Zoology* 53 (1975): 590–613; and E. H. Miller, "Walrus Ethology II: Herd Structure and Activity Budgets of Summering Males," *Canadian Journal of Zoology* 54 (1976): 704–15. Also of interest: R. E. Salter, "Site Utilization, Activity Budgets, and Disturbance Responses of Atlantic Walruses during Terrestrial Haul-Out," *Canadian Journal of Zoology* 57 (1979): 1169–80; and A. R. Wyes, "The Walrus Auditory Region and the Monophyly of Pinnipeds," *American Museum Novit.* 2871 (1987).

FRANCISCO LÓPEZ

# Blind Listening

Many nature recordings as well as some current sound art embody an aesthetic that is governed by traditional bioacoustic principles, which emphasize procedural, contextual, or intentional levels of reference. Whenever there is such a stress on the representational/relational aspect of nature recordings, the meaning of the sounds is diminished, and their inner world is dissipated.

Counter to this trend, I believe in the possibility of a "blind" listening, a profound listening that delves deeply into the sounds and is freed as much as possible from such constraints. This form of listening doesn't negate what is *outside* the sounds but explores and affirms all that is *inside* them.

In my sound work I am not attempting to document or represent a richer and more significant world. My compositions are offered as openings through which the listener can access and focus on this inner world of sounds, the transcendental dimension of the sound matter *itself*. My piece *La Selva*, for example, was not meant to be a representation of La Selva, the reserve in Costa Rica. While it certainly contains elements that could be construed as representational, this sound work is rooted in a sound matter paradigm rather than having a documentary intent. Structurally, *La Selva* follows a prototypical day cycle of the rainy season, beginning and ending at night. This was a compositional decision. *La Selva* was conceived and created as a musical composition. My apprehension of sound matter itself, and not any possible *intention* of documenting the place, dictated all editing and montage decisions.

The sounds of many animal species are included in the recordings that constitute my work *La Selva*, and they have even been identified, but none of them has been singled out in the processes of recording and editing. With traditional bioacoustics, the calls, songs, or other sounds of a certain species are usually isolated from the "background" sound of its environment in both the recording and the editing processes, and the contrast between the foregrounded species and its background is even further enhanced.

In *La Selva* the sound-producing animal species appear together with other accompanying biotic and nonbiotic components that inhere in the sound environment. Any resulting distinction between foreground and background was not arranged purposefully but emerged incidentally, due to the location of the microphones, as might occur with our ears. My attention was "focused" on the sound environment as a whole, which is one of the reasons why there are no indexes on the CD. I wanted to discourage a focal listening centered on the entrances of species or other sonic events.

The habitual focus on animals as the main elements in a sound environment is particularly limiting. Not only are nonbiotic sound sources evident in many nature environments (rainfall, rivers, storms, wind), but there is also a type of sound-producing biotic component that is usually overlooked and exists in almost every environment: plants. In most cases — especially forests — what we tend to refer to as the sound of rain or wind might more aptly be called the sound of plant leaves and branches.

If our reception of nature sounds were more focused on the environment as a whole, rather than on the organisms we perceive to be most similar to us, we would be more likely to take the bioacoustics of plants into account. Further, a sound environment is the consequence not only of all its sound-producing components but also of all its sound-transmitting and sound-modifying elements. The birdsong we hear in the forest is as much a consequence of the trees or the forest floor as it is of the bird. If we listen attentively, the topography, the degree of humidity of the air, or the type of materials in the topsoil become as essential and definitory of the sonic environment as the sound-producing animals that inhabit a certain space.

Addressing the call to widen our scope of attention from individual species to the whole environment, Bernie Krause has offered his "niche hypothesis," in which different aural niches are basically defined in terms of the frequency bands of the sound spectrum that are occupied by different species. This approach interests me because of its explicit intention of expanding classical bioacoustics from an auto-ecological (single-species) to a more systemic perspective, considering assemblages of sound-producing animal species at an ecosystem level. But this hypothesis is still indebted to the field of bioacoustics in that its approach is the analysis of sound and, more important, because it focuses on the differentiation of the biotic sources of sounds.

In my work with nature sound environments, I have moved away from rationalizing and categorizing these aural entities. I prefer this environmental perspective not because it's more "complete" or more "realistic" but because it encourages a perceptual shift from the recognition and differentiation of sound sources to the appreciation of the resulting sound matter. As soon as the call is in the air, it no longer belongs to the creature that produced it.

The recordings that are featured in *La Selva* have not been modified or subjected to any process of mixing or additions. One might say that this work fea-

FRANCISCO LÓPEZ

tures "pure" nature sound environments, as is often claimed on commercially released nature recordings. But I believe this obscures a series of questions that have to do with our sense of reality and our notions about its representation in sound recordings. In some of the nature recordings that attempt to convey an easy sense of naturalness, various animal vocalizations are mixed over a background matrix of ambient sound. As in the case of traditional bioacoustics, in which the sounds are isolated, we could criticize this artificial mixing approach of massive inclusion as being unreal, or even hyperreal. Yet we should then consider on which grounds we are criticizing this tricky departure from reality.

Since the advent of digital recording technology (with all its concomitant sound-quality improvements), it has become all the more evident, in our attempts at apprehending the sonic world around us, that the microphones we use are not only our basic interfaces, they are non-neutral interfaces. The way different kinds of microphones "hear" varies so significantly that they could be considered as a first transformational step in the recording process. The consequences of the choices made regarding which microphones will be used are more dramatic than, for example, a further re-equalization of the recordings in the studio.

Yet even if we don't subtract or add anything to the recording, we cannot avoid imposing on it our version of what we consider to be reality. Attempts have been made to circumvent this problem by means of technological improvements. The ambisonics surround sound system, for example, has been promoted as a means of *reproducing* soundscapes, conveying a more realistic sense of envelopment and an illusion of "being there." Although I appreciate the palette of new sound nuances and the "spaceness" facilitated by these technological developments, it isn't "realism" that I'm after in my work. But this evocation of place seems frequently to be an objective in the creation of nature recordings.

Only I don't think "reality" is being reproduced with these techniques; rather, a hyperreality is being constructed. The carefully recorded, selected, and edited sound environments that we are able to comfortably enjoy in our favorite armchairs offer an enhanced listening experience, one that we would likely not have if we were hearing those sounds in the "real" world. Ironically, it is often these nonrealistic effects that give this kind of sound work its appeal, as they satisfy our expectations of how "the real thing" sounds.

Sound editing seems to be another unavoidable obstacle in the attempt to portray aural reality. Whereas the "microphone interface" transfigures the spatial and material characteristics of sound, editing affects its temporality. This process has already begun to take place during the act of recording in that there is always a start and an end for the recording. In most cases, further "time windows" are created in the editing process when a new start and a new end are established for the sound fragment. Also, when we have several sound fragments, we create a montage.

If it is naturalness that we are after in our sound work, what kind of editing makes a piece sound more "real"? David Dunn has challenged the decision often made in nature recording to eliminate human-made sounds. He contends that the elision of sound fragments of natural environments that contain human sonic intrusions (aircrafts, road traffic, etc.) — by not recording them or by editing them out — is a "false representation of reality" that "lures people into the belief that these places still fulfill their romantic expectations."

But I think the problem goes beyond the issue of phonographic falsification. Our bodies and imaginations engage in sonic transcription and reproduction more than the machines we have invented for these purposes. For instance, we can have a much more striking perception of such a human sonic intrusion than does a microphone, or not perceive it at all, both in the moment it is heard and in the traces it has left in our memory. Do we always realize when there's some distant traffic noise if our attention is focused on an insect call? Do we remember the nearby voices of people when we are recalling a day we enjoyed the sound of the rain in the forest? If not, was our experience — or what we have retained of it — false? Even if our level of conciousness includes both the traffic and the insect, do we have to embrace both of them in representing reality? Because this perceptual ambiguity is at the basis of our apprehension of "reality," I don't think a recording that has been "cleaned up" of human-made sounds is any more false than one that hasn't.

I don't believe there is such a thing as the objective apprehension of sonic reality. Regardless of whether or not we are recording, our minds conceptualize an ideal of sound. And not only do different people listen differently, but the very temporality of our presence in a place is a form of editing. The spatial, material, and temporal transfigurations exist independently of phonography. Our idea of the sonic reality, even our fantasy about it, *is* the sonic reality each one of us possesses.

Most of the works that deal with nature sound environments seem to have a documentary agenda. Among them are those made by the Nature Sounds Society, which regularly organizes field recording workshops. Their goal has been expressed as follows: "to provide an aural window into places that many people might never visit." The documentary perspective of these works is reinforced with accompanying descriptions of nonsonic relational elements and sound content.

I find it striking that nature sound recordists so rarely refer to the sonic matter they are supposedly dealing with. Instead, they mention the nonsonic elements that were experienced in the place at the time the recording was made.

FRANCISCO LÓPEZ

This is a paradoxical convolution that tends to relegate the recorded sounds to a role of documenting or referring to a certain space.

The richness of the sound matter in nature is astonishing, but to appreciate it in depth, we must both challenge and free ourselves to listen profoundly. We have to shift the focus of our attention and understanding from representation to being.

Acousmatics, or the rupture of the visual cause-effect connection between the sound sources and the sounds themselves, can contribute significantly to achieving the "blindness" of profound listening. La Selva, like most tropical rain forests, is a dynamic example of what we could call "environmental acousmatics." There are many sounds in the forest, but one rarely has the opportunity to see the sources of most of those sounds, and not only because most of the animals are hidden in the foliage. The foliage also obscures itself, concealing myriad plant sound sources, caused not only by wind or rain but also by falling leaves and branches — a frequent occurrence in that forest.

Many of the animals in La Selva live in this acousmatic world, in which the rule is not to see their conspecifics, predators, or preys but just to hear them. This acousmatic feature is best exemplified by one of the most characteristic sounds of La Selva: the strikingly loud and harsh song of the cicadas. During the day, this is probably the sound that typically would most naturally stand in the foreground of the sonic field. There you hear it with an astonishing intensity and proximity, but you never see its source.

Nature sound environments are often characterized as tranquil places, peaceful islands of quietude in a sea of rushing, noisy, human-driven habitats. While this notion might be true for certain natural environments and under certain conditions, I think it contributes to a restricted and bucolic view of nature. Like many other tropical rain forests, La Selva is quite a noisy place. The diverse sounds of water (rain, watercourses), together with the sound web created by the intense calls of insects or frogs and plant sounds, make up a powerful broadband sound environment of thrilling complexity. The textures are extremely rich, with multiple layers that periodically merge with each other and then reveal themselves, challenging one's perception and also the very notion of what an individual sound might be.

This contributes to expanding our aural understanding of nature, not by denying stillness but by embracing a more inclusive conception, freed of our judgment and reductive categorization. I'm certainly in favor of defending the "pristine" sound quality of natural environments, but for this reason: I think we should avoid the sound intrusion that leads to sonic homogenization, thus conserving the diversity of sounds in the world. In that spirit, I also support the preservation and enhancement of the diversity of human-made sound environments and devices.

I consider *La Selva* to be a piece of music, but not in the classical sense of the word. Nor do I subscribe to the traditional concept of what is considered to be musical in nature, or how nature and music have been coupled — for example, the search for melodic patterns, comparisons between animal sounds and musical instruments, or "complementing" nature sounds with "musical" ones. To me, a waterfall is as musical as a birdsong.

I believe in expanding and transforming our concept of music through nature (and through "non-nature"), not in the absolute assignment of sounds to music (either in any restricted traditionally academic sense or in the Cagean universal version). Rather, it is my belief that music is an aesthetic (in its widest sense) perception/understanding/conception of sound. It's our *decision* — subjective, intentional, non-universal, not necessarily permanent — that converts nature sounds into music. We don't need to transform or complement the sounds. Nor do we need to pursue a universal and permanent assignment. It will arise when our listening moves away and is freed from being pragmatically and representationally oriented. And attaining this musical state requires a profound listening, an immersion in the *inside* of the sound matter.

DAVID TOOP

# From *Exotica*

Exotica is the art of ruins, the ruined world of enchantment laid waste in fervid imagination, the paradox of an imperial paradise liberated from colonial intervention, a golden age recreated through the lurid colors of a cocktail glass, illusory and remote zones of pleasure and peace dreamed after the bomb. Nothing is left, except for beaches, palm trees, tourist sites with their moss-covered monuments, shops stocked with native art made for the invaders, beachcomber bars, and an absurd perception of what may once have been.

Just ruins and a spell, repeated endlessly to provoke fading memories: lust and terror, chainsaw bikers, sultry tropical airs, Aztec spells, x-ray eyes and hot pants, sunken cities, lost cities, singing sea shells, electric frogs, bustin' bongos, wild stuffed bikinis, jungle jazz, sacred idols, space escapades, switchblade sisters, pits and pendulums, tabu, taboo, tabuh, tamboo, taboo, tabuh, tamboo, tabuh-tabuhan.

### The Vending Machines

The French author and translator, Arthur Mangin, published a romantic study of wilderness in 1872. *The Desert World* defined its subject as "all the regions where man has not planted his regular communities or permanent abodes; where earth has never been appropriated, tilled, and subjected to cultivation; where Nature has maintained her inviolability against the encroachments of human industry."

This may have been true in the nineteenth century, particularly for Mangin, who promoted the colonial view: "[the] one incontestable fact, the superiority of those races that have acquired civilisation over those which are incapable of so grand a work." In our time, wilderness is a place where the grand works of the civilized races have done their worst. I found myself in such a wilderness, stumbling into a central encampment during the dry season. Was encampment the word? I don't think so. This was a city, but a city like none I had ever seen. Loud, complex, fluid, terrifying; a city of extraordinary possibilities. Before entering the inner walls, I took my bearings. In one direction, the suburbs, surrounded by whipping fences armed with deadly voltage. Blackened animals sat

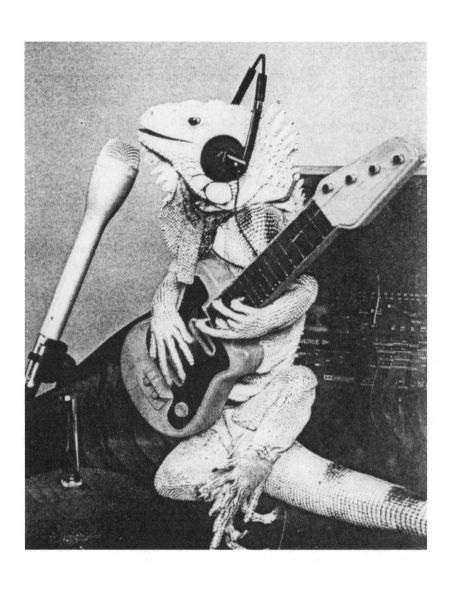

at electrical throwing distance from these banshee defenses and wondered why they had died.

In another direction, sand without boundaries, chaotic with strange life-forms. There were legends of a subsonic boom that paralyzed sidewinder snakes as it rolled across the dunes, hurling trapdoor spiders out of their burrows and high into the air and causing instantaneous diarrhea in all two- or four-legged creatures unlucky enough to be caught without nappies.

In the encampment, pornographic raconteurs delivered circadian monologues from open-fronted shops, thin plastic microphones held delicately between thumbs and forefingers in the manner of lounge singers. Speaking quickly, without pause, in disconnected fragments, they described colorful incidents of bestiality, torture, exotic auto-erotic devices, industrial accidents, the histories of dismemberment and cannibalism. Their listeners — children and old people, dogs and empty chairs — accumulated a mass of dismembered knowledge. Their dreams were disturbed by the arcana of the raconteurs, a rich brew of sexual fantasy fortified by references to Samoyed hand-cutting spirits, Mayan priests playing flutes and rattles to decapitated heads resting in pots, the bat god Tlacatzinacantli with his skulls and gourd rattles, itinerant Tantrics conversing with the dead through skull drums.

As the monologues droned on past the witching hour, nocturnal cult ceremonies weaved through the streets, faces of the initiates hidden behind masks beaten from obsolete household labor-saving devices. These were known variously as the Flashing Night Spirits, the Society of Faces, the Spore Diviners, the Boneless. Their secret speech mixed borrowed expressions from so many different languages, all transformed through partial understanding, that even the cult leaders found themselves lost in a sea of alien tongues.

I had arrived, I discovered, at the moment preceding a burial rite. No child was exempt from the forage during these rites. More than fifty cavity beetles had to be collected. Their mating song was unique. They would burrow backwards into the sand until vertical, then open their abnormally wide mouths and wait for the wind to catch the edges of their jaws.

For those few travelers who had heard it, the sound was said to be as haunting as a wolf howl. I was reminded of the potoo or wood nightjar, an ugly bird cursed with a body like a fungus and a gaping mouth like a surgical operation. Found in the West Indies, Haiti, and South America, the potoo has contributed to local mythology and spirit lore. In Trinidad, for example, its eerie cries are said to be the carriers of criminal souls.

I imagine something similar must have occurred with the cavity beetles. For the burial, they were mounted in fishbone glue, upright and separated according to sex. Hidden behind a screen, their eerie singing was interpreted by noninitiates as the sound of spirits caught in string-woven ghostcatchers as they tried to break through into the world of humans.

## A Dog's Life

In 1889, an eighty-year-old sound recordist named Ludwig Koch recorded the song of an Indian Shama thrush. More than a hundred years later, the technology has evolved from wax cylinder and wire recording into the digital domain, yet this urge to document and enjoy nonhuman music has grown into a fascinating minor industry. Is this evidence of technology's role in the synthetic reproduction of nature, purchased to compensate for the loss of wild places, the systematic reduction of biodiversity?

I asked Lassie.

"Within the New Age or Spoken Word sections of music hypermarkets," she barked, "you can find a growing number of environment, relaxation, and bioacoustic CDs: tropical rainforests, dolphins, howling wolves, primates, seashore and country garden, rainfall and thunderstorms. Extracts can be sampled on the in-store touch 'n' listen displays, demonstrating that this is an impulse-shopper niche. Superficially, this is a slice of the stressbuster market: a pair of headphones, a 60-minute recording of waves rolling gently onto a beach, a subtle underpinning of digital synthesizer drones and the urban info-warrior is fortified for the next battle."

"Good girl," I said.

Clearly piqued by my patronizing address, she fixed me with one of those dog stares that precedes a bite. "The history of wildlife and environment recording," she continued, "adds another aspect to this demotion of whalesong CDs to the level of goldfish videos, hypnosis cassettes, and do-it-yourself meditation manuals. Like television and photography, sound recording is an unstable mixture of documentation and entertainment. Tape recorders have proved to be a vital tool for bioacousticians investigating the mechanics and meaning of animal vocalization. Many early commercial discs of animal and bird sound were structured to appeal to a market of amateur scientists. So species would be introduced by a suitably sober narrator, Latin names would be given, habitats described."

I recalled a personal favorite in my own collection. A 1957 Folkways album — *Sounds of North American Frogs* — was narrated in an unwittingly comical, froglike voice by amphibian specialist Charles M. Bogert. Bogert's croak may lack the surreal dimension at the outer limits of the Folkways catalogue, but his album typifies the humor that lurks wherever bioacoustic sound is emitted. For the ultimate in scientific endeavor collapsing into hysteria, I listen to a 1968 LP — *Sounds In the Sea* — produced by the Electro-Marine Sciences Division of Marine Resources Inc. Following recordings of sperm whales, drum fish, sonar signals, torpedo launches, and an unidentified boing, comes a recording of Commander Scott Carpenter and his crew singing "Goodnight Irene" 250 feet below the surface in Sea Lab II, their voices Smurfed into the stratosphere by helium.

As if it were a favorite slipper, Lassie tugged the conversation back to her favorite subject. "As television coopted this audience of wildlife enthusiasts with its exotic journeys of zoological voyeurism," she growled, "so the scientific narration guiding them through animal sound albums took on a travelogue feel. By aspiring to the condition of TV, they moved towards the current idea of soundscape as virtual environment. But do we need a Crocodile Dundee in the wilderness if we're sitting in an armchair in the suburbs?"

"Ah, the armchair traveler," I interjected. "Some discs began to acknowledge that there are two kinds of traveler: the guided tourist and the free spirit. *The Swamp In June*, produced in 1964 by Droll Yankees Inc., gave you one side with narration, complete with 'comments on swamp life,' and a reverse side of uninterrupted flies, frogs, birds, and beavers. You could just feel yourself being bitten by the mosquitoes. Others followed, like the Saydisc label's *Antarctica*, with its fabulously flatulent Weddell seal recordings and creaking ice floes. But the major breakthroughs were Dr. Roger S. Payne's *Songs of the Humpback Whale*, released by Capitol at the beginning of the 1970s, and Syntonic Research Inc.'s *Environments* series.

"The prominent trademark symbol appended to the title of this series suggests that Syntonic Research Inc. (whatever syntonic means) knew they were on to a moneyspinner with their soothing nature backgrounds. 'Turn your hi-fi into a psychoacoustic device,' they instructed on the cover alongside endorsements from psychiatric technicians and songwriters. The success of these two American projects — serious science and pseudo science overlapping the psychedelic diaspora — was linked to a growing environmental movement."

"So who, or what, got the royalties?" snarled my canine friend.

"Fair point," I agreed. "Particularly from your perspective. In the laudable case of Payne's recordings, the creatures themselves, since his intention was to create whale awareness and to fund research and conservation projects from the massive sales of the two whale records. Elsewhere the profit margins were huge, relatively speaking.

"But the ecology movement was descended from a spiritual hunger that had been expressed in very different ways by Henry David Thoreau, Jack Kerouac, and Jimi Hendrix. Immune to the lure of post-hippie psychobabble, some recordists stuck to the idea of bird song as music, a notion that is surely as old as music itself. In France, the records in Jean C. Roché's *L'Oiseau Musicien* series were presented as continuous concerts, beautifully recorded and edited. The standard is maintained with his current Sitelle series of *Natural Con-*

*certs.* This is a world of rich, strange sounds — a voyeuristic plunge into the intimacies of potoos, peppershrikes, lemurs, bearded seals, and belugas."

Lassie had fallen asleep, I noticed. Undeterred, I continued. "By 1973 Roché was abandoning the concept of sound guide for some discs, instead evoking the atmosphere of remote environments. With the advent of digital compact discs, this concept of the wilderness packaged into substitute environment, sonic therapy, or complex sound field was matched by the appropriate technology. No more confusion between vinyl imperfections and the high frequencies of insect stridulation; no more mix-ups between turntable noise and the low rumbles of marine mammals; no need to get up and turn the record over. Just lie back and be transported.

"Inevitably, this evolved into abominations: float tank soporifics and whale banalities. Mysteries — or, at the very least, gastric rumbles — once conveyed by humpback whale songs have been drastically cheapened by anthropomorphism and overexposure. This new-age notion that nature is all beauty and peace is nonsense. Listen to the screaming racket that sea birds make; the crackle of Alaskan krill; the harsh signals of insects such as the gratte-coui locust from Guadeloupe; the noisemaking birds — the mangrove cuckoo, the lesser Antillean grackle, the giant coua of Madagascar, the black-headed oriole, the trumpeter hornbill, the black-winged stilt. All of them sound like cogs and scrapers pulled from a Futurist noise machine.

"We only need one major earthquake or typhoon to remind us that wilderness is not a benign, shock-free backdrop that decorates earth solely for the benefit of alienated humans. The best atmosphere CDs acknowledge this. Rykodisc's *Thunderstorms* even comes with a safety warning: 'If you feel your skin tingle or your hair stand on end, squat low to the ground on the balls of your feet.'"

Crocodilian in her sudden menace, Lassie opened one eye in response to this human-centered assumption that all feet have balls. "Interestingly," she growled, "a bitch might argue that bioacoustic recordings anticipated the pathetic human obsession with alien kidnappings."

"Are you familiar," I said, ignoring the provocation, "with music that manipulates bioacoustic sounds? Graeme Revell's *The Insect Musicians*, for example? 'And perhaps the ultimate horizon of technology is nature itself,' Revell wrote. Does that fit your theory . . . the idea that nature is an extraordinarily complex, unknown world, an alien world in fact, and technology can only aspire to that complexity?"

"I can't listen to that stuff," groaned Lassie. "It hurts my ears."

"Tough being a dog," I rallied. "In my opinion, Revell undermined his project by using insectiverous sounds to play melodies that were distressingly human. The true fascination of these signals is not just the sound quality or

DAVID TOOP

what they may communicate, but their alien structure. The best description of these patterns I have come across is outlined by an anthropologist and musician named Steven Feld. In *Music Grooves*, a book he co-wrote with another musicologist, Charles Keil, Steve illuminates the possible meanings of lift-up-over-sounding, an awkward yet remarkably resonant phrase used by the Kaluli people who live in the tropical rain forest of Papua New Guinea's Southern Highlands. 'For me, intuitively,' Steve writes, 'lift-up-over-sounding creates a feeling of continuous layers, sequential but not linear; nongapped multiple presences and densities; overlapping chunks without internal breaks; a spiraling, arching motion tumbling slightly forward, thinning, then thickening again.'"

Lassie cocked her head on one side, one ear bent, a quizzical look in her eyes. I pressed on with my main theme. "For many years I've been fascinated by the unusual rhythmic, seemingly random relationships that can be heard in call-and-response duets sung by African bou-bou shrikes and trumpeter swans, a chorus of tree frogs, or from the ensemble flute playing of Amazonas, Central African Republic, Ethiopia, and Papua New Guinea. There are similarities to hocketing — the medieval music hiccup — or church bell change ringing, though these are predictable, systematized forms. It's something to do with wind, breath, unpredictable complexity, though bird duets can be remarkably precise in their timing. Sometimes two birds take one of the parts, creating a three part duet; in a pair, after one bird dies, the surviving partner continues to sing both parts of the duet. I've tried to duplicate the effect in the studio with some success, using randomized overdubbing, but the sustained interest comes from listening to a group performance in which the component parts sound totally integrated yet perpetually out of synch.

"Feld describes the essence of lift-up-over-sounding as 'part relations that are in synchrony while out of phase.' For the Kaluli people of New Guinea, unisons are anathema; interest comes from staggered entries or multiple densities. 'Part of the stylistic core of lift-up-over-sounding,' Feld explains, 'is found in nuances of textural densification — of attacks and final sounds; decays and fades; changes in intensity, depth, and presence; voice coloration and grain; interaction of patterned and random sounds; playful accelerations, lengthenings, and shortenings; and the fission and fusion of sound shapes and phrases into what electroacoustic composer Edgard Varèse called the "shingling" of sound layers across pitch space.'"

"Do you get it now?"

"Does he object to you quoting these meaty chunks of his work?" asked Lassie. "Where can I hear his stuff?"

"These are important ideas," I blustered. "What Feld and Keil call fat thoughts. Listen to the CD he recorded — *Voices of the Rainforest*. Interestingly enough, Steve's personal stash of music tapes didn't crank the handle for his New Guinea hosts when he was living with them. The exception was *Nefertiti*, by the Miles Davis Quintet. The subtle textural shifts and staggered, overlapping echoes of the Quintet 'made sense to Kaluli because it sounds like their kind of groove.' Imagine what might grow out of these ideas: textural and rhythmic microworlds elevated to their rightful place in our aesthetic value system; we might even discover a more grounded awareness of our own insecure place in the thick, exotic rain forest of mediated, marketed, MIDI music. Among the Kaluli, Feld had discovered a way of classifying the world that was totally different to ours. Think of it; a taxonomy based on sound."

Lassie sniffed the air. A long pause followed. Faintly, from a distant ranch, I heard the self-pitying lament of Don Gibson's "Sea of Heartbreak," or was it La Monte Young singing a never-ending cowboy song to the cicadas? I saw a shadow in the trees, maybe a man from the city, armed with a gun. "So what you're saying," said Lassie, a sly look in her eye, aware of the shadow long before I was, "is that I'm more in tune with this subject than you are."

My throat tightened, dry as a sand lizard's belly.

DAVID TOOP

# From *Brother of Sleep*

*Robert Schneider's novel* Brother of Sleep *tells the story of young Elias Brender, a musical prodigy who grows up in a remote mountain village at the tail end of the eighteenth century. He hears music in the earth reverberate through his bones. This excerpt describes the moment when he first learns of his great gift.*

Sounds, noises, timbres, and tones arose, the like of which he had never heard before. Elias not only heard the sounds, he also saw them. He saw the air incessantly contracting and expanding. He saw into the valleys of sounds and into their gigantic mountain ranges. He saw the hum of his own blood, the crackle of the tufts of hair in his little fists. And his breath cut his nostrils in such shrill whistles that a raging summer *Föhn* would have sounded like a murmur in comparison. The juices of his stomach churned and clattered heavily around. An indescribable diversity cooed in his intestines. Gases expanded, hissed, or blew apart, the substance of his bones vibrated, and even the water in his eyes trembled with the dark beating of his heart.

And again his range of hearing multiplied, exploded, covering the patch of ground on which he lay like a vast ear. Listened down into landscapes hundreds of miles deep, listened out into regions hundreds of miles across. Against the sonorous backdrop of his own body noises, ever more powerful acoustic scenarios passed with increasing speed: storms of sound, tempests of sound, seas and deserts of sound.

All at once, out of this huge mass of noises, Elias discerned his father's heartbeat. But his father's heart beat so arhythmically, so out of harmony with his own, that Elias, had he been in command of all his senses, would have despaired. But God, in his endless cruelty, did not stop his display.

In unimaginable streams, the storms of sounds and noises fell upon Elias's ears: a mad tohubohu of hundreds of beating hearts, a splintering of bones, a singing and humming of the blood of countless veins, a dry brittle scratching when lips closed, a crashing and crunching between teeth, an incredible noise of swallowing, gurgling, snorting, and belching, a churning of gall-like stomach juices, a quiet splash of urine, a swish of human hair and the yet wilder swish of animal hair, a dull scrape of fabric on skin, a thin singing of evaporating sweat, a whetting of muscles, a screaming of blood when the members of animals and men grew erect. Not to mention the crazed chaos of voices and sounds of men and creatures on and under the earth.

And deeper went his ear, into all the screams, jabbers, squawks, into all the talking and whispering, singing and groaning, screeching and yowling, yammering and sobbing, sighing and coughing, slurping and slapping, right into the sudden silence where the vocal cords were really still violently vibrating with the sounds of words just uttered. Even the droning of thoughts was revealed to the child. The range of his hearing grew ever more powerful, and he saw ever more picturesque sounds.

Then came the indescribable concert of sounds and noises of all the animals and all of nature and the endless mass of soloists. The mooing and bleating, the snorting and whinnying, the rattle of halter chains, the licking and tongue-whetting on salt blocks, the clapping of tails, the grunting and rolling, the farting and blowing, the squeaking and peeping, the meowing and barking, the quacking and crowing, the twittering and wing-beating, the gnawing and pecking, the digging and scratching. . . .

And he saw yet deeper and farther. He saw the beasts of the sea, the song of the dolphins, the gigantic lament of dying whales, the chords of huge shoals of fish, the clicking of plankton, the spiral of ripples when fish expelled their roe; saw the resonance of the waves, the collapse of subterranean mountains, the luminous metallic stridency of streams of lava, the song of the seasons, the foam on the sea, the hissing of the thousands of tons of water sucked up by the sun, the crashing and bursting explosion of gigantic cloud choirs, the noise of light. . . . What are words?

# IV
## Many Natures, Many Cultures

JOHN LUTHER ADAMS

# The Place Where You Go to Listen

*Songs are thoughts which are sung out with the breath when people let themselves*
*be moved by a great force, and ordinary speech no longer suffices.*

*When the words that we need shoot up of themselves, we have a new song.*
— Orpingalik, a Netsilik Eskimo elder

They say that she heard things.

At Naalagiagvik, The Place Where You Go to Listen, she would sit alone, in stillness. The wind across the tundra and the little waves lapping on the shore told her secrets. Birds passing overhead spoke to her in strange tongues.

She listened. And she heard. But she rarely spoke of these things. She did not question them. This is the way it is for one who listens.

She spent many days and nights alone, poised with the deep patience of the hunter, her ears and her body attuned to everything around her. Before the wind and the great sea, she took for herself this discipline: always to listen.

She listened for the sound, like drums, of the earth stirring in ancient sleep. She listened for the sound, like stone rain, as rivers of caribou flooded the great plain. She listened, in autumn, for the echo of the call of the last white swan.

She understood the languages of birds. In time, she learned the quiet words of the plants. Closing her eyes, she heard small voices whispering:

"I am *uqpik*. I am river willow. I am here."

"I am *asiaq*. I am blueberry. I am here."

The wind brought to her the voices of her ancestors, the old ones, who taught that true wisdom lives far from humankind, deep in the great loneliness.

As she traveled, she listened to the voices of the land, voices speaking the name of each place, carrying the memories of those who live here now and those who have gone.

As she listened, she came to hear the breath of each place: how the snow falls here; how the ice melts; how, when everything is still, the air breathes. The drums of her ears throbbed with the heartbeat of this place, a particular rhythm that can be heard in no other place.

Often she remembered the teaching of an old shaman who spoke of *silam inua* — the inhabiting spirit, the voice of the universe. *Silam inua* speaks not through ordinary words, but through fire and ice, sunshine and calm seas, the howling of wolves, and the innocence of children, who understand nothing.

In her mind, she heard the words of the shaman, who said of *silam inua*: "All we know is that it has a gentle voice like a woman, a voice so fine and gentle that even children cannot be afraid."

The heart of winter: She is listening.

Darkness envelopes her — heavy, luminous with aurora. The mountains, in silhouette, stand silent. There is no wind.

The frozen air is transparent, smooth, and brittle; it rings like a knife blade against bone. The sound of her breath, as it freezes, is a soft murmuring, like cloth on cloth.

The muffled wing beats of a snowy owl rise and fall, reverberating down long corridors of dream, deep into the earth.

She stands, motionless, listening to the resonant stillness. Then, slowly, she draws a new breath. In a voice not her own, yet somehow strangely familiar, she begins to sing . . .

JOHN LUTHER ADAMS

# Nature and Music

*Translated by Yoshiko Kakudo and Glenn Glasow*

## I

This summer [1962], walking through the fields of Hokkaido, I could not help thinking that my own thoughts have come to resemble the sidewalks of a city: rigid and calculated. Standing there in a field with an uninterrupted view for forty kilometers, I thought that the city, because of its very nature, would someday be outmoded and abandoned as a passing phenomenon. The unnatural quality of city life results from an abnormal swelling of the nerve endings. In this way, though, seemingly active, hasn't it also become helpless?

A lifestyle out of balance with nature is frightening. As long as we live, we aspire to harmonize with nature. It is this harmony in which the arts originate and to which they will eventually return. Harmony, or balance, in this sense does not mean regulation or control by ready-made rules. It is beyond functionalism. I believe what we call "expression" in art is really discovery, by one's own mode, of something new in this world. There is something about this word "expression," however, that alienates me: no matter how dedicated to the truth we may be, in the end when we see that what we have produced is artificial, it is false. I have never doubted that the love of art is the love of unreality.

Facing the silence of the old trees I could not help thinking about my own work. My truth, however, is found only in the act of creation. And it is in that act that self-criticism arises and I feel alive. There is nothing profound about that.

Although I think constantly about the relationship of music to nature, for me music does not exist to describe natural scenery. While it is true that I am sometimes impressed by natural scenery devoid of human life, and that may motivate my own composing, at the same time I cannot forget the tawdry and seamy side of human existence. I cannot conceive of nature and human beings as opposing elements, but prefer to emphasize living harmoniously, which I like to call naturalness. To be sure, this contradicts fleeing to "the narrow road to the deep north." In my own creation naturalness is nothing but relating to reality. It is from the boiling pot of reality that art is born.

In Hokkaido I met some tourist Ainu who continue to wear their traditional garb — not by choice, but out of their own weariness from resisting outside forces. I also talked to some young white-shirted Ainu who looked down on the tourist Ainu. These young people held as an ideal the preservation of their culture in a pure state. They regarded the carved wooden bears and artificial crafts produced by the tourist Ainu as distortions of their culture. That may be true, but I was irritated and frustrated by the distance between the reality of the tourist Ainu and the ideals of those youths. Listening to their talk I despaired and felt like letting the whole Ainu culture die.

But there at the deserted lake, enchanted by the deep blue of the water, I could not forget those strong impressions that nearly caused me to lose my own identity: the Ainu woman crouching by the roadside with averted face, the shabby and somewhat smelly village. No, I do not underestimate the value of preserving a tradition. But those Ainu youths and I must remember one thing: as long as we live we must produce something. That is the natural thing to do.

I wish to free sounds from the trite rules of music, rules that are in turn stifled by formulas and calculations. I want to give sounds the freedom to breathe. Rather than on the ideology of self-expression, music should be based on a profound relationship to nature — sometimes gentle, sometimes harsh. When sounds are possessed by ideas instead of having their own identity, music suffers. This would be my basic rule, but it is only an idea and naturally I must develop a practical method. One way might be through an ethnological approach. There may be folk music with strength and beauty, but I cannot be completely honest in this kind of music. I want a more active relationship to the present. (Folk music in a "contemporary style" is nothing but a deception.)

Because the writer of popular tunes looks at his world with too much detachment, it falls to the composer to deal with the real thoughts and emotions of his time. In this welter of contemporary life it is only through his own sense of worth and by proving himself that a composer is able to relate to tradition in the most faithful sense.

## II

I found Chikuhō had become an area of abandoned mines. An earlier vivid image of it as a place of bitter labor disputes was now replaced by the reality of abandoned miners' shacks standing pitifully weathering in the wind. An algae-laden crater lake and a tailings pile were only a pattern of deserted ruins. I stood there uneasily taking in the scenery as everything merged into a lyrical landscape. There were layers upon layers of heavy silence and I was beginning

TORU TAKEMITSU

to feel that it was fruitless to resist it. I have never seen the ruins along the Nile River, but I wondered if those ruins and the scene I was facing shared the same qualities. I don't know. But it seems to me that for human beings, living is nothing but piling up the stones of ruins.

The story of Socrates rolling the stone to shut off the light of the sun is really the story of humankind. The true nature of history is something that could not be planned because it is only through living that a human being verifies his own life.

I can do nothing but walk on the track left by Socrates' stone. Everyone plods this fruitless road, treading out the path of history. This unfolding of humankind's history has nothing to do with fatalism or eternal principles.

There, confronting it, I resolved to face that silence as long as I can endure it. That is discipline.

Within our Western musical notation the silences (rests) tend to be placed with statistical considerations. But that method ignores the basic utterance of music. It really has nothing to do with music. Just as one cannot plan his life, neither can he plan music.

Music is either sound or silence. As long as I live I shall choose sound as something to confront a silence. That sound should be a single, strong sound.

I wonder if the task of the composer should not be that of presenting the basic unaltered form of music.

I would like to cut away the excess to be able to grasp the essential sound.

On the way back from a contemporary music festival I stopped at the Moss Garden in Kyoto. It appeared simple, but in its technical accomplishments I found it far removed from my taste. I do not like self-conscious artificiality. Even in composing, techniques are required to build up sounds and shape a piece of music. But even here, the appearance of effortlessness is considered an advanced technique. At the same time, a strikingly brilliant technique is not the mark of a master and is not to be admired. But this is all quite unnatural. The term "anti-virtuoso" appears to have a profound spiritual depth but in reality it is closely related to the intellect, and in the end it is really rooted in the notion of human superiority over nature. This is not the way to confront silence. We cannot avoid the silence of death that awaits us. For this reason I spoke earlier of the gentleness and cruelty of nature. If a work depends on technique it will be picked bare by nature, its bleaching bones left to become part of the landscape. Neither the edifice of history nor tradition readily reveals itself. Both are like the track left by Socrates' stone: invisible, delicate.

I wish to discard the concept of building sounds. In the world in which we live silence and unlimited sound exist. Painstakingly I wish to carve that sound with my own hands, finally to reach a single sound. And it should be as strong a sound as possible in its confrontation with silence.

October 6. . . . Heard *gagaku* [court music] at the Imperial Household Agency.

Certainly I was impressed by the ascending sounds that towered toward heaven like a tree. While the soundwaves of the music float through the air and by necessity exist in time, my impression of *gagaku* was that of a music that challenges measurable time. The Western method of capturing time in graphic form (using measured notation) and that of *gagaku* are completely different in their nature.

*Gagaku* lacks the concept of beat in Western terms. Of course, a certain rhythm is present, woven by specific percussion instruments — namely, *kakko, taiko* — and the *shō* [mouth organ]. However, they serve only to embroider the gossamer curtain of intricate sound. The symbols suggest a rhythm, but it is certainly far removed from the human pulse. As a pattern it is static. Occasionally it shoots sharply toward heaven like an arrow, as if to show the direction of the spirit. In this arena of sound even the basic primitive character of the instruments contributes to the creation of a mysterious harmony, resembling in this way nature's own workings. There is even a sensual quality about the delicate intervals that resist being classified by the usual means. Heterophony is present like splashes in the stream of sounds, and yet it sounds appropriate.

The most important instrument here is the *shō*. My impression of ascending sounds and the secret of immeasurable metaphysical time seems to be based on the sound of this instrument. Sound on the *shō* is produced by inhaling and exhaling. The resultant sound, continuous and without attack, does not generate external beats, but awakens an internal latent rhythm. Delicately swaying clusters of sound reject the concept of everyday time. I now recall Pierre Reverdy saying, "Only silence is eternal."

Creating sound by inhaling and exhaling results in an unbroken continuity. While the pauses in a Noh drama possess a certain feeling of liveliness, the stream of sounds from a *shō* has an eternal repose about it. *Gagaku* reveals a strong Buddhist influence. In hearing the stream of sounds it is possible to imagine the concept of transitoriness but not necessarily that of lifelessness. Indeed, inhaling and exhaling are the history of life.

There is also something in the pauses in a Noh drama that has to do with eternity. Also, much of our traditional music aims at an immeasurable metaphysical sense of time. The unique qualities of this music would be lost if one began flirting with external form, but I need time to explore the real substance of that idea.

Western music has been carefully classified within a narrow system of sounds, and its presentation has been systematically notated. Rests within a score tend to be placed with mathematical compromises. Here the sound has lost its strength within the limitation of functionalism. Our task is to revive the basic power of sound. This can be done only by a new recognition of what sound really is. I do not know if *gagaku* satisfies that requirement, but I do know that in this stream of sounds that is *gagaku*, a richness of sound undivided by rigid classifications can be recognized.

I have referred to the "stream of sounds." This is not only an impressionistic description but a phrase intended to contrast with the usual method of construction in music — that of superimposing sounds one on another. This is not a matter of creating new space by merely dividing it, but it does pose a question: By admitting a new perception of space and giving it an active sense, is it not possible to discover a new unexpected, unexplored world? This is the same as recognizing sound as an object. Listening to the *shō* I began to think of a basic creative approach to negative space.

The external and internal world is full of vibration. Existing in this stream of infinite sound, I thought that it is my task to capture a single defined sound. The revival and reinstatement of *gagaku*, which has miraculously survived for such a long time, would be anachronistic in this modern world. And I myself have no particular desire to promote such a revival. I do, however, want to give serious thought to some of those things that *gagaku* suggests to contemporary music.

## IV

In former times the Confucian ideas that music was ceremony held sway.

Ceremony has to do with refined procedures, at the same time eschewing the direct expression of emotions. Without saying things directly one tries to tell about himself through allegorizing. Such an approach was regarded as dignified. The distance between the German *Ich-Romanen* [fictionalized autobiography] and the Japanese *shishōsetsu* [Japanese novel in which the author is the central figure] may also be seen between the Western music-as-expression and the traditional idea of music-as-ceremony. The bells of Westminster Abbey speak in terms of first-person singular: they have an individual motive with a distinctive statement. The Japanese temple gong, however, speaks without personal identification: its sound seems to melt into the world beyond persons, static and sensual.

Yukio Mishima wrote:

The Japanese language consists of sentences that easily eliminate the subject. *The Tale of Genji*, for example, has many passages where the subject is very obscure. In the case of the *shishōsetsu*, once the person "I" is established it can be understood by the reader without any problem. This is also true

*Nature and Music* [ 187

of "he." This simplifying technique, which includes the elimination of the third person and the mixing of "he" and "I," places the novel in the reader's own spiritual world at the expense of social and human relationships.

I wonder if the deep impression of the *shishōsetsu* might not be that of the beauty of denial of self. It impresses, not by confession, but by the restraint in denying one's self, which, while it limits and narrows the world, is at the same time emancipating. That is what creates the deep impression. Words are transformed into the fourth-dimensional passage between this world and the pure land of the future.

In all Japanese music I think *gidayu* holds the strongest expression of violent emotions, although it is at the same time highly restrained in its use of the voice. There is no other example as vivid as this.

Does one express himself through his own suppression? Or is the reverse true? Either way a simple comparison of Japan and the West is meaningless.

I hope to define the characteristics of something Japanese, then, with those characteristics — personally confront something European of comparable value. At this point in my generation such confrontation of the two traditions should not be impossible. Whatever contradiction results may provide the basis for discussion.

V

Toshi Ichiyanagi expressed the following ideas:

> Result is a thing of the past. If you are concerned with results no vital action exists because the present is not known. Motivation and process are the important things. When a composer puts meaning into sound and invents fixed forms he objectifies himself through his own ego. Through his attitude one is removed from his own time quality. The Self is there without inventing it. And that entity of Self includes everything.
>
> It is not necessary to build fictitious reality.

I don't question the ideas expressed here; in fact, I rather agree with most of them. I wish to develop my "nature and music" by dealing with these matters in my own way. I must not ignore my doubts about the falseness of this so-called "expression" — they will never be resolved. But by confronting the imperfect act of expression a composer can turn it into a productive one. Could not the beginning of expression be the recognition of that part of one's self that cannot bear expressing? Expression is not the world giving meaning to me, but me giving meaning to the world. By doing so I reassure myself of my own existence in the world.

One does not regard the naming of the five fingers as expression. But grasp-

TORU TAKEMITSU

ing and pointing are expression. And fingers are part of the hand, and the hand is part of the arm, and the arm is part of something you call yourself. I can be only a hand. And that hand is certainly part of myself. The something that makes me alive could be myself. Just because I am only a hand doesn't mean we can say that my hand could not be a tree.

Expression never means separating myself from other things.

The world is immediately with me, but when I am aware of it, it retreats. Therefore, in talking to the world you are really only talking to yourself. Walk your own path, avoiding the influence of the senses, which often deceive you. It is only this path that will lead you to the richness of the world.

All art ends in artificiality; in that sense it is false. But what is it that gives it the ring of truth? I do not wish to make the invisible part of art fictitious.

Ichiyanagi says that when a composer puts meaning into sound he objectifies himself, but I don't think I really understand that. To me the world is sound. Sound penetrates me, linking me to the world. I give sounds active meaning. By doing this I am assured of being in the sounds, becoming one with them. To me this is the greatest reality. It is not that I shape anything, but rather that I desire to merge with the world.

## VI

Discouraged, I retreated into what resembled a cell in a beehive, sealed, without fresh air. No flags fluttered there. I had sold my soul for an easy system that had the superficial attraction of an insect specimen box. Actually, there were flags there, each on a straight pin, classifying the specimen and assigning it to its place in such a way that the desiccated specimen became even more real than the living creature. But it was a world without peace of mind. . . . I could not sing . . . no decay . . . no deterioration . . . time stood still.

A beautifully organized exterior without true substance!

But the stream of history flows on, carrying with it pollution as well as precious life.

Now that I have captured this concept of sound I must make it live rather than abstracting it into lifelessness. I must smash this glass specimen box, exposing my own fundamental error in pasting those classification labels on the realities of history. Never mind the shattering glass — my own wounds will mark the beginning of "life."

Circumstance and reality combine to shred my thinking. I must boil down this relationship to the point where "reality is nothing but sound to me." Reality is all around me offering the "tomorrow" I need to assure the promise of a future.

I have been trying to research the problem of the Japanese tradition in music. But I should be careful about making easy pilgrimages into the past.

*Nature and Music*

Some time ago among the ruined mines of Chikuhō, I stood watching the frightening scenery in which nature reclaimed its own, bringing everything back into a sentimental landscape. Why was that so frightening to me? It was the fear of something man-made crumbling back into nature. Even an extremely well-crafted intellectual construction can crumble. Is it only geology that teaches us this?

To the human being nature is anonymous. Its scattered elements exist, potentially defined by their own names. True rapport between nature and human beings begins when we name things. It is then that the real exchange between things and man begins. When one sees a humanized tree, that tree truly exists. In other words, I strive to create an unnatural environment in my world. That is really a *natural* thing to do. For me, the naturalizing through allegory and metaphor that one finds in Japanese folk songs is completely *unnatural*. On numerous occasions I have written about the reconciliation of the Japanese people and nature. But now, by turning away from such thinking, I want to try to understand it in a new way.

What I have been saying is that we must give meaning to sound by returning it to its original state as a naked being. Sounds themselves, their movement as personalized beings — that is what we must discover and continue to discover anew. Organized sound is merely a subjective creation of the human being and is not the personalized sound I am discussing. My phrase "give meaning to sound" refers to something other than mere naming and differentiating. It concerns a total image. Both my acceptance and my suspicion of "chance music" stem from this point of view.

I want to carve away the excess to expose the single real existence. I must continue to work, striving always for precision and clarity.

## VII

Some time ago, right after his *Nirvana Symphony* was published, the composer Toshirō Mayuzumi wrote an article about his profound attachment to the Buddhist temple gong. I expressed a kind of disapproval of what he had written because I could not bring myself to believe that the electronic analysis of a Buddhist gong was a prerequisite for the creation of that piece. Certainly the sound of a Buddhist gong might give a composer some new ideas and techniques. I would not deny that. But there should be a great distance between the sound of a gong and the utterances of a composer.

I have no criticism of Mayuzumi's scientific analysis of the Buddhist gong and his attempt to reduce it to general musical terms. On the contrary, I approve. And his own subjective re-creation of the gong sound is not the issue. If that were the case the problem would have been simple for me. What does concern me is the way Mayuzumi tried to explain that piece of music by means of the gong. I also had this feeling about *Samsara*, a recent work of Mayuzu-mi's in which the Buddhist idea of the transmigration of the soul is reduced to nothing but the role of a narrator, leaving me with the impression that the composer was imitating the idea with sounds. What is more, that simple explanation seems to be the basis of the general popularity of that piece. This is not intended as a criticism of the actual work. In fact, I have no doubt that at least the *Nirvana Symphony* is a masterpiece of symphonic literature.

In my opinion that gong effect in the *Nirvana Symphony* is not the most crucial part of the work. While Mayuzumi's article has a certain descriptive accuracy about it, there is something in the music that goes beyond the sound of the gong. That something is what I would call true expression, that special element that cannot be explained.

What was important was the way the sound of the gong, described by Mayuzumi as a "campanology effect," captured space and time beyond everyday life, shaping and moving according to the will of the composer. The actual gong sound ceased to be important. I believe that is the most honest approach a man can take toward the gong-nature, if one can presume to speak of the gong as having a nature. I feel the same way when Olivier Messiaen talks about bird songs, after he has pointed out that it is silly to transcribe nature in a slavish way.

> The words in poetry are something like iron filings on a sheet of paper: they can be arranged by a magnet and be made to rise, all pointing in one direction. Once a certain vital power penetrates words, the words themselves are abandoned, transformed by that power. Each word begins to show a magnetic character. Words gain direction.

The quotation above is from a study of poetics by Makoto Ooka. I include it here because I think it is meaningful to think about the conditions he describes in terms of sounds. The excitement music provides goes beyond verbalization. And that is the reason we find meaning there.

That time when we are truly impressed by a human being occurs when we see great power working within a small humble person. This is also true of words. That is, we are impressed, not by description, but by something elevated to "expression."

### VIII

I think it is important, not only in words but also in my own music, to grasp the concrete sound that, in its confrontation of silence, should have strength and integrity.

While differences may exist between so-called spoken and written language, I do think that spoken words are stronger than written words. But this may be my own conviction as a composer. I have been using the term "utterance" to cover the physical and expressive sides of speech, and I have suggested that it is a symbol for "life." What does this term "utterance" really mean?

In the private quarters of the Rakanji Temple in Meguro I had a chance to hear some old *biwa* music. Hirata Kyokushu of the Chikuzen school of *biwa* playing once said to me, "Since my voice is low it is not suited for the brilliant polished melodies of Chikuzen. Because of that personal problem I had to learn to sing from my heart much more than other singers."

What is it to "sing from the heart"? It was only after hearing a performance that I really discovered the significance of those casual remarks.

Generally it is rare to find individual invention within the singing of Japanese music. The music itself is highly polished and refined within the limitations handed down through generations. Technical experiments may appear but they too are restricted. In the performance of *jōruri* or other traditional styles we sometimes invoke the name of a specific virtuoso, as if seeking to reach his level of virtuosity. Why? Are we aspiring toward such divine singularity? If so, where is individuality in this traditional world of music? Of course technique is respected, but in this case respect has a significance far beyond the usual sense of the word.

There is a Japanese word, [*iki*], which may mean "stylishness," "breath," or "to live." A superb technique is not stylish [*iki*], not to be respected. On the other hand, virtuosity, which has the technique of making a long tradition live *iki*, is respected as the superior one. That Chikuzen art is Hirata's own, but, paradoxically, at the same time it is not his. Most certainly it is Chikuzen. When the old melodies come alive through Hirata, is that not something beyond technique? That is what moves us.

Within the limiting, yet timeless, conventions of Japanese music, starting from the individual's breathing, it goes beyond the personal to merge with the pulse of "life," to become free. For me this has important implications.

Naturally the utterance of sound is not restricted to the voice. One has to have a direct physical relationship to the creation of that sound, otherwise wouldn't "singing from the heart" become a meaningless idea? Rigorous training is required for traditional Japanese music for a good reason, and it is not only for purposes of technique. Such training is really directed at uniting the musician's breathing with the immense "life" in nature.

As far as traditional Japanese music is concerned I am an outsider. But there are moments when I feel a sensual refinement in the old virtuoso arts, which goes beyond their being mere venerable masterpieces, a kind of distilled sensuality, something concrete. That is the quality we should not miss.

The quality I have been discussing is certainly utterance. At the same time it is something we might call a vision of life.

STEVEN FELD

# Lift-Up-Over Sounding

*Because knowledge can never replace respect as a guiding principle in our ecosystemic relations,*
*it is adaptive for cognized models to engender respect for that which is unknown, unpredictable,*
*and uncontrollable, as well as for them to codify empirical knowledge. It may be that the most*
*appropriate cognized models, that is, those from which adaptive behavior follows, are not those*
*that simply represent ecosystemic relations in objectively "correct" material terms, but*
*those that invest them with significance and value beyond themselves.*
— Roy Rappaport, *Ecology, Meaning, and Religion*

One way to imagine the potency of "nature" as a cultural construction is to imagine the appropriateness of the word "aesthetic" in each place where Roy Rappaport[1] uses the word "adaptive" in his essay on ecology and cognition. To do that I will review two intertwined dimensions of a mutualism of adaptation and aesthetics among the Kaluli people of Bosavi in Papua New Guinea: the ecology of natural sounds as a human musical ecology; and the conceptualization of place as a cartography of human song and lament. In the first instance the mutualism begins with the natural soundscape of the Papuan rainforest in the Bosavi region. Here the calls of some one hundred and thirty species of birds, as well as the sounds of many frogs, the rhythms of cicadas and insects, the sonic presence of creeks, streams, waterfalls, pools, and other waterway formations are obvious quotidien presences. For Kaluli people, these sound patterns are indexically heard as the time of day, seasons of year, vegetation cycles, migratory patterns, heights and depths of forest, and many other markers of place as a fused human locus of time and space. What Kaluli perceive and know about natural diversity in their world articulates often through attention to these sounds, and through elaborate conceptual and cognitive indicators of the centrality of sound to experiential truth.

At the same time, Kaluli vocal and instrumental musical sounds are inspired by, modeled upon, and performed with these environmental sounds. And the evocative powers of these musical performances, as well as their interpretation and affective response, are modeled from the same pervasive perceptual and epistemological primacy of sound. Here ecological and aesthetic co-evolution means that the music of nature is heard as the nature of music. Moreover, this iconized or constructed "naturalness" is brought into alignment by an over-arching cosmological framework for the interpenetration of nature and culture. This framework is located in the dualism of birds, who both coordinate the local natural historical sense of being in space-time, and whose presence continuously announces the presence of spirits. To each other the birds appear as people, interacting as such and sounding out through talk. To Kaluli, birds "show through" as a metaphoric human society whose colors, behaviors, and sound categories (whistling, singing, talking, saying their names, crying, making noise) thoroughly fuse the "natural historical" and "symbolic" dimensions of imagination and engagement.[2]

Turning to the ways physical place, sensed and sensible, is imaginatively coded in a cartography of songs and lamentations, the emphasis will shift to how Kaluli song and lament texts are organized as maps of placenames. The sequences of these names are textually co-articulated with names of trees and vegetation, creeks and waterways, and birds. Here we can concretely understand how places are quite literally "placed" in memory, and how their codification and evocation in the formal genres of song and funerary lament poetics intensifies the expressive relationship between the biographical, feelingful, experiential dimension of cultural identity, and the adaptive dimensions of ecological knowledge and awareness.

### Acoustic Ecology As Aesthetic Adaptation

*Does it require deep intuition to comprehend that man's ideas, views and conceptions, in one word,*
*man's consciousness, changes with every change in the conditions of his material existence,*
*in his social relations and in his social life?*
— Karl Marx and Frederick Engels, *Manifesto of the Communist Party*

A commonplace orientation of cultural ecology is to the processes by which societies adapt to environments. Generally this entails understanding how cultural configurations emerge, transmute, reproduce, change, and sustain. Emphases on technology, economics, and the control and regulation of resources are central to these concerns, as is the role of ecological interactions within a broader understanding of the biological and cultural interface of adaptation. One rarely sees or hears talk of aesthetics within these discourses on cultural ecology, co-evolution, and adaptation, matching the equally scant attention to cultural ecology in the discourses on cultural expressive systems. Indeed, among all domains of ideational, symbolic, and hermeneutic approaches to culture, materialists and ecologists have tended to view the aesthetic-expressive lens as superstructural and epiphenomenal. And for their own part, cultural aestheticians have equally tended to view the ecological and adaptational lens

STEVEN FELD

as reductionist and positivist. Such caricatured discursive polarization has had intellectually unproductive consequences. And even if that point is widely recognized and acknowledged by many more anthropologists than it was ten or fifteen years ago, there is still little work that takes the ecological-aesthetic interface beyond a low-level "reflectionist" paradigm toward an intellectual challenge worthy of extended theoretical or empirical scrutiny. Parallel polarizations can be found as easily in discourses on geography as in cultural anthropology. Even within the diverse literatures of humanistic geography, rapprochement of systematic and experiential perspectives is admired more than achieved.

One way to pose the challenge of a new dialogue is through clarification of how an approach to aesthetics in a cultural and phenomenological framework can articulate with ethnographic and materialist agendas. Aesthetics is here taken, to use Robert Plant Armstrong's phrase, as an ethnographic location of "form incarnating feeling,"[3] and specifically where works of what Armstrong called "affecting presence"[4] are witnessed as "a direct presentation of the feelingful dimension of experience."[5] Like Armstrong and other phenomenologists, my approach here sidesteps aesthetics as an asocial philosophical discourse aimed at abstractly illuminating conditions of virtuosity, excellence in execution, and beauty. Rather, the ethnographic intrigue is to locate what Kaluli find affecting and moving about mundane and intensified experiences; to explore the vicissitudes of what they interpret as powerful and nonordinary, whether deriving from casual or heightened realms of sociability. Aesthetic here means to recall the Greek notion of "sensuous perceptions," albeit ethnographically formulated as fully articulated social facts.

Reviewing similar issues from a more materialist stance, Raymond Williams traced the limiting dimensions of "aesthetic" as a historically specific discourse in the West:

aesthetic, with its specialized references to art, to visual appearance, and to a category of what is "fine" or "beautiful", is a key formation in a group of meanings which at once emphasized and isolated subjective sense-activity as the basis of art and beauty as distinct, for example, from social or cultural interpretations. It is an element in the divided modern consciousness of art and society: a reference beyond social use and social valuation which, like one special meaning of culture, is intended to express a human dimension which the dominant version of society appears to exclude. The emphasis is understandable but the isolation can be damaging, for there is something irresistibly displaced and marginal about the now common and limiting phrase "aesthetic considerations," especially when contrasted with practical or utilitarian considerations, which are elements of the same basic division.[6]

Williams' own attempt to create a more suitable analytic category, under the rubric "structures of feeling,"[7] formulates a more socially situated aesthetics as the concepts and practices that animate senses of evocation. "Evocation" illuminates a universal dimension of human existence: that all people sense and mark certain experiences as special, acknowledging the ways they evoke behaviors, moods, and feelings heightened in awareness yet centered in a local sense of identity. Transposed to any local situation, one may empirically investigate what is found compelling in expressive forms and their performed presentations, and how such practices are rationalized, valued, and internalized as core experiences. Such embodiments, local premises of style, are central to understanding an aesthetic imagination in action.

The central circumstance in such an exploration of how Kaluli aesthetics challenges an ecological perspective concerns the local imagination and performance of linkages between poetic, musical, choreographic, and visual-material expressive systems on the one hand, and on the other, perceptions of the structures and contents of the rainforest environment. Three continuously intersecting patterns organize such linkages; in simple terms: inspiration, imitation, appropriation. Inspiration involves imagining and creating expressive forms symbolically interpenetrated with environmental knowledge and appreciation. Imitation involves the mimesis or the iconic or indexical suggestion of actual elements — usually more referential or overtly identifiable features — of the environmental sensorium in expressive forms and their associated perceptual reception. Appropriation is the more thorough incorporation or conventionalized stylization in expressive forms of larger patterns of either formal structures or evocative features of environmental order. The structures of such transcorporation usually invite application of the notions of metaphor or trope.

In an attempt to systematically explore these patterns among Kaluli people, my research has explored these three ecological nature-expressive culture linkage patterns across four general areas of musical and verbal arts, these being (1) myth, (2) song texts and vocal style, (3) instrumental sounds and performance style, and (4) musical theory and verbalization. In the case of myth this work has concerned the representation of the voice of weeping as the voice of a fruit dove; with text it turns to song.

In the area of song texts and vocal style the work has illuminated how and why Kaluli sing with, to and about birds, water, insects. Emergent sound play and a poesis of onomatopoeia directly relates to singing with nature as well as about it and like it, interlinking ethnoecology and ethnopoetry. In the area of instrumental sounds and performance style the work has analyzed how drums literally and metaphorically incorporate bird voices and through them become the voices of spirit children. Refraction of the bird voice through the spirit/drum voice uncovers an elaborate set of ideas about the spatialization

STEVEN FELD

and density of natural and instrumental sound. In the area of theory and verbalization, centrally the linguistic mediation of musical concepts vis-à-vis actual musical practices, the work has analyzed the technical metalanguage and polysemy linking the semantic fields of water and sound, as well as the broader range of conceptual metaphors, like the notion of "flow," related to style and performance. It is in this last area that the conceptual and practical dimensions of aesthetics are more poignant in their cross-modal significance, linking musical thought to realms of the visual, verbal, and choreographic, and, as well, back to ecological modelling of the rainforest.

One of the key notions in this area, central to grasping a Kaluli aesthetics, is *dulugu ganalan* — "lift-up-over sounding."[8] This is the term that prescribes and describes natural sonic form for Kaluli, and given my primary interest in the realm of sound, I first thought that it was a notion that referred exclusively to that domain. Instead, this term is a spatial-acoustic metaphor, a visual image set in sonic form and a sonic form set in visual imagery. By calling attention to both the spatial ("lift-up-over") and temporal ("sounding") axes of experience, the term and process explicitly presuppose each sound to exist in fields of prior and contiguous sounds. In practice this is quite the case because the antithesis of "lift-up-over sounding" is unison. All "lift-up-over sounding" sounds are dense, heavily blended, layered; even when voices or sound types momentarily coincide, the sense is that the unison is either accidental or fleeting, and indeed, it is entirely by chance.

The essence of this "lift-up-over sounding" idea involves two components. One is part-relations that are simultaneously in synchrony while out of phase. "In synchrony" means that the overall feeling is of togetherness, of consistently cohesive part coordination in sonic motion and participatory experience. Yet the parts are also "out of phase," that is, at distinctly different and shifting points of the same cycle or phrase structure at any moment, with each of the parts continually changing (even competing) in degree of displacement from a hypothetical unison.

A second component concerns timbre, the building blocks of sound quality, and texture, the composite, realized experiential feel of the sound mass in motion. Timbre and texture are not mere ornaments; a stylistic core of "lift-up-over sounding" is found in nuances of textural densification — of attacks and final sounds; decays and fades; changes in intensity, depth and presence; voice coloration and grain; interaction of patterned and random sounds; playful accelerations, lengthenings, shortenings; and the fission and fusion of sound shapes and phrases.

In the forest, sounds constantly shift figure and ground; examples of continually staggered alternations and overlaps, at times sounding completely interlocked and seamless, are abundant. One hears no unison in nature; presence and absence of sound and changes in direction and dimension coordinate space as intersecting upward and outward. For Kaluli this is the naturally coherent model for soundmaking, whether human, animal, or environmental: a constant textural densification constructed from a "lift-up-over sounding" that is simultaneously in synchrony yet out of phase. Interlock, alternation, and overlap, as a fused locus of natural and human sound production, embodies simultaneous icons of competition and cooperation. In other words, sounds constantly interact in a tense quest for primacy, for one to momentarily stand out from the others, while at the same time conveying the sense that any primacy is fluid, momentary, and as quickly lost as it is gained.

Kaluli apply this acoustic figure/ground idea not just to the "naturalness" of the rainforest soundscape and to the vocal and instrumental music they create that is of a piece with it. In the realm of visual form, the face painting styles associated with Kaluli ceremonial costume masks involve a singular figure and ground principle realized in both a shiny/dull texture contrast and black/red color contrast. These contrasts visually mirror sonic "lift-up-over" and are discussed in that way. Comments on color pictures taken at earlier ceremonies or from other parts of Papua New Guinea also spontaneously elicited this conceptual designation and idea. Hence we have in face painting a visual homology-resemblance to the sonic principles of "in synchrony yet out of phase" and "textural densification."

A similar homology is evidenced in ceremonial costumes. Costumes mix many types of materials, layering possum fur, frame headpiece with white cockatoo feathers; painted body (face, arms, stomach, legs) in red, black, and white; shell necklace surrounded and centered by woven cross bands reaching under the arm; flapping feathers strung from bamboo in arm, belt and knee pieces; waist belt with attached crayfish-claw rattle in rear, emerging through palm streamers densified with cordyline top pieces. Costumes project layered density. The sound emanates from shells and streamers in motion as the dancer bobs up-and-down, "lifted-up-over" by the drum and rattle or by voices and rattles. The performer's voice "lifts-up-over" the costume-as-waterfall so as to sound like the voice of a bird that dances in place by a waterfall. Thus there is a visual-bodily-sonic interaction of textural densification in costume, dance, and sound that merges with a visual-bodily-sonic in-synchrony and out-of-phase sensation.

A final "lift-up-over" touch that completes costumes is called the *tamin*, a single white cockatoo feather, or a pair of same, placed in the top center of the dancer's headdress. This *tamin* feather (a name derived from the verb for "lead" or "go first") is attached to the end of a long pliable piece of bamboo that springs up from the headdress. As the dancer bobs up and down, the *tamin* swings backwards and forwards in a long arc continuously outlining a

STEVEN FELD

backward then up-and-over pendulum. This swaying arc flows in synchrony directly with the dancer's vertical movement, but is also out of phase by virtue of mapping the opposite (horizontal) motional plane. The *tamin* then "lifts-up-over" the rest of the costume both materially and motionally. It completes the sense that all costume materials are in layered multiple visual-sonic-motion figure/ground relationships. Hence we have another homology linking the "lift-up-over sounding" of the dance costume to that of body painting.

When applied to the sound world of the rainforest, "lift-up-over sounding" refers to the fact that there are no single discrete sounds to be heard. Everything is mixed into an interlocking soundscape. The rainforest is like a world of coordinated sound clocks, an intersection of millions of simultaneous cycles all refusing to ever start or stop at the same point. "Lift-up-over sounding" means that Kaluli people hear their rainforest world as overlapping, dense, layered. Whether it is the more specific overlapping of avian antiphony (like the dueting of the New Guinea Friarbird and Brown Oriole) or the way forest heights and depths are signaled by the swell of cicadas and constant refiguring of creek and river hisses wherever one walks, Kaluli often note, both on the trail or in the longhouse area, that the forest is "lift-up-over sounding." And Kaluli apply the same principle to their own music when they say that their voices "lift-up-over" like the trees of the forest canopy. Or that sounds of drums or axes "lift-up-over" like tumbling waterfalls into swirling waterpools.

In sum, the "lift-up-over sounding" idea takes in nature (birds, insects, water), human music (vocal and instrumental form and performance style), body painting and costume (figure/ground shifts and textural density), choreography (sound and costume in motion), work and interactional sociability (overlapping speech and song coordination; the term for "conversation" in Kaluli is "lift-up-over talking"). And it unites them such that visual, motional, and sonic (musical, verbal, natural) dimensions of style are conceptually and practically united through active engagement and participation, linking feelingful experience and everyday knowledge and action.

To turn to the significance of this pattern, two notions, of trope and synaesthesia, are helpful for understanding the cohesive sensory, perceptual, emotional, feelingfully practical dimensions of aesthetics packed into the Bosavi concepts and practices of "lift-up-over sounding." Moreover, these notions are helpful to understanding the naturalization of music as an ecologically modeled system and the culturalization of nature as an aesthetic system. Roy Wagner speaks of trope as "a single phenomenon or principle [that] constitutes human culture and cultural capacity . . . the phenomenon is coherent and pervasive, organizing conditions for the perception of meaning over the whole scale-range of cultural forms."[9] Likewise, Lawrence Marks glosses synaesthesia as "intersensory correspondences . . . the transposition of sensory images or sensory attributes from one modality to another."[10] "The synesthetic, like the metaphoric in general, expands the horizon of knowledge by making actual what were before only potential meanings."[11] Synaesthesia and trope concern concomitant sensation, simultaneous joint perceptions. An analogic icon for Kaluli ceremonial and artistic synaesthesia thus might be the experience of the rainforest itself, where in a sensually involuntary and culturally conventional manner, features of sound, texture, space, and motion are interrelated. In the tropical rainforest height and depth of sound are easily confused. Lack of visual depth cues couple with the ambiguities of different vegetation densities and everpresent sounds, like water hiss, to make depth often sensed as height moving outward, dissipating as it moves. "Lift-up-over sounding" precisely yet suggestively codes that ambiguous sensation: upward feels like outward.

What of course is central in all this connection is the mysterious world of Bosavi birds, which is the world of Kaluli spirit reflections; of "voices" that are also "gone reflections" (*ane mama*) between visible and invisible worlds. The primacy of sound in the rainforest makes music the domain of nature for which Kaluli have so much natural historical, mythological, and ornithological interest. Thus it seems fitting that in Bosavi there was a tendency for prolific composers to also be expert ornithologists. Notions like this, inextricably linking the transformative play of nature and culture, are in no way singular to Bosavi, and various commentators on Papua New Guinea have reported them in a variety of ways for a wide range of societies. Perhaps one of the most-repeated renditions comes from an anecdote, reported in the voice of quaint colonial journalism, by Colin Simpson, an Australian writer who produced a well-known trilogy about Australian exploration in Papua New Guinea. In the opening to a chapter about birds of paradise, he writes:

> Between the natives and the birds there is a marked and intimate relationship — though it is perhaps too predatory on the native side to be called an affinity. The native ornaments himself with bird plumage. In his dancing he imitates some of the postures of the birds that perform courtship dances. In his songs some of the birds' calls are recognizably introduced. And the natives make dancing lawns which — particularly at Mt. Hagen where trees are planted and buttressed in much the same way as the bird surrounds a sapling with a circle of built-up moss — resemble the playgrounds of the Gardener Bower Bird. This was pointed out to me by Fred Shaw Mayer who has more first-hand knowledge of the birds and animals of New Guinea than anyone I have met or ever hope to meet.
>
> He once said to a man at Mt. Hagen, "You people must have copied your dancing grounds from the Gardener Bower Bird."
>
> "Oh, no," the native said. "The bird copied us."[12]

## The Cartography of Song and Lament

*The events of one's life take place, take place. How often have I used this expression, and how often*
*have I stopped to think what it means? Events do indeed take place; they have meaning in relation to*
*the things around them. And a part of my life happened to take place at Jemez. I existed in that*
*landscape, and then my existence was indivisible with it. I placed my shadow there in the hills, my*
*voice in the wind that ran there, in those old mornings and afternoons and evenings. It may be*
*that the old people there watch for me in the streets; it may be so.*
— N. Scott Momaday, *The Names*

A humanistic and artistic appreciation of the universal prominence of place in human lives and activities may still be most easily found in literary expression, and indeed, forcefully indicated in the literary works of indigenous peoples, like American Indian author N. Scott Momaday. And while such accounts present alternative, complementary, or oppositional discourses to ethnographic writing, the general tendency to recognize the special significance of place has come to be more taken for granted in academic discourses of anthropology too, even though ethnographers lag far behind humanistic geographers in actually theorizing place. Heidegger's theory of dwelling, a "topology of being,"[13] is well figured in geographical versions like Yi-Fu Tuan's *Topophila* (1974), but has only more recently been taken up in ethnographic studies, like James Weiner's *The Empty Place* (1991). From such an ethnographic standpoint the key issues around the prominence of place are how spaces are transformed and "placed" through human action, and, more crucially, how places embody cultural memories, and hence are substantial sites for understanding the construction of social identities.

The issue here is as much in the theorization of memory as of place. Edward Casey's phenomenological study of remembering argues that vicissitudes of memory go considerably beyond temporal recall and retrospection to a significant second dimension, that of place. He analyzes how place memory has been greatly overlooked both in philosophical discourses and in cognitive psychology.

It is the stabilizing persistence of place as a container of experiences that contributes so powerfully to its intrinsic memorability. An alert and alive memory connects spontaneously with place, finding in it features that favor and parallel its own activities. We might even say that memory is naturally place-oriented or at least place-supported. Moreover it is itself a place wherein the past can revive and survive; it is a place for places, meeting them midway in its own preservative powers, its "reservative" role. Unlike site and time, memory does not thrive on the indifferently dispersed. It thrives, rather, on the persistent particularities of what is properly in place; held fast there and made one's own.[14]

Casey views place as reflexively locative and evocative: "place is selective for memories; that is to say, a given place will invite certain memories while discouraging others . . . memories are also selective for place; they seek out particular places as their natural habitats . . . places are congealed scenes for re-membered contents; and as such they serve to situate what we remember."[15] Moreover, "this 'down home' sentiment is not only a matter of feeling at ease in a given place but of feeling at ease in a place that has become one's own in some especially significant way. 'One's own' does not imply possession in any literal sense; it is more deeply a question of appropriating, with all that this connotes of making something one's own by making it one with one's ongo-ing life."[16]

But there is more than holding and appropriating, for place too has its posi-tion in and as "affecting presence." Like Armstrong's "form(s) incarnating feel-ing(s)," Casey sees potentials for place as evocative embodiment.

> The relationship between emotion and expression is close indeed, and it is therefore not surprising to discover that the expressiveness of landscapes is linked to their inherent emotionality. This link is especially evident in the case of "special places," which bring with them, as well as engender, an un-usual emotional claim and resonance. The power of such places to act on us, to inspire (or repel) us, and thus to be remembered vividly is a function of such emotionality — but only as it finds adequate expression in the features of landscapes.[17]

Moving to the more specifically poetic dimensions of place, Keith Basso's recent writings provide several keys to locating these broader philosophical no-tions of place, memory, and biography within a linguistic and ethnographic approach to place through placenames. He writes, "place-name terminologies provide access to cultural principles with which members of human communi-ties organize and interpret their physical surroundings."[18] Basso illustrates how Apache placenames are not just descriptions of locations but are always replete with allusions to activities, danger, historical events. As such, Apache place-names do more than just narratively anchor events and people; "instead of describing . . . settings discursively, an Apache storyteller can simply employ their names and Apache listeners, whether they have visited the locations or not, are able to imagine in some detail how they might appear."[19] Recalling Edward Sapir's notion of Algonquian verb stems as "tiny imagist poems" and remarking on how Western Apache placenames are simultaneously so dense and compact, descriptive and evocative, Basso cites a Western Apache acquain-

STEVEN FELD

tance, Benson Lewis, who made this comment about a place he visited: "Its name is like a picture."[20]

Locating the resourceful and poetic potential of placenames, Basso notes:

> Placenames are arguably the most highly charged and richly evocative of all linguistic symbols. Because of their inseparable connection to specific localities placenames may be used to summon forth an enormous range of mental and emotional associations — associations of time and space, of history and events, of person and social activities, of oneself and stages in one's life. And in their capacity to evoke, in their compact power to muster and consolidate so much of what a landscape may be taken to represent in both personal and cultural terms, placenames acquire a functional value that easily match their utility as instruments of reference.[21]

Moreover, "Poets and songwriters have long understood that economy of expression may enhance the quality and force of aesthetic discourse, and that placenames stand ready to be exploited for this purpose."[22]

The affective quality and aesthetic force Basso speaks of can also be coded poetically in more vague or sparse place imagery. For example, Melvin Dixon's book on geography and identity in African-American literature discusses oppositional creations, uses of place to alter displaced marginality. Images of journeys, conquered spaces, imagined havens, wandering, wilderness, underground, mountaintops, and places of refuge are part of an expressive transformation from rootless to rooted. These images break down the physical realities of "settlement" and reinvent, in their stead, a placed identity. "The wilderness, the underground, and the mountaintop are broad geographical metaphors for the search, discovery, and achievement of self. They shape Afro-American literary history from texts that locate places for physical and spiritual freedom."[23]

Dixon's perspective on slave songs illuminates how place is ultimately about position, in this case, options for where to be located when insider and outsider positions are set in the key of domination and power. Aloneness, alienation, integration and linkage are thematically part of this way that placeness and personness are critical literary constructs.

> Music creates a landscape, defines a space and territory the singer and protagonist can claim. The slave songs initiate pilgrimages and other self-creating acts, including resistance and escape, that ultimately defeat the inertia of place and identity upon which the institution of slavery had thrived. By seizing alternatives through poetry and music, slaves charted journeys to many kinds of freedom. The symbolic geography in the slave's religion told where and how to reach the territory of freedom.[24]

The range of issues raised by Casey, Basso, and Dixon figure prominently in genres of song and lament in Bosavi. Placenames, what Kaluli generically call *hen wi*, or "land name," and imagined symbolic geography, what Kaluli call a *tok* or "path," operate throughout songs sung in both ceremonial and everyday leisure or work settings as well as in laments, sung-wept at funerals and other moments responding to intense loss. Each genre of Kaluli song involves different contexts for performance, occasions for use, ceremonial and instrumental regalia, elaborateness of staging. All of these genres involve, as a key textual common base, paths of placenames that feature prominently in the text.

Song paths may start far away and end where you are singing, or start where you are singing and lead far or close by. They may circle the land vaguely or closely. They may be dense with names of places and sparse with corresponding trees and creeks. Or they may only name particular progressions of waterways, or small shrubs. Some just insert the sounds of those waterways in place of the names. Song paths may follow the course of bird flight paths, meander alongside creeks, stick to more major walking paths, or just follow the course of hills, ridges, and high places.[25]

There are a great variety of strategies for poeticizing the movement through place in Kaluli songs. But all songs have "paths," and in the approximately one thousand songs that I have recorded over the last sixteen years there are about six thousand places named, prominently lands, waters, mountains, and valleys. Simple songs, like those of the *heyalo* genre, can have a minimum of perhaps three or four named places in a given text. Complex songs, like those of the *gisalo* genre, will tend to have between ten and thirty-five placenames to a song.

Like these composed songs, the other major Bosavi vocal genre, *sa-ya:lab*, improvised laments sung and wept by women during funerals, also compress a great deal of knowledge and feeling. In performing *sa-ya:lab* Kaluli women become known for their ability to improvise textual lamentation maps of places they shared with a deceased person. *Sa-ya:lab* give voice to landscapes of memory. These are projective blue-printings of socially affective space onto the physical space of the environment.[26] Like poetic song, *sa-ya:lab* weeping is more than a vehicle of memory. Voicing and witnessing are active modes of expressing and constituting memory, literally "placing" it, and this involves a merger of practical and aesthetic knowledge and judgment, a way of imagining and enacting belonging, identity. The pain of dissolving social relations, of forgetting them and giving them up, takes place through the activity of constituting and reconstituting them, of remembering. The imagistic qualities of placenames and their sequence extends their uttering and witnessing from the sense of maps to the sense of journeys. A song or weeping text that travels a *tok*, a path of *hen wi*, placenames, is itself a particular kind of performance, one that is an indexical icon of the journey to/from/in/and around-about those places.

STEVEN FELD

It is an intensified microscopic grand tour of the feelings and experiences engrained in those places.

The time of the song or the weeping, literally its precise duration as a performance, creates a time-space for immersion, a momentary witnessing linked to the time of travel and experience, the durations of travel, of movement, of journeying. Here the journey is completely in the listener's head rather than out along those lands, but it is a journey nonetheless, and a powerfully integrative one because of the compact, corporeal durative moment. What makes the moments from the start to the close of the song or weeping particularly powerful is this framing of introspective space, a space that is placed in lands and their relationships, a space that senses the experience of journey as the experience of biographical review. Knowing where you are is knowing who you are, and this is one of the ways in which place is an integrative site for memories, and hence a truly transformative locus of naturalized culture and culturalized nature in Bosavi expression.

## Notes

1. Roy Rappaport, *Ecology, Meaning and Religion* (Berkeley: North Atlantic Books, 1979), pp. 100–101.

2. Steven Feld, *Sound and Sentiment: Birds, Weeping, Poetics and Song in Kaluli Expression* (Philadelphia: University of Pennsylvania Press, 2nd ed., 1990), pp. 44–85.

3. Robert Plant Armstrong, *Wellspring: On the Myth and Source of Culture* (Los Angeles: University of California Press, 1975), p. 11.

4. Robert Plant Armstrong, *The Affecting Presence: An Essay in Humanistic Anthropology* (Urbana: University of Illinois Press, 1971).

5. Armstrong 1975, p. 19.

6. Raymond Williams, *Keywords* (London: Fontana, 1983), p. 33.

7. Raymond Williams, *Marxism and Literature* (New York: Oxford University Press, 1977), pp. 128–35.

8. Steven Feld, "Aesthetics as Iconicity of Style, or, 'lift-up-over sounding': Getting into the Kaluli Groove," *Yearbook for Traditional Music* 20 (1988), pp. 74–113 and cassette.

9. Roy Wagner, *Symbols that Stand for Themselves* (Chicago: University of Chicago Press, 1986), p. 126.

10. Lawrence Marks, *The Unity of the Senses: Interrelations among the Modalities* (New York: Academic Press, 1978), p. 8.

11. Ibid., p. 254.

12. Colin Simpson, *Adam in Plumes* (Sydney and London: Angus and Robertson, 1954), p. 183.

13. Martin Heidegger, *Being and Time* (London: Basil Blackwell, 1962).

14. Edward Casey, *Remembering: A Phenomenological Study* (Bloomington: Indiana University Press, 1987), pp. 186–87.

15. Ibid., p. 189.

16. Ibid., pp. 191–92.

17. Ibid., p. 199.

18. Keith Basso, "Western Apache Place-Name Hierarchies," in Elizabeth Tooker, ed., *Naming Systems* (Washington, D.C.: American Ethnological Society, 1984), p. 79.

19. Keith Basso, "'Stalking with Stories': Names, Places and Moral Narratives among the Western Apache," in Edward Bruner, ed., *Text, Play and Story: The Construction and Reconstruction of Self and Society* (Washington, D.C.: American Ethnological Society, 1984), p. 32.

20. Ibid., p. 27.

21. Keith Basso, "Speaking with Names": Language and Landscape among the Western Apache," *Cultural Anthropology* 3/2 (1988), p. 103.

22. Ibid.

23. Melvin Dixon, *Ride Out the Wilderness: Geography and Identity in Afro-American Literature* (Urbana and Chicago: University of Illinois Press, 1987), p. 3.

24. Ibid., p. 14.

25. On paths, see Steven Feld, "Waterfalls of Song: An Acoustemology of Place Resounding in Bosavi, Papua New Guinea," in Steven Feld and Keith H. Basso, eds., *Senses of Place* (Santa Fe: School of American Research Press, 1996), pp. 91–135.

26. On lament and memory, see Steven Feld, "Wept Thoughts: The Voicing of Kaluli Memories," in Ruth Finnegan and Margaret Orbell, eds., *South Pacific Oral Traditions* (Bloomington: Indiana University Press, 1995), pp. 61–87.

STEVEN FELD

ERIC SALZMAN

# Sweet Singer of the Pine Barrens

The song of the hermit thrush is exquisite, some say the most beautiful bird music there is. The time and place, the last light of day and the most solitary woodland, are an essential part of the appeal. We used to have a favorite spot in the Long Island pine barrens where, in the fading light of a spring evening, we would go to hear the hermit thrush sing.

A highway came right through the spot.

It is not easy to find singing hermit thrushes on Long Island anymore, but the beauty of the music, the rarity of the bird, and the need to preserve its pine barrens environment gave us compelling reasons to look.

*Catharus guttata*, the spotted sweetsinger, is not a rare bird in most places, but it is usually noticed in migration or, on occasion, in winter. But if you want to hear the exquisite cantilena, you must go to its breeding grounds.

In nesting season, the hermit thrush generally lives up to its name, preferring the great forests of the north and west, but it also summers in the pine barrens of Long Island and eastern Massachusetts, where small, relict populations survive, separated from the main centers of hermit thrushdom by many miles of swelling urban sea.

Walt Whitman, who grew up in Suffolk County, used bird song in his work more than once. *Out of the Cradle Endlessly Rocking* is a poem about a lost mockingbird — a rarity on Long Island in his day (it is extremely common today). The poem follows the pattern of repetition and variation found in the mockingbird's song; the effect is both formal and emotional. *When Lilacs Last in the Dooryard Bloom'd* incorporates the hermit thrush song in a similar way. Although everyone knows that this poem is an elegy to the martyred President Lincoln, the evocation of the hermit thrush and its song — an essential ingredient of the work — is now obscure to most people who have never heard of the bird.

When Whitman was growing up, Long Island was certainly a more bucolic place than it is now, but it was hardly a wilderness. Most of its hardwood forests had been cleared for farming and grazing or cut over many times for

cordwood and charcoal to be shipped to the New York market. The pine barrens, too sandy to till, too barren to graze, and too piney to cut for cordwood,
were considered worthless and were then, as now, a backyard wilderness.

Whereas other American poets imitated the bards of Old England, Whitman
was the first to hear a purely New World music; the prose of ordinary American speech, the hum and bustle of cities, the clash and clatter of enterprise and
industry can all be heard in his singular verse. But he was not solely an urban
poet; he heard the melodies and tunes of fields and woods as clearly as the percussion of the city. Let other poets write about Old World larks and nightingales; Whitman heard the music of his native woodland and gave it life in his
poetry.

"It is," he once said about the hermit thrush, "the sweetest, solemnest of all
our singing birds." It is through the song of the bird and its continuity in the
landscape that Whitman comes to terms with the death of Lincoln:

> And the singer so shy to the rest receiv'd me,
> The gray-brown bird I know receiv'd us comrades three
> And he sang the carol of death, and verse for him I
>      love.
> From deep secluded recesses,
> From the fragrant cedars and the ghostly pines so still.
>
> *
>
> To the tally of my soul
> Loud and strong kept up the gray-brown bird,
> With pure deliberate notes spreading filling the night.
>
> Loud in the pines and cedars dim,
> Clear in the freshness moist and the swamp-perfume . . .
>
> Passing over the song of the hermit bird and the
>      tallying song of my soul,
> Victorious song, death's outlet song, yet varying ever
>      altering song,
>
> As low and wailing, yet clear the notes, rising and
>      falling, flooding the night,
> Sadly sinking and fainting, as warming and warming, and
>      yet again bursting with joy,
> Covering the earth and filling the spread of heaven . . .
> Sing on, sing on you gray-brown bird,

ERIC SALZMAN

Sing from the swamps, the recesses, pour your chant
from the bushes,
Limitless out of the dust, out of the cedars and
pine . . .
Sing on dearest brother, warble your reedy song,
Loud human song, with voice of utmost woe.

O liquid and free and tender!
O wild and loose to my soul — O wondrous singer!

Now, this is not merely good poetry; it is also good ecology and a wonderful evocation of the hermit thrush song, which indeed rises and falls in a long series of variations on a simple pattern ("varying ever-altering song"), starting with a low and "pure deliberate note" and then bursting up "liquid and free and tender" to a high warble or trill. The ascending tones are produced as two-note chords, giving a reedy effect. The song, typically delivered in the gathering dusk from a low perch inside the forest, is quite ventriloqual and far-carrying, seemingly amplified and enriched by the surrounding trees and the dense evening air.

The presence of the hermit thrush in the Long Island pine barrens is a living annotation to geologic history. Like the mosses and lichens in the Long Island woods, the heath plants in the bogs, the ruffed grouse and the red crossbill, the hermit thrush is a living relic of the last ice age.

The glaciers, by carting the rubble and debris of half a continent and dumping it on a southern shore, created Long Island. After the ice retreated — only a geological heartbeat ago — Long Island had a climate much like present-day Labrador or Newfoundland, and the land still stirs glacial memories: the look of a bog or a frozen kettlehole pond surrounded by pines and cedars, the taiga-like Dwarf Pine Plains near Westhampton. But things are changing fast. These days the Virginia opossum prowls these woodlands, and the cheery whistles of the cardinal redbird or the moonlight serenades of the mockingbird are now heard in latitudes where, only a short time ago, they were unknown or very rare. The species *Homo sapiens* itself is, biogeographically speaking, a recent intruder from the south.

The advance of southern flora and fauna, aided and abetted by a palpable warming of the climate (attribute it to what you will), is very evident on Long Island. Southern herons, gulls, terns, and shore birds are colonizing at a remarkable rate, and brown pelicans are now regular summer visitors. The wood thrush, formerly rare as a breeding bird on Long Island, has taken over the moister woods and more settled garden areas, limiting the hermit thrush to the most remote backwoods — not something that Long Island has a great deal of anymore. In spite of the current campaign to save what is left of the pine barrens, the hermit thrush is highly threatened on Long Island.

The Long Island pine barrens, similar to the better-known ones in New Jersey, used to cover most of the central portion of the island; there are perhaps 100,000 to 125,000 acres remaining. These barrens sit astride the central, or Ronkonkoma, moraine. Considered in a wider sense, they include many oak and oak-pine as well as pure pine communities. Most of this landscape is dry and sandy, but there are also some very distinctive wet areas where swamp maples and white cedars dominate.

Fire and water are the twin keys to the ecology of the pine barrens. The vegetation of this ecosystem is maintained and even nourished by periodic wildfires. When one of these brush fires breaks out in New Jersey or Long Island, the local fire department and the press invariably attribute it to arsonists, but there have been burns in these woods for a long time, and fire is an integral part of the ecosystem. The "fire climax" community is now a well-known and well-studied phenomenon; the vegetation, full of resinous oils, has actually evolved to encourage fire, which weeds out competition and releases needed nutrients into the poverty-stricken soil. Lightning and spontaneous combustion in the leaf litter ignite brushfires if human activity does not. The cycle is remarkably predictable.

Water is mostly underneath. Rainfall does not run off, but filters through the sandy soils to form a remarkably pure underground aquifer. In certain places (and for various reasons), water collects, seeps, or bubbles to the surface, creating springs, bogs, ponds, swamps, or creeks — wet oases amid the dry sand.

When compared to moist forests, pine barrens do not have a lot of biological diversity. Life here is not easy, but those species that manage to cope with the stresses in the environment — the pine barrens specialists — can be extraordinarily successful. Besides the pitch pine itself and half a dozen species of oaks, the members and close relatives of the heath family are particularly notable: blueberries and huckleberries, bearberries, cranberries, wintergreen, trailing arbutus, laurels and azaleas, and a whole list of obscure swamp plants. Extensive fruitings of berries and cherries attest to a remarkable fertility in these so-called barrens. In season, flocks of songbirds enter the pine barrens to feast on these fruits. The heath hen, or eastern prairie chicken, which fed on the fruits and buds of these plants and was so absurdly tame that it was easily exterminated by hunters, used to strut its stuff here.

Some of the most unusual and endangered animals of the pine barrens are insects, and the most spectacular of these is the black, white, and red buck moth. The mating flights of this moth take place, quite improbably, on brisk October days in spectacular numbers, providing another good example of a rare species that is common in the right time and place. One could say that most often it is not so much the species that is threatened as its habitat.

Perhaps the most surprising avian inhabitant of the pine barrens is the eastern bluebird, which breeds in knotholes or old woodpecker holes in areas that have been opened up by fire. More common residents are the whippoorwill, bobwhite, pine and prairie warblers, great horned owl, red-tailed hawk, great crested flycatcher, eastern wood pewee, ovenbird, rufous-sided towhee and several common and uncommon species of sparrow, all of which are still quite abundant. In the Dwarf Pine Plains and the areas around Westhampton Airport, the endangered northern harrier breeds along with the upland sandpiper, eastern meadowlark, prairie warblers, and grasshopper and vesper sparrows; most of these species were once common on Long Island and elsewhere but have become rareties.

Although it is the unusual quality of the biota that interests biologists and conservationists, it is the purity of the underground water supply that wins political support for pine barrens preservation. These areas are all in the direct path of the development juggernaut that on Long Island has been slowed but by no means halted. If large areas of pine barrens are not set aside, the days of the Long Island hermit thrush are indeed numbered.

In 1964, John Bull of the American Museum of Natural History estimated that fewer than one hundred pairs of hermit thrushes remained on Long Island. Perhaps this was a low estimate, but given the apparent need of this species for territorial size and remoteness, it would be hard to know where to fit in one hundred pairs today. Little by little, the hermit thrush is disappearing from most of its former haunts, its presence and music missed only by the few who took the trouble or had the luck to know it.

The hermit thrush used to be placed with the wood thrush in the genus *Hylocichla*, but now, along with our other northern thrushes, it has been classified with the nightingale-thrushes of tropical America as a *Catharus*. The pine barrens bird is not a race or subspecies; there are birds in the pines on the Massachusetts mainland that make the transition to the north woods form. In a technical sense, this is not an endangered bird. But it seems a sad fate that the exquisite voice of an unexpected wildness should disappear with such inevitability. The fate of the hermit thrush and the fate of these woods are inextricably tied together; hence the intensity of our search for survivors.

*Catharus guttatus* is a neat little bird. It is a touch more impressive than its more famous European relative, the nightingale. Like the nightingale, it has a brownish (or brownish gray) coloration and a reddish tail. Unlike the nightingale but like many other thrushes, the hermit sports a spotted breast and has a habit of flicking or twinkling its wings and of pumping its tail up and down in more or less the same measured tempo that it prefers in its music. It feeds and nests on the ground, making it extremely vulnerable to predation by dogs and cats, a fact that by itself would explain its devotion to the more remote corners of the woodlands.

At first glance and at first hearing, the hermit and wood thrushes appear to be very much alike (even so astute an observer as Thoreau was confused). The wood thrush is bigger, carries reddish tints on its head, not its tail, and sings a lower-pitched and altogether friendlier, more conventionally musical song. Hermit thrush music seems to pass right up through and even beyond the range of human hearing, a wood-note wild that literally aims high. It may escape us a bit at first — the way unfamiliar music from another time and place often does.

Any music is hard to describe, but I will try to give an impression of the hermit thrush song. Our earth-colored bird has a glinting, ethereal melody that begins with a single pure note followed, in a very calm, measured cadence, by ascending silvery trills. These trills are actually quite complex. More than one pitch is sounded simultaneously, and these chords (for that is what they are) are quickly alternated or trilled with other tones or chords; each sound is itself a reedy, shimmering harmony. The ascent is not in a straight line but rather appears to climb in a series of steps or spirals.

Our human metabolism is a good deal slower than that of birds; we live longer and at a slower pace, a quarter the speed and a couple of octaves down. Not surprisingly, we miss the high fine points, and to catch them, we must record these songs and play them back at a lower speed, bringing them down into the center of our hearing range and resolving details in a slow tempo. Only then do we become fully aware of the richness and complexity that lie hidden inside these dulcet harmonies.

Nevertheless, even at the risk of missing the subtleties, I would argue that the hermit is best appreciated, not from recordings (at any speed) and certainly not from descriptions, but live on its native grounds. Nothing suits the bird and its incomparable song as well as its favored solitary woodland. Though they are hardy enough to winter occasionally on Long Island and even farther north, they display their musical talents only on their breeding grounds and, even then, only for a short season.

At least that's what it says in the books. The Long Island birds, who do not seem to have read these books, have a definite and full-throated resumption of song in midsummer, apparently after the first brood is safely launched. Although the basic habitat is pine barrens, they often seem to prefer the oak areas that are mixed in with the pines. In the north, they are said to prefer wetter woods, and if some of Whitman's references are correct, they may also have bred in the Long Island wetlands. Today that habitat has been taken over by

ERIC SALZMAN

two other thrushes, the wood thrush and the veery; hermits are found mostly in drylands. They are very well adapted to the dark forest understory, and like the nightingale, they sing in the dim light of dusk and dawn. But, again contrary to the books, they also sing commonly in the heat of the summer midday from the top of a tree — admittedly, not a very high or grandiose perch in these stunted woods.

Even in suitable territory, hermits seem to be thinly and patchily distributed. As if in compensation, their silvery music carries over long distances, traveling through the forest understory enhanced by woodland echo (amplification by tree trunk), which imparts a dreamy, ventriloqual quality to the song.

This song is deliberate in tempo and, although far carrying, not very loud. Compared with the brilliant inventions of the mockingbird or brown thrasher (or, for that matter, the nightingale or European song thrush), it is rather set in form. The other thrushes are baroque artists, constantly elaborating, reworking, and adding to their showy repertoire. The hermit thrush is a classicist, working on the principle of less is more, *multum in parvo*. Constantly changing variations appear within a simple, firm musical framework. Complex chords and high overtones climb and resonate between the tree trunks to create a sense of space and depth: a song in three — no, four — dimensional space that seems to speak of eternal things.

The pine woods in early June are poised between spring and summer. An old sand road winds between pitch pine and scrubby oak, lady slipper and lupine, the first fragrant swamp azalea blossoms and the last of the mountain laurel bouquets. An oriole is still heard whistling, but the brown thrashers have abandoned concertizing for homemaking. The insect wheeze of the blue-winged warbler rides on the cool of the evening, although the bird is all but indistinguishable from the oak leaves dappled yellow by an almost horizontal late sun.

The time of the hermit thrush is between the light and dark hours. The last thrashers and towhees climb up on their perches to sing a round or two before packing it in. An early whippoorwill tunes up a note or two and then falls silent. We strain to hear the glint of a fairy-tale music, something beyond the far-off barking dogs and the distant rush of traffic. Somewhere there is a far-off song hanging in the translucent evening air. A hermit? A wood thrush? To check it out, we would have to crash through the brush in the gathering darkness, but reluctantly abandon the idea. Darkness in the forest does not fall; it rises up from the ground, quickly enveloping us. It would be embarrassing but perfectly possible to become lost in these Long Island woods and have to spend the night.

Suddenly, a small gray-brown bird streaks out from under a pine in a clearing next to the trail. Instead of disappearing, it hovers nervously and uncertainly well inside a nearby thicket, refusing to identify itself. There is a nest here, artfully tucked away under a shrub in the pine duff, with three flecked greenish blue eggs inside. We feign departure and try to use a dense shrub as a blind, but the bird sees through our clumsy charade and stays away. It will not return to its nest as long as we are watching, and loath to create any further disturbance, we decide to leave.

The last edge of daylight dissolves above as we retreat; fortunately, the white sand road, which has now given up almost all the accumulated heat of the day, still holds enough light to guide us home. As we trudge back in silence, a bird begins to sing — an ancient hymn rising from the dark forest floor to an almost empyrean height, where the last embers of the sky still glow over the woods.

The hermit thrush is with us still.

ERIC SALZMAN

# Where the Sounds Live

### I

I worked with the Nez Perce in Idaho and central Washington in the late sixties and early seventies, recording oral histories, music, and natural ambient sound. Many of the Elders, wishing to have their traditions preserved, generously permitted us to record their stories. These exchanges of family histories played an important role, establishing a mutual trust over a period of many months. One member we interviewed, tribal Elder Angus Wilson, suddenly became very pensive and quiet one afternoon when I told him, among other personal revelations, that I was a musician. "You white folks know nothing about music," he said, half-serious, half-teasing with a confrontation unusual in his culture. "But I'll teach you something about it if you want."

Early the next morning, we drove from Lewiston to Lake Wallowa, one of the many campsites in northeastern Oregon where Chief Joseph had lived and where the Nez Perce had lived and hunted for many centuries. Wilson led my colleague and me to the bank of a small stream, the east fork of the Wallowa River, and motioned for us to sit quietly on the ground. In the chilly October mountain air, we sat huddled in fetal positions, arms wrapped tightly to our sides, trying to keep ourselves warm for the better part of an hour. Every now and then, we glanced in the direction of Angus, who sat stoically and motionless about fifty feet upstream. For a long while, except for the calls of a few jays and ravens, we heard nothing. After what seemed like a long time, a slight breeze came from up the valley and began to stir the branches of the aspen and fir trees. Suddenly, the whole forest burst into a cathedral of sound! Like a huge pipe organ with all the stops out, a giant cacophonous chord echoed from everywhere throughout the valley. Angus, seeing the startled looks on our faces, walked slowly in our direction and said, "Do you know yet what makes the sound?"

"No," I said, shivering and irritated. "I haven't the slightest idea."

Without another word, he walked over to the bank of the stream and, kneeling low to the water's edge, pointed to the reeds that had been broken different lengths by wind and ice. Slipping a hunting knife from the leather sheath hanging at his belt, Angus cut one of the reeds at the waterline, whittled some holes, and, without tuning the instrument, brought the transformed reed to his lips and played a melody. After a long while, he stopped and said quietly, "This is how we learned our music."

II

Essentially, the relationship of humans with the natural world and its wonders has a history of being adversarial and isolated. This is especially evident when we try to replicate aspects of the wild natural in our natural history museums and aquaria. In many of these spaces, animals are lumped together in contained areas: African species mixed with Asian, estuary with open ocean. The audio media used to reproduce this material is not much better. Frequently set up in reverberant or noisy outdoor spaces and competing with other events, the sound is often boring and hard to hear. Video material is also of poor quality. And many museums, zoos, and aquaria are still using antiquated push-a-button, hear-a-sound (or see-an-event) systems. For me as a visitor, nothing much is gained from these encounters, as they are so far from useful experience. As part of my own work, I have gone to lengths to address these problems through the development of new technologies that play back sound as it would be heard in a natural state. When these systems are used to play back excellent field recordings, the visitor is able to experience a bit of the wild. In doing so, we've begun to address the art of re-creating natural environments more realistically. Other forms of sound art, however, still lag behind.

For instance, what has happened to Western musical expression and our so-called connection to the natural? Our art forms have become so detached from our direct experience with the wild that, while aspects of music attempt to emulate or express nature, none I've heard sounds particularly convincing. Some composers may take the melodious voice of a thrush or warbler and be inspired to write a symphony as a result. However, the articulation of the bird through the limits of Western instrumental voices, elaborate compositional techniques, or computers doesn't begin to capture the dramatic aural complexities and textures one experiences in natural habitats. Yet some of us still fool ourselves into thinking we are able to capture its essence. As Claude Lévi-Strauss wrote in his recent book, titled *Look, Listen, Read*, "an uninformed listener cannot say that it is the sea in Debussy's composition of the same name . . . but once the title is known, one visualized the sea on hearing . . . *La Mer*."

I suspect that we are functionally incapable of reaching back far enough in time to be able to make the important distinctions between what we have composed or orchestrated and what really exists in the wilderness. Long ago, we acquired our musical heritage largely from the animal world, of which we were once a collective and integral part. We now earn our musical certification by degree at institutions like Juilliard, Eastman, the Paris Conservatory, Yale, or through a grant from the NEA. Having experienced more than a little of both worlds, it is my impression that modern music education does not appear to be linked in any way to the natural world. Roy Lichtenstein once said, "artists try to tell you that what they do comes from nature, and I'm always trying to tell you that what I do is completely abstract." To me, it is the sound from the unaltered natural world that is the real music I love most.

Paul Shepard, in his book, *The Others: How Animals Made Us Human* (Island Press, 1996), reminds us of the Greek tale of Orpheus, "who created music and taught it to the astonished beasts." He then goes on to say that the Greeks had it backwards. It was the animals who first made music, and it was our ancestors who listened. "When humans uttered their first words," he continues, "birds, frogs, and insects were already whistling, dancing, drumming, and trilling." One evening, while on a field trip to Africa commissioned by the California Academy of Sciences, I heard what I thought was a group of these amazing creatures chorusing in a kind of harmonious synchronicity — a cohesive and precise animal orchestration that was special to that particular habitat. This biophony was a revelation that began to challenge some tenaciously-held Eurocentric notions I had believed for so long.

In my own life, I have been recording natural sound and utilizing the results as components of orchestration since 1968, when I first began this odyssey. I love the task of recording and creating, and I can't imagine doing anything else more blessed in this life. I like to think of myself as a fairly competent naturalist, field recordist, and producer who, until very recently, spent an average of seven months a year in the field, often alone. I don't fear the natural world, its creatures, or the events I encounter. However, I have come to greatly respect it and have learned its dangers firsthand. Nevertheless, I feel much more comfortable and safe when I'm alone in a rainforest or a desert at night than I do when walking around the streets of Manhattan, Los Angeles, or Paris in broad daylight, or enduring the pitfalls of academia or the business world. The apparent contradiction here is that I prefer living in the presence of wildness, in the ecotone where *uncertainty* is the expectation. At least, there, the limits of uncertainty are knowable. Yet my Western conditioning is so strong that I am always reluctantly and sadly drawn back to the "civilized" world I have grown up knowing. Psychologically, I am unable to make the final break, so at best, my relationship with the wildness is more or less tenuous. At the same time, there is a kinship to the wild (perhaps genetic) that I cannot escape no matter how hard I try. And so I live in two worlds: romantically desiring to be in one (evidenced by my work), and inevitably being sucked back into the sullen realities of the other (also evidenced by my work).

One of the things I like best about wildness is the profound lack of judgment. A creature either thrives or it doesn't. I am either prey or a predator, and I have learned enough to distinguish between the two and to make certain choices about my behavior in the presence of the Others. Without a serious weapon, I become simply one of the many — certainly more equal — and the experience has taught me a kind of humility that I was quite unlikely to learn living primarily in cities, the rural countryside, or at any university. Ego counts for zip in the bush.

As a recordist, though, I am a voyeur, taking what I can for the moment within the limitations of my equipment. I used to think that what I captured on tape was "authentic." I know better, now, and have become much more modest with my claims. The abstractions I capture with current technologies, be they music or ambience, are nothing more than a mere shadow, much like the phantoms that once played out their hour on Plato's cave wall — a kind of delusion, a speculation void of context and meaning that is further distorted as we confine those iterations to compact discs. I realize that the very act of recording these habitats means to dissect the natural — carefully selecting for time, place, dynamic creature performance — then further choosing one small aspect to create new contexts akin to an ideal expression of whatever aural vision momentarily comes to mind. I've traveled long distances to collect what John Cage somewhat disparagingly referred to as "found compositions." Like most of us, he missed the point. But, there still remains a viable context where human-created music is directly connected *with* "nature." In some of the few forest-dwelling groups of people whose music, stories, and culture still resonates with birdsong and the throbbing choruses of frogs at dawn or dusk, the tenuous synapse remains.

Shortly after my 1983 trip to Kenya, where I first considered the niche hypothesis, I had an opportunity to visit both Australia and southern Ecuador, where I encountered the Pitjantjara and Jivaro groups, respectively. The Pitjantjara of central Australia move through what, to us, may look like completely flat and undifferentiated terrain. To them, however, it is described to a significant degree by sound definitions of their ancient routes (songlines): "Travel along this route as long as you hear the green ants sing, then, when their song ends, head toward another voice (and so on) until you get to your destination."

The Jivaro were former headhunters who continued to rearrange the skull sizes of their adversaries until the late sixties. In 1599, after wiping out a Spanish-controlled town of around 20,000 inhabitants, they were considered to be so fierce that they earned a reputation as the only South American tribe to effectively repel these Iberian invaders. On one visit, when I was allowed to accompany a group of men on a night hunt, I was astounded to discover that they found their way through the densest foliage without the aid of torches,

BERNIE KRAUSE

guided primarily by subtle changes in forest sounds. With amazing accuracy, they were able to describe unseen animals far down the path by the slightest variation of insect and frog articulation. Their music, too, seemed to reflect a notable relationship to the sounds around them and often appeared to be driven by the "mood" of the forest daytime or evening sounds.

Unfortunately, I was too focused on separating human sounds from those of the forest at that time and did not think to record the music and forest ambience together. So I was able to capture the forest on tape and left behind one of the more relevant links in a fit of ignorance. I deeply regret this oversight but honestly didn't know better. Other discoveries, however, are beginning to reveal new evidence of links we have long dispensed with in our own culture.

There has been a great deal of work done recently by people like Louis Sarno, who has been living with the Babenzélé (Bayaka) Pygmies in the rainforests of the Central African Republic. Sarno suggests that music and language of the Bayaka arises from the biophony of their respective environments, among many other influences. The relationship between the music of the Bayaka and sounds of the forest seems so strong that they often appear to use the environmental sounds as a kind of natural karaoke orchestra to which they perform. He adds that one of the most robust links is an association to the forest and its creature voices that is strongly spiritual and social, where their music becomes at once both a replication and reflection. Other anthropologists suggest that it is too simplistic to offer that music and language are *directly* influenced by the sounds of the forest. That may be. However, Sarno and I both feel that there may be some areas that have previously been overlooked *precisely* because they are so elusive and difficult to quantify.

In Sarno's book/compact disc, *Bayaka: The Extraordinary Music of the Babenzélé Pygmies* (Ellipsis Arts, 1995), sounds of the forest can be heard mixed with the music in a representative way. After I finished the production, samples were sent to Sarno to play for the Bayaka singers and instrumentalists. They were asked to pay special attention to the relationship between the ambient sounds and music. With the exception of a comment about the shortness of a particular "Boyobi" performance (a ceremony which is normally performed over a period of many hours or even days) the work was universally accepted by those who created it.

There are, of course, other models of this interdependent phenomenon of natural sound directly influencing music. Some Native American music of North, Central, and South America, for instance, is still joined to its respective environment in ways more or less similar to that of the Bayaka. However, this marvel is disappearing at a rate linked to that of habitat destruction combined with the impact of Western religious missions. Luther Standing Bear (1868–1939) expressed this forcefully:

Only to the white man was the natural world a "wilderness" and only to him was the land "infested" with "wild" animals and "savage" people. To us it was tame. Earth was bountiful, and we were surrounded with the blessings of the Great Mystery. Not until the hairy man from the east came and with brutal frenzy heaped injustices upon us and the families we loved was it "wild" for us. When the very animals of the forest began fleeing from his approach, then it was that for us the "Wild West" began.

The missionaries were very late in realizing that the souls of the Yup'ik (Eskimos) in Eek, Alaska, were worth saving. Mostly, there was a scarcity of valuable economic resources in the remote territories of southwestern Alaska. Fur seals were some distance away, and other furbearing animals were not as plentiful as in other areas. Gold was nowhere nearby, and fish, moose, and bear, their staples for food, clothing, and shelter, were not terribly useful on the open market. However, when the "robed ones" finally arrived just after World War I, bans were immediately imposed on "pagan" ritual music and dance, forcing it immediately underground for over half a century. Fortunately, Chuna McIntyre's grandmother survived well into her nineties and passed on to him a wonderful legacy of traditional song, dance, ritual, and prayer that he has re-created in his album, *Drums Across the Tundra*, which I produced in 1993. The reverential expressions of the natural world and animal references in this tape are remarkable, and the material is currently being reintroduced into the tribal ceremonies and culture. Finally, after seventy years, this rich heritage of music from the wild is reluctantly tolerated by resident churches.

When the question is readdressed, "What does either the Bayaka, the Pitjantjara, the Jivaro, and some Native American music have to do *with* 'nature'?" a different answer begins to emerge. In most instances, to me, the relationship is palpable if not directly correlated. However, where it still exists, it is because the point at which the two elements merge is seamless. There is no conflict. No contradiction. It is bonded to the lives of these humans in fundamental ways I can only dream about for ourselves.

The natural world will reveal its mysteries to us when we begin to think of ourselves as an integral part of the whole — when we think of it not simply as an economic resource but as a font of spiritual renewal. Westerners, in our daily rush to reinvent or validate ourselves, haven't given much time to this consideration. Consequently we, as a culture, no longer have any close spiritual ties to the natural world. From the changes in myself during the course of my work, it has become clear that this nexus is a fundamental ingredient we will have to learn to accept once again. In addition, to comprehend the relevance of birdsong, we must come to know the voices of insects, frogs, and mammals vocalizing at the same time and learn the myriad complex ways in which they all relate to one another. Otherwise, the "facts" we have learned will not necessarily provide the insights we need. We can no longer separate creatures from the complex structure where they live and vocalize in and hope to learn very much about them. And for true spiritual renewal, we need to give ourselves time in the wild. A week or ten days in the field won't suffice because time in the forest is necessarily experienced differently. A digital wristwatch beeping off the hours has no relevance. Animals don't meet at any fixed hour to sleep, forage, or hunt. Instead, intervals are determined by the cycles of seasons, the right amount of morning light to trigger birds and insects into song, the passing cells of weather, the dappled shadings of light on the forest floor as the day progresses, and the distinct fragrances that arise at various parts of day or night. Of course, true wildness manages to evade capture on audio tape, film, or any other medium. They simply cannot be *explained*. After being present below the canopy of an equatorial rainforest for a very long time, the tactile, aural, and visual constituents eventually unite, and the creature voices become both unified and distinctive. Only at that point do I begin to hear tiny fragments of what might possibly inspire the hunter-gatherers who live nearby to begin an ancient chant. The forest becomes my place of worship, and my mind begins to imagine what it must have been like to be part of that creature world we have so long ago forsaken and devalued. How would our music sound if, given all the wonderful experience and technologies we possess, we could only find a way to reconnect once again with the Others for one brief moment?

I cannot presently see Western music, or for that matter, any art form, as being linked *with* "nature." It is the intricate and resonant music of the Bayaka, the Jivaro, the Kaluli, or the Yup'ik Eskimos that I long to hear over and over again, precisely because it springs from the sounds of natural environments and is not yet severed from its origins. When I wish to hear the voice of a bird, or a wolf, or a whale, I'll take the time to visit where it lives. At the same time, I'll listen hard for the songs of neighboring humans whose lives are intimately bound to that which sustains them. I'm willing to take the risk that these performances just might occur in ways I'm unlikely to hear in an urban concert hall or on a well-packaged compact disc.

Only much later in my life, after many reinventions of myself and when I was well into middle-age, did I realize that the sounds of the natural world created a robust music of their own — one that I would come to love and would come to use as a palette for my sound sculptures and musical orchestrations. Often, when I can do nothing to improve on the raw field recordings, I sit alone and play them softly, trying to imagine the enchanted moment of their creation. When I'm in a creative state, I'm in a no-man's land between life and death. We all find our own path whether it be toward our own voice or tethered to that of an Other. Sometimes it's a combination of both. Either way, I make the choice to leap into the unknown.

## III

I learned to listen by sitting quietly for long periods of time in natural, quiet places and trying to hear as non-humans might. To do this, I have built extensions to my ears out of paper and Scotch tape and tried to use them as a cat might — first focusing both in one direction, then another, then turning each one in different directions. To hear worms moving under the surface of the soil, I placed a hydrophone (underwater microphone) on the surface of the ground where a robin had been focusing its attention just moments before. To hear sand dunes sing, I have stood at the crest of the Kelso Dunes in the Mojave on Kelbaker Road, just north of Interstate 40. These are some of the actions that have changed my life and guide the ways in which I choose to enjoy each day. However, it hasn't freed me from resistance from some colleagues and peers.

Because I know that most of us are confused about what we experience and how to portray what we think we see or hear, I'm usually not bothered by such criticism. But there are times. One day, after making a presentation on the subject of natural sound, I played some music I had composed entirely with animal voices. Because this was largely an academic audience, several folks were outraged by the process and the result. "You're doing violence to animals!" said John Cage, the late composer, writer, and artist. "And you've changed their sound," added one of his colleagues. Feeling like some kind of biological felon, I waited until all the criticisms were expressed, most of which had to do with changing the sound so radically.

"First of all," I pointed out, "most of the sounds weren't changed. It's just that none of you sitting here have moved far enough away from your insular environments to really hear what's out there in the forest or below the surface of the water near a coral reef." Fully prepared for this response, I pressed on, saying that no recording represents an "authentic" sound any more than an Ansel Adams photograph of "Half Dome" *is* Half Dome, or a Marty Stouffer wildlife film with a predator-prey scene happens as he contends.

In my field, every microphone, every cable through which the electrical impulses travel, every component of every recorder, digital or otherwise, is calibrated with enough difference to create a distinctive variance between discrete recorded representations of the same material. Each type of microphone, for instance, gathers sound in a specific kind of pattern. Some mics, called omnis, pick up sound with equal sensitivity coming from all directions. A shotgun mic, on the other hand, picks up sound coming from a very narrow pattern based on the direction it is pointed, tending to eliminate most other audio information. There are many kinds of patterned mics in between those extremes, as well as different ways in which mics are powered to receive sound.

Most importantly, a sound, once recorded in the field and then brought into the studio, is completely out of context. Typically, sound is presented in stereo. Coming out of only two speakers, it is reduced once again to a narrower field. So in order to create the illusions of depth and moment, there needs to be a great deal of processing, mixing, and editing to make the sounds translate from one medium (the natural world) to another (artificial spaces). The birdsong is not *exactly* the bird. Aesthetically, it is a poor representation and not nearly as exciting as when it's heard in the context of the forest along with the tactile and visual cues. The elaborate equipment we humans have developed is often regarded by us as being omnipotent and without fault. But, at best, it is limited and replicates our world poorly and in far fewer dimensions than we have been conned into believing.

Furthermore, with our world turned upside down, we have learned to hear mostly what we see. Standing by the seashore, we gaze at the water lapping at our feet; it is only then, as we concentrate on the image, that we hear the tiny bubbles in the sand fizzle all around us. Our attention then shifts to the breakers thirty or forty yards offshore as they surge, curl, and crash. We no longer hear the bubbles, as our attention has shifted. Then, as we peer down the beach at the breakers, we hear the low roar of many waves and are almost totally unaware of the sounds just inches away from our ears. One cannot go the ocean shore, set up a microphone, and hope to record waves. The technology simply won't allow a successful replication of the sound. To accomplish the illusion, an audio naturalist must combine recordings of near-field, mid-field, and far-field elements just to begin to approach the experience of being at the shore. Gregory Bateson once observed, "The map is not the territory." Nor do the utterances we hear on tape represent the biophony of the forest. It's simply impossible to capture God's choir in a recording.

# From "A Portrait of Shunkin"

*In Junichiro Tanizaki's tale "A Portrait of Shunkin," Sasuke falls in love with his teacher, the blind shamisen master Shunkin, and eventually pierces his own eyes to share her precise sensory world. But still she is not satisfied with him. This harsh bind of teacher to student is echoed in master Shunkin's explanation of the way nightingales are trained to bring wildness into the rooms of civilization. It is no easy leap.*

When a woman is blind and never marries, there are limits to her extravagance. Even if she has expensive tastes in food and clothing, and indulges them, the sums involved are not likely to be very great. However, Shunkin's household included half a dozen servants, and the monthly expenses were substantial. As to why she spent so much money and kept such a large establishment, it was chiefly because she was a bird fancier, with a weakness for nightingales.

Today, a nightingale that sings beautifully will cost up to ten thousand yen; no doubt that was true even in Shunkin's time. Meanwhile, bird fanciers seem to have changed their tastes somewhat; but in current practice the most valuable nightingales are those which, apart from their natural call of *hōhokekyō*, can sing both the "valley-flying call" of *kekkyo-kekkyo* and the "high notes" of *hōkiibekakon*. Wild nightingales cannot produce these two melodies. At best, they may achieve an unpleasant *hōkiibecha* — to become capable of the lovely, lingering bell-like note of *kon* they require intensive training. Baby nightingales must be caught before their tail feathers are grown, and then trained by another nightingale, a "teaching bird." If their tails are already grown out, they will have learned the unmelodious calls of their parents, and nothing more can be done.

Teaching birds are trained from the beginning in this artificial way, and famous ones have names, such as Phoenix or Eternal Companion. So when it is learned that a certain gentleman has a marvelous nightingale, other nightingale fanciers come from far and wide, bringing their own birds to be "given a voice" by it. This training usually occurs early in the morning, and goes on day after day. Sometimes a teaching bird is taken out to a special place, and its pupils gather around it, like any singing class. Of course each nightingale has its own unique qualities, its own kind of song: there are infinite degrees of skill at turning a melody, or holding a long, trailing note, even when it comes to producing the same call. First-rate nightingales are hard to find, and, in view of the profit from training fees, command a high price.

Shunkin gave the finest of her nightingales the name Tenko, or Drum of Heaven, and loved to listen to it from morning till night. Tenko's voice was really superb. Its clear, ringing high notes made one think of some exquisite musical instrument: it was a voice of steady, sustained power, as well as of great charm and sweetness. And so, Tenko was handled with meticulous care, every precaution being taken as to its diet. Now, a nightingale's feed is prepared by parching soy beans and unpolished rice, grinding them together, and adding rice bran to make a "white meal," after which a "carp meal" is made, by grinding up dried carp or dace or other fresh-water fish; then the two are mixed (in equal parts) and thoroughly blended with the juice of grated radish leaves. And besides all this, which is trouble enough, the bird must be given a few insects every day — the insects living in the stem of the wild grape vine are the only ones that will do — in order to improve its song. Shunkin had about half a dozen birds that required this sort of care, and one or two of her servants were kept busy looking after them.

Since nightingales never sing while people are watching, they are housed in special cages of paulownia wood, closely fitted with sliding paper screens which admit only a faint glow of light. These screens have decorative panels of rosewood, ebony, or the like, elaborately carved, or worked in gold lacquer and inlaid with mother of pearl. Some of the cages have considerable artistic value — even now people often pay large sums of money for them. Tenko's cage was fitted with handsome panels, said to have come from China: the frames were rosewood and the lower part was set with jade plaques of landscapes and palaces in delicate relief. It was a very elegant piece.

Shunkin kept this cage in the window beside the alcove in her sitting room, where she could listen to Tenko whenever it sang. Since Tenko's lovely voice always put her in a good humor, the servants would do their best (even dashing water over it) to get the bird to sing. It sang best on sunny days, so that Shunkin's mood brightened with the weather. Tenko's voice was heard most frequently from late winter through spring; by summer its silences began to lengthen, and Shunkin became more and more gloomy.

Nightingales are often long-lived if properly cared for, but they require constant attention. Left to an inexperienced person they soon die. As pampered as it was, Tenko died at the age of seven, and Shunkin, like most owners who lose their birds, tried to find a worthy successor. After several years she managed to train another splendid nightingale, which she also called Tenko and prized as highly.

JUNICHIRO TANIZAKI

Tenko the Second, too, had a voice of such marvelous beauty that it might have sung in Paradise. Shunkin loved the bird dearly and kept its cage by her side night and day. She used to make her pupils be quiet when it sang, and then admonish them in this fashion:

Listen to Tenko, all of you! It was only an ordinary fledgling at first, but you can see what long training has done for it. No wild nightingale has a voice as beautiful as that. Some people may say that it is merely an artificial beauty; nothing is more lovely, they will tell you, than the song of the wild nightingale bursting suddenly out of the mist over a stream, as you wander through deep valleys looking for the flowers of spring. I cannot agree with them. It is only the time and place that make the call of the wild nightingale so moving; if you stop to listen, you realize that its voice is far from beautiful. But when you hear a bird as accomplished as Tenko, on the other hand, you are reminded of the tranquil charm of a secluded ravine — a rushing stream murmurs to you, clouds of cherry blossoms float up before your eyes. Blossoms and mist alike are within that song, and we forget that we are still in the dusty city. This is where art rivals nature. And here too is the secret of music.

Often she would make the slower pupils feel ashamed, asking derisively if even the little birds had not penetrated the mysteries of art.

"You are really no match for them," she would say.

To be sure, there was a degree of truth in what Shunkin said. Still, Sasuke and the other pupils must have found it trying to be so often — and so unflatteringly — held up for comparison with a bird.

# V

## The Disc of Music and Nature

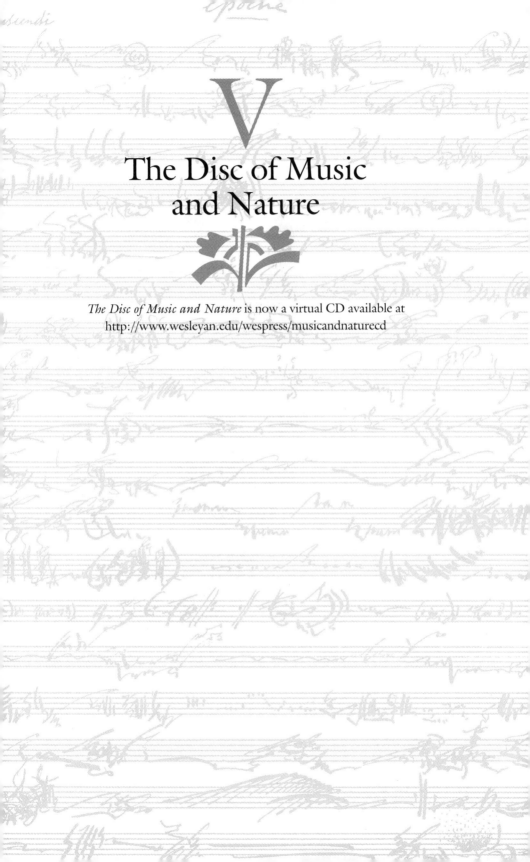

*The Disc of Music and Nature* is now a virtual CD available at
http://www.wesleyan.edu/wespress/musicandnaturecd

DAVID ROTHENBERG

# The Disc of Music and Nature

"To search for models in nature is . . . to seek the most effective use of freedom, the measure of this effectiveness being joy, whose conquest is one of music's missions, and which is nothing but power over oneself and one's things." So writes François-Bernard Mâche in *Music, Myth and Nature* (Harwood Academic, 1992), one of a handful of existing books on our theme. Finding music in nature lures us into experiencing the echoing wonder of the world, how beautiful it can be, how much meaning can be heard in the most unusual of places. I'm not sure I'm comfortable with calling it power. I would instead prefer to think of it as a gentle sense of mastery: knowledge tempered by humility—admitting that there is only so much we can know. But without knowing exactly what they're trying to tell us, we can play and improvise and make music with the world's sounds. That's the most at home music can make us feel.

Any compilation CD is a risky affair, a mixing and matching of excerpts and short cuts from many different musical places and sonic worlds. Works of music can go on for many minutes or many hours, and certainly nature follows no rigorous clock like the bounds imposed by a seventy-four-minute disc. We want to surprise you and make you pause—draw you into disparate natures, places on earth where human song blends into the surrounding mix.

Much of this music is constructed out of natural sounds, and the rest of it tries in various ways to interpret the Cagean dictum—to imitate nature in its manner of operation. Don't sound like nature, but work like nature! Those who believe in a naturalized aesthetic might think the best music already does this. It will be up to you, the listener, to decide when the method works, and when it doesn't. Close your eyes, turn on the machine, come to your senses.

### I. **Dawn Solo from *Pied Butcherbirds of Spirey Creek***
#### Recorded by David Lumsdaine

Of the hours of nature recordings I listened to for this project, this one truly stands out. It would convince even the staunchest skeptic that there are more than human musicians out there in the world. Why? This is a bird singing, but it sounds like human music. The pied butcherbird sings a recognizable melody, easily perceivable by human ears. Then he varies it slightly, returns to the theme, then changes it again, all with a logic and form that can easily be discerned. We don't have to slow it down, speed it up, or change the pitch to grasp the tune. This bird is a musician. He's improvising, playing around. We could join in.

It's music, pure and simple. Does it matter whether it is a bird or a flutist? Listening to it makes me feel part of nature. This piece convinces me at once that there *is* music in nature. If we admit this, we can partake in the wonders of the real world. Here is what David Lumsdaine says about this work:

> My soundscapes are studies in rhythm, harmony and texture in the sounds of the natural world. To use Lévi-Strauss's convenient distinction, their essential stuff is raw as opposed to the cooked stuff which we usually call music. But to speak of anything as "a piece of music" is to indulge in a convenient fiction. Music is not a score on a library shelf, it's not the sound produced by a piano or an orchestra or a computer. Music is an activity, a particularly creative way of listening. The words "composer," "performer," "audience" enable us to distinguish different roles or perspectives within the context of this activity, but they must never distract us from the essentially creative contribution of each participant.
>
> For me, composing is usually the notation on paper of a listening which goes on "inside" my head. By contrast, these soundscapes are recordings of a very active listening which, we may say, has gone on "outside" my head. In the making and editing of these recordings I'm organizing my listening; that's to say, I'm composing it. The techniques I've used for recording the material in these soundscapes differ somewhat to those used in making specimen recordings of individual species. Rather than recording foreground solos, I have tried to capture solos and groups of solos in the context of their community, and to explore the perspectives of the sound stage from the closest to the most distant events.
>
> In composing the soundscapes I've tried to create the least distortion, in time and space, of the original events in order to retain the integrity of each locality. I've also tried to retain a sense of the rhythm of the original scene. Temporal condensation of the material has been made as tactfully as possible, the longest sequences representing those periods of the greatest sonic activity. Inconspicuous edits are used for minor condensation of the material, but hard edits are used to mark changes of perspective and larger changes of time. (There is no mixing of events recorded at different times in order to make a passage "more interesting.") Most importantly: for environmental and musical reasons, I try to create a minimal disturbance in the field. Still, however much tact and cunning I may use, I'm inescapably a

DAVID ROTHENBERG

participant in the field of action I'm observing. Equally, I can't avoid shaping what I hear. The microphones were directed by one pair of ears, and no other pair of ears would have heard these sounds in the same way.

The pied butcherbird song which you can hear on the CD accompanying this *Terra Nova* book is an excerpt from a much longer soundscape, *Pied Butcherbirds of Spirey Creek*. East and West Spirey Creeks rise high in the southeast of the Warrumbungle mountains and meet to create an open valley. This valley is the home of the pied butcherbirds who were recorded between 15 and 17 September 1983.

Pied butcherbirds live in family groups. Both sexes sing and their music is fundamental to communication and bonding between members of the group. The most consistent clues to recognizing the voice of a pied butcherbird are the quality of the voice and the style, or character, of its singing. The members of any group will have a number of calls which they share with other pied butcherbirds, but the musical content of the songs varies from one area to another, even between neighboring territories. Essentially, their territory seems to be defined by the family songs which they learn from their parents and siblings, that is, by means of a musical tradition which each generation may take over and use in its own way.

The pied butcherbird music most commonly heard consists of short antiphonal duos and trios which are sung throughout the day. The much longer, and more developed song — usually a solo — may be heard at night and at dawn in the breeding season. Because the pied butcherbird's song is delivered slowly, and well within the human audio spectrum, it is easy for us to follow it both in detail and broad outline. It is also easy for us to appreciate its harmony.

The pied butcherbird is a virtuoso of composition and improvisation: the long solo develops like a mosaic, through the varied repetition of its phrases. In the course of the song, some elements remain constant, some elements transform through addition and elimination. The bird is a virtuoso of decoration: there is an extraordinary delicacy in the way it articulates the harmonic course of its song with microtonal inflections, or places its cadences with a bird's equivalent of tremolandi and flutter-tonguing.

I've made a number of recordings of pied butcherbirds, and many of them are technically better than this set; but, beautiful as they may be, none of them matches the performance by these particular birds. Serendipity plays a large part in determining the musical quality of a soundscape; there are no retakes in the wild.

In composing the original Spirey Creek soundscape, I placed the pied butcherbirds at its center; their songs were my pathway into the valley, but the music really begins when we hear the whole valley singing with them.

## 2. Making Sago
### Ulahi
### Recorded by Steven Feld

Ethnomusicologist Steven Feld spent many years living with the Bosavi people of New Guinea and has studied and documented their uniquely musical ecological theory of life. The Bosavi conceive of themselves as fitting into and interacting with nature in a particular way, which they call *dulugu ganalan*, loosely translated as "lift-up-over sounding." You can hear that philosophy in action in this piece, as women sing along with birds while cutting up a sago palm tree to extract its root for food. Listen how easily the forest sounds make room for human laughter and work. Here's what Steve Feld wrote about the music the Kaluli (one subgroup of the Bosavi) make among themselves and with the birds as they prepare sago from palm trees:

> As you listen picture this: I'm standing in a very shallow creek by a grove of sago palms, the kind of tree from which the Kaluli extract their staple starch. Directly across from me, on the other side of a plit palm ready for scraping, sits Ulahi. She is surrounded by her daughter Yogodo, her youngest sons Bage and Wano, and Wano's friend Sele. Some other young women, Siegiba and Haidome, are also sitting nearby.
>
> As she works, Ulahi sings in a melodic style called *koluba*. Haidome echoes with a rhythmic whistled breathing. They scrape the pith with stone pounders, swung overhead like an ax. The scrapers never hit in unison; their rhythms overlap in the lift-up-over sounding of voices and percussion.
>
> Ulahi has composed many *koluba*. The first one she sings is about the trees from which resin torches are made. The second concerns her older brother, who has gone to live in a distant place. She sings *ni adeyo-e*, "my older brother," calling out, imagining how she might see him again.
>
> What you're hearing is endangered music. Why? Because the people of this area have been intensely impacted in recent times. Evangelical missionization took a heavy toll on music and traditional culture in the seventies and eighties. But the heavier blow is being dealt right now by mineral exploration and the devastation of the rainforest itself.

It is true that this culture is threatened. Big American mining concerns are moving into the area, and villagers are tempted to work in the mines and learn the meaning of money. With the help of Mickey Hart, drummer for the Grateful Dead and long a tireless promoter of world music, Steve Feld recorded their music and released it widely to the world in 1991. Profits from the CD found their way back into a foundation for the Bosavi, and the people learned that their traditional way of life has economic value in the world market. This might be the only way to convince them that it is worth saving.

Note: When Feld's CD was first released, The Nature Company, a retail store, refused to carry it because it depicted a nature in which people were also present. That wasn't the nature they wanted to sell. I believe by now they have changed their tune.

### 3. The Butterflies of Jumla
Ram Saran Nepali, *sarangi*
Recorded by Hans Weisethaunet
Mixed by Jan Erik Kongshaug

This utterly sublime solo performance, recorded live on a hillside outside Kathmandu, features wandering minstrel Ram Nepali, who moved from village to village in Nepal bowing his *sarangi*, a vertically held small stringed instrument, for anyone who would pay with a meal, some change, or some grains of rice. This particular piece evokes a remote place in far western Nepal, peaceful, the air awash in fluttering wings. Nepali said this before he began: "My nature, where I am born — the forest, the birds, and so many butterflies, nice rivers, and the mountains: this is music. What you need to find out is that this is music. Sometimes birds are dancing, sometimes there is fog, sometimes it is cloudy. This is all music." It could be played only outdoors, only at dawn.

Here's what ethnomusicologist Weisethaunet says about the work in *The Performance of Everyday Life: The Gaine of Nepal* (Scandinavian University Press, 1998):

Ram Saran Nepali was an outstanding Gaine musician whose friendship I was privileged to enjoy from our first meeting in the spring of 1991 until his death, five years later. "The Butterflies of Jumla," in which Ram explores combinations of sounds derived from natural soundscapes as well as cultural elements of the Nepalese place-world, gives us a sense of his aesthetic views on the significance of nature to music. An improvised meditation based around a few motifs, this music "came to him," he explained, when he was visiting Jumla, a place that lies in the Karnali Zone of the Inner Himalayan range.

The musicians of the Gaine caste think of their profession as an obligation given through the law of karma and reincarnation. A Gaine is born to be a musician. His life is to travel from village to village playing music and making a living from the food he is given in exchange for his performance. Like most of the Gaine, Ram started out at an early age traveling from village to village with his father, learning local customs, songs, and the indigenous sounds of the various places they visited.

The traveling Gaine attempts to capture the local sounds in such a way that the specific local voice — in speech and song — and sound qualities will be recognized in performance and associated with experiences of the local place-world. Since the listeners' aesthetic experience lies in their making sense of the musical sound, without this local sonic knowledge, the musical sounds would not produce the locational and associational moves of local participatory experience. Ram frequently stressed that the musician must learn that the forests, the birds, the butterflies, the rivers, and the mountains are music — that all nature is music.

In what Ram considered to have been a direct revelation or mediation of nature, the music for this piece came to him as he was sitting alone with his sarangi by the banks of a river in the far western village of Jumla. All of a sudden a cloud of butterflies appeared, dancing on the top of the water as the water surged around and around, drifting up and down from the water's surface: "It was all silent. And the sight of the dancing butterflies was so beautiful. And I started to play this music."

Ram Saran Nepali was definitively a musician who was very concerned about the sound of his instrument and music. Listening to and discussing the final recording, he was particularly pleased with this piece, since, as he said, it captured the sound of his sarangi without the addition of other in-

DAVID ROTHENBERG

struments, or massive use of reverb that characterizes some of his locally released cassette recordings.

It should also be mentioned that this recording was further refined in Rainbow Studios in Oslo by the legendary engineer Jan Erik Kongshaug, whose careful ears have shaped the spacious, environment-filling recordings on the ECM label that have defined a European jazz sound for many years, often a purely instrumental music that speaks of a natural quiet, with a carefully constructed aural sense of place surrounding the sound.

### 4. The Concert of Noises (excerpt)
Pierre Schaeffer
Recorded fragments of an orchestra tuning and J. J. Grunewald,
piano improvisations

"Having come into the studio to make noises speak, I stumble onto music," wrote Pierre Schaeffer in 1948, the year this piece was composed and recorded. If it sounds like an old and faded recording, that's because it is. If it sounds strangely startling and fresh, that's because something about it remains prescient to this day. Schaeffer was the pioneer of musique concrète, the notion of building music concretely out of sonic material, moving beyond the notion of composers writing and musicians playing. Despite that goal, we chose this particular piece because it blends the performed and the assembled, and because the improvisatory nature of the piano part, first live, then gradually transformed into the mix, does not deny the living sense of music as something participatory, alive, moving, and human, reaching out into a field of warbling sounds.

The transformations of the music are quite subtle here, especially given the time it was made. With the background of tuning strings, the orchestra becomes not a vehicle for ideas, but an environment of all possible musics. You hear it literally at the beginning and at the end; and throughout it offers some grounding tonality with which the pianist improvises. The piece that emerges is not random but clearly French, grounded in an impressionistic style, a bit like Poulenc's written *Improvisàtions* for solo piano. This music that is rooted in its era reaches out to nature as the home of all sonic possibilities. Listen to it as a harbinger of so many generations of concrete musics to come.

Musique concrète is above all about listening. It starts with the sounds of the real world, be they natural or artificial, and encourages us to listen as carefully as possible to appreciate the raw sounds of the world as something of aesthetic worth. As a method, Schaeffer's is thus a primary inspiration for much of the work we present here on this disc. It is related to but not the same as the

Cagean dictum to open up your ears and take in the rich opportunities the world's breathing sounds offer us. Where Cage is meditative, motivated by a Zen kind of elegance in subtle concentration, Schaeffer is exact, meticulous with an engineer's kind of intelligence. He kept careful track of his working methods, as demonstrated in this excerpt from his *Traité des objets musicaux*, chapter 19, "Les structures sonores naturelles: L'écoute musicienne" (Editions Seuil, 1966):

> One must stop passively hearing just a part of the music and open one's ears like a conductor to grasp the whole orchestra. When one listens musically, a focusing of sound occurs. . . . The orchestra constantly attracts and eludes the ear with its astounding richness and variety. . . . The same methods of musical perception can be applied to a body of sound that is not "musical" — sound that is in fact outside of any musical system. . . . Imagine a listener in a noisy place. This place could be an amusement park, a fair, or simply a large group of people chatting beside an aviary. They are at the seaside, next to trees rustling in the wind. The listener's highly *musical* ear does more than to just identify each sound it hears — birds chirping, neighboring voices, sound of ocean waves, or *ritornello* of a Barbary organ. The ear does not confuse these sounds, as even the most advanced computer would do. Instead, in its own way, it segregates the sounds, creating a unique musical score (in the etymological, not the symbolic, sense), and giving each sound source its own part and its own *continuum*.

### 5. Beneath the Forest Floor (excerpt)
#### Hildegard Westerkamp
#### Composed of Vancouver Island old-growth rainforest sounds

Hildegard Westerkamp's music is remarkable for the subtlety in which concrete and engaging music is shaped out of raw natural sound material. The piece has logic, movement, swells, and rhythm. It does not claim to represent an environment "out there" but is clearly a carefully composed work, made not by instruments or out of notes but out of natural sound. Every sound in this work has a certain organic feel to it — from the creaking of trees rubbing against each other in the wind, to the whooming threat of the clear-cutting chainsaw.

Here is what Westerkamp says about the work, which is recognized as one of the premier soundscape compositions of our time:

> *Beneath the Forest Floor* is composed from sounds recorded in old-growth forests on British Columbia's western coast. It moves us through the visible forest, into its shadow world, its spirit, into that which affects our body, heart, and mind when we experience *forest*.

DAVID ROTHENBERG

Most of the sounds were recorded in the Carmanah Valley on Vancouver Island. This old-growth rain forest contains some of the tallest known Sitka spruce in the world, and cedar trees well over a thousand years old. Its stillness is enormous, punctuated only occasionally by the sounds of small songbirds, ravens, jays, squirrels, flies, and mosquitoes. A few days in the Carmanah creates deep inner peace — transmitted, surely, by the trees that have been standing in the same places for centuries.

*Beneath the Forest Floor* is attempting to provide a space in time for the experience of such peace. Better still, it hopes to encourage listeners to visit a place like the Carmanah, half of which has already been destroyed by modern industrial forestry. A visit ought also to transmit a very real knowledge of what is lost if these forests disappear — not only the trees but also the inner strength they transmit to us, a sense of balance and focus, new energy and life. The inner forest, the forest in us.

### 6. Ikebukoro/Madrid/4
#### Brian Eno

In the early seventies, Brian Eno pioneered a kind of surrounding ambient music that does a remarkable job of attuning us to hear the sounds of the world around us. By not threatening the environment, it leaves room for the environment. Listen to the strange background intrusions in this piece. Doesn't it make you wonder if that's on the disc, or outside your window? The boundary is meant to be unclear. You are meant to live inside this music.

Ambient music is bigger today than ever, part of a new category in the record store called electronica, a blur between the experimental noises and the regular beats of pop. Just when you thought you could dismiss it as New Age Muzak, it has become the latest trend in music, with trip-hop and jungle beats spinning in late-night chill rooms and clubs.

It may sound like nature, it may be constructed like nature, but most of all, if played softly enough, it ought to *attune* you to nature, and to all the sounds around you that solidly melt into air. As Eno says, "I don't want this music to evoke landscape. It *is* landscape."

### 7. Women Gathering Mushrooms
#### BaBenzélé Pygmies
#### Recorded by Louis Sarno in the Central African Republic
#### Ambient sounds added and mixed by Bernie Krause

This delicate recording is a seamless blend of human voices and forest sounds. Sarno has lived for more than ten years with the Pygmies, not as an academic but as a foreigner who just loves their music and their lifestyle. Here is his description of the moment when this song was recorded:

Early one morning seven women went a short way from a recently established forest camp to gather some mushrooms they had discovered the evening before. Mushroom gathering lends itself especially well to lyrical accompaniment, for it is not in the least bit strenuous and often takes place in beautiful and spacious primary forest. On this occasion in 1993, the women sang melodies from a *boyobi* ceremony they had sung the night before. I recorded from a short distance away. Afterward we all returned to camp and had a delicious mushroom breakfast.

The acoustics of the primary rainforest bestow on the human voice a special richness of tone. Yodels — calls or cries in which there is a transition between chest and throat voice — are the most natural and effective way to use the voice in this environment because the voice resonates through the trees, both high and low notes hang in the air at the same time. A single voice thus creates a chord. For some reason yodels carry farther in the forests than ordinary shouts or screams.

Bernie Krause is one of the acknowledged masters of soundscape recordings. He took ambient sounds indigenous to the Ituri forest and blended them in with the human chorus, creating a smooth environment where human rhythms play off of insect rhythms. Krause comments: "The intent was to demonstrate the relationship between the forest sounds and the music. Since they came to us as separate elements, we had no choice but to mix them together. Like all recordings, it's both concept and illusion."

All these pieces, and this one in particular, are compositions, not simple documents of what is out there. That is, they are art, not nature. But it is art that reveals nature as a home to human emotion, not a cold place indifferent to us and our music.

Just how ancient is the music of the Ituri forest Pygmies? One should recall that in 1961, when Colin Turnbull asked a group to sing the oldest song that they knew, what came out was a strange version of a most familiar tune: "Clementine." On the other hand, Steve Feld writes that the ancient Egyptians were already borrowing from Pygmy music to add some exotica to their pop songs a few thousand years back. No culture is any more primitive than any other. And music gets around.

### 8. **And God Created Great Whales (excerpt)**
Alan Hohvaness
Seattle Symphony, conducted by Gerard Schwartz

Hohvaness's 1970 work makes use of recorded whale songs as accompaniment and inspiration for this partly aleatoric work, a rare but successful opportunity

DAVID ROTHENBERG

for orchestral musicians to improvise in the midst of a symphonic movement. Here's how Hohvaness describes it: "Free rhythmless vibrational passages suggest waves in a vast ocean sky. Each string player plays independently. Undersea mountains rise and fall in horns, trombones, and tuba. Music of whales also rises and falls like mountain ranges. Song of whales emerges like a giant mythical sea bird. Man does not exist, has not yet been born into the solemn oneness of Nature."

Hohvaness could be considered a transition figure between Aaron Copland and modern mystics like Arvo Pärt and John Taverner. Many of his pieces have a certain orientation toward nature, including his best-known symphony, *Mysterious Mountain* (1955). But Hohvaness decided that to deal with material as otherworldly-sounding as whale songs, he had to make his orchestra do unconventional things, with more openness, more improvisation, and more of a reach toward nature's manner of operation.

### 9. Borbangnadyr: Overtone Song and Rushing Stream
Anatoli Kuular, throat-singing and jew's harp
Recorded live in Tuva by Ted Levin and Joel Gordon

What separates this recording from the many others now available of the remarkable throat-singing music of Tuva, a small semi-autonomous country between Mongolia and Siberia, is the fact that this record was made in the habitat where the music originates, emphasizing its relationship with the sounds of that habitat. The goal is "to present as vividly as possible the wonderfully permeable border between sounds of the nonhuman world, human imitation of that world, and musical constructions involving those imitations," writes Gordon. Levin describes just how the occasion of recording the song with the water came about:

> One evening just before dusk while walking on level grassland, we
> came upon a small stream. I asked Anatoli, who is in his early thirties
> and polished his virtuoso throat-singing abilities as a Soviet-style concert
> performer of Tuvan "folk music," whether he had ever heard, or heard
> of, older herders singing along with flowing water. Anatoli nodded.
> "*Borbangnadyr*," he said, naming a style of throat-singing that imitates
> the sound of something rolling or flowing. When Anatoli jumped into
> the rocky streambed, we noticed that, when he produced a harmonic
> melody of just the right rhythm, pitch, and timbre, his vocal harmonic
> melded with the dancing harmonics produced by the rushing stream. . . .
> Tuvans like to hear streams that "speak," or "sing," like the English notion
> of the "babbling brook." Too great a rate of flow is unappealing because it

produces white noise without identifiable patterns, while streams with too little flow lack the constantly shifting sonic drama which holds a singer's interest. . . .

Indeed, for animists, a sensitivity to the subleties of timbre provides the most essential and intimate tool for interacting with the natural soundworld.

10. **In The Wilderness**
Lucky People Center
Johan Söderberg, percussion and production
Lars Åkerlund, sampled sounds of Sarawak rain forest, Bruno Manser,
and a Penan elder
Sebastian Öberg, electric cello

The Swedish multimedia ensemble Lucky People Center is a performance group and a kind of grassroots artistic political movement, whose happenings and raves draw thousands of fans and supporters in their native Sweden. Their film, a collaboration with visual artist Erik Pauser, is called *Lucky People Center International*, a kind of hip *Koyaanisqatsi* with contemporary music and new millennium spiritual preoccupations.

This piece is taken straight from the film soundtrack, a section that depicts the plight of the Penan people of the Sarawak rain forest on the island of Borneo. The first voice heard is that of Bruno Manser, the Swiss activist who lived among the Penan for many years, returning to the West only to plead that something be done to save these people, who depend on the forest for their subsistence, from the pressures of forestry and development being inflicted on them by the Malaysian government. Later in the song we hear the words of a Malaysian official, spoken in English, who claims that the government allows the Penan to live freely, however they like, but hopes that they will choose to join modern civilization. A Penan elder speaks his mind, in his native language. Here's an English translation of what he says:

> My ancestors came here at the beginning of time.
> The land is ours, we have not left it.
> The logging companies came
> The government came.
> They said:
> Here's a map with all the paths and rivers.
> But that is not our map.
> We know the land.
> We know the paths and rivers
> and where to find poison for our arrows.

DAVID ROTHENBERG

We don't need that map.
The government said: "This is our land."
They told us: "You have no right to it."

I would be happy if they left.
Then I wouldn't be angry anymore.
I don't want anything they want to give me.
Where will my children go?
Where will my woman go?
There will be no forest left.

The voices resound over a steady electric cello rhythm layered upon the sounds of the Sarawak forest. Also featured in the sonic palette are the sampled cries of a Maori spirit-healer and Japanese Kodo drumming.

Lucky People Center makes music that comments on our environment through specific messages blended with sound and image. It's powerful and explicit, an example of the kind of intertextual art we will be hearing much more of in the near future.

## 11. **Sonora**
### Richard Lerman
Richard Lerman, piezoelectric Sonoran desert field recordings
David Rothenberg, bass clarinet

Richard Lerman is the populist of field recording technology. He makes inexpensive (under $1) microphones out of piezoelectric disks (small, flat pieces of metal), attaches them to blades of grass, and lets raindrops fall on them. Sometimes he lets hundreds of ants walk all over them in the desert. The sounds he produces and assembles are immediate, shocking, intensified, and brilliant. His work expands the infinitesimal sounds of the natural world into noises that are wide and surrounding, changing our human sense of scale. The bass clarinet improvises a place in the midst of this vast and enhanced soundscape.

In the midst of this piece you will hear rain on the needles of fire-charred saguaro cactus, wasps spinning around in the sand, carpenter bees boring into long-dead trees, and the rustle of small red weeds in the dry wind.

What's most special about Lerman's work is the quality of the sounds themselves and the overall aesthetic vision that holds them together. He never claims to represent the world the way it sounds "out there," but neither does he consider his specially gathered sounds as raw musical material. The sounds instruct the form — through them a vision of how the music ought to be assembled comes to life.

Anyone can afford this inexpensive recording technology, and Lerman will gladly tell you how to assemble piezoelectric microphones out of materials you can pick up at any electronics store: pzo.lerman@asu.edu.

### 12. La Selva (excerpt)
#### Francisco López
#### Composed entirely of Costa Rican forest sounds

López's essay above offers detailed insight into the compositional process of this piece, composed entirely of sounds recorded in a Costa Rican forest. Through careful composition and blending, López still wants the sounds to speak for themselves, following an approach that he describes below as being closer to the experimental searching of Pierre Schaeffer and a departure from the solace-in-nature perspective he finds too often in much of the soundscape literature, which posits silence as a respite from the awful noises of our life and times. For López, instead, the forest is a noisy place, booming, buzzing, swarming with activity and possessing an almost symphonic potential:

> The idea of sound object (*objet sonore*) developed by Pierre Schaeffer summarizes the main achievement of *musique concrète*: the conception of a recorded sound as something with its own entity by itself, independent of its source. This experience has only been physically possible since the technical development of electromechanical means of fixation and reproduction of sound. It is this technological isolation, and not the use of sounds from the environment, that defines the idea of "concrete."
>
> I am a professor of ecology, and I have been recording and composing with sound environments for more than fifteen years. Although I am quite aware of the obvious relationships between all the properties of a real environment, I think it is an essential feature of the human condition to artistically deal with any aspect(s) of this reality. . . . The "abstractionism" of the *art des sons fixes* is precisely a "musicalization" and — somewhat paradoxically in this comparison — quite the contrary to the abstraction in music, i.e., a concretization. It can obviously close doors in the experiential description of sounds and their sources, but it opens new doors of artistic creation. To me, the latter are much more essential and relevant to the human condition than the former.

*La Selva*, a one-hour musical piece with no subdividing indices on the CD, is presented not as a documentary of the forest in Costa Rica in which it was recorded but as a musical composition. A phenomenology of listening guides López's creative process: "I believe in the possibility of a 'blind' listening, a profound listening that delves deeply into the sounds and is freed as much as

DAVID ROTHENBERG

possible from such constraints. This form of listening doesn't negate what is *outside* the sounds but explores and affirms all that is *inside* them."

It isn't where this recording was made that is the focus, nor which specific insects, frogs, and birds are heard or what they might represent. Take in the sounds. Listen.

### 13. **Visions, Part 1: Mystère**
Toru Takemitsu
Tokyo Metropolitan Symphony Orchestra

The late Toru Takemitsu was Japan's greatest contemporary composer. Trained first in Paris as a "Western" composer, later in his life he found ways to place traditional Japanese instruments, timbres, and structures into his music. The text excerpt from *Confronting Silence* above shows how central nature is to Takemitsu's thought process. This piece, the first movement of a two-movement suite for orchestra, demonstrates just how well he blends impressionist elements of Claude Debussy, birdlike calls à la Olivier Messiaen, and a desire to explore stasis and balance characteristic of Japanese music. If it works as nature works, there is no need to imitate or to be descriptive. That is the mystery; that is the vision.

### 14. **Toothwalking**
Douglas Quin: field recording, sound collage
David Rothenberg: clarinet, cloud chirpers, keyboard bass

I jumped at the chance to collaborate with Doug Quin, who has spent many years questing for the world's most exotic sounds in far-off and perilous locales. This collaboration took place in the raw virtuality of today's world, with DAT tapes FedExed back and forth across the continent, e-mail queries beaming from McMurdo Sound to Newark, Sonoma to Cold Spring.

I asked Doug to work with the sounds he had recorded on his Alaska trip (described in his article) to create a piece on which there would be room for me to experiment. Here is how he describes the process:

> In assimilating my experiences and contemplating the musical potential of what I had heard at Round Island, I was drawn further into the extraordinary realm of walrus vocalization and acoustic display — for their sounds are remarkably diverse and complex. On one occasion, I had the opportunity to witness a group of males form what Sue described to me as a "rosette." While maintaining stationary positions in the water near the surface, they all faced a large rock at close range; their bodies radiated in a loose circumference, like fat spokes from a hub. The performance involved

rounds of gonging, a sort of free-form gamelan. I watched their necks inflate and tension being released — making sounds aimed to reflect back from the rock face beneath the waves.

Gonging and teeth clacking are heard frequently underwater. The latter is produced by jaw action and does not involve the tusks. As a musical premise, I wanted to explore a sense of place connected with this particular species and to evoke some of the oneiric quality of multiple perspectives that I had felt as I dozed off to sleep in my tent. The process of composing from and with natural sound engenders a spirit of inquiry. I revisited the bioacoustic analyses that I had done as part of my report on disturbance. The harmonic aspects of certain sounds and the wonderful rhythms that I had scrutinized suggested directions.

Gong sounds are particularly rich and complex, with many overtones reaching from the lower frequencies to the upper threshold of human hearing (18 KHz). After making samples from the field recordings, selections were processed using digital and analogue filters. The latter were set to resonate, or feedback, slightly at different harmonic intervals — "sweet spots" in the original overtone series and around the first four formants. Other recorded material, particularly from birds on the surface and snapping shrimp underwater, was processed using predictive linear deconvolution algorithms, or noise reduction filters. Residual harmonic artifacts were emphasized and remixed with the field recordings. By weighting or coloring the noise in the percussive banging of teeth, I was able to bring out different and often indeterminate pitches which related well to the resonance of gong formants. The apparent contraction and expansion of aural spaces reflects some of the unique qualities of each cove where the field recordings were made. I juxtaposed various samples with artificial reverb in a spatial counterpoint. The music is a composed set of acoustic images of walruses and their habitat — facts, artifacts, and fabrications as they relate to these unusual creatures. Coo Coo Ca-joo . . .

After listening to Quin's sonic take on the journey to Round Island, I considered what I could add to the spectacle. Answer: not much. A few careful background sounds to intensify the overtones. But who can tell they are not secret walrus cries? The clarinet joins as a raucous seabird, or a discarded instrument of driftwood, making songs far from its original Zanzibar home, where the *mpinga* tree out of which it is formed grows.

It was a major risk to go for tonality, to add a minimalist bass line toward the end. But I didn't want to be afraid. After all, I've been listening to a lot of this ambient material in preparation for this collection. I wanted to be swayed, not afraid to relax. No reason simplicity cannot ask for a few seagulls. Clacking

DAVID ROTHENBERG

walruses or changing chords, it's all part of the soundscape into which we can improvise our essential place.

### 15. Poem for Change (excerpt)
Pauline Oliveros, composer, voice, accordion
Klaus Schöning, production

> Change
> Change one thing
> Change something
> Change nothing
> Change everything
> Change two things
> Change the same thing
> Change many things
> Change a few things . . .

Pauline Oliveros, one of the true modern masters of twentieth-century music, has worked for years on participatory pieces that combine open-ended instruction — careful, attentive, deep listening — with a guiding, spiritual structure. This work, composed for West German Radio in Cologne with the assistance of Klaus Schöning, combines Oliveros's whispering voice with her delicate accordion playing and sampled sounds of our troubled contemporary world.

This concluding piece poses the questions that will incite our further exploration to show how finding music in the world around us might really lead us to a new kind of world — a place more sensitive, more aware, and more alive — long into an uncertain future.

> Listen! Not with your ears with your feet.
> Listen! Not with your ears with your blood.
> Listen! Not with your ears with your ancestors.
> Listen! Not with your ears with your future.
> Listen! Not with your ears with your training.
> Listen! Not with your ears with your ears.
> Listen! Not with your ears with your elbows.
> Listen! Not with your ears with your spleen.
> Listen! Not with your ears with your brain.

CONTRIBUTORS

Composer JOHN LUTHER ADAMS lives outside Fairbanks, Alaska. His works are heard throughout the world, and his recordings include *The Far Country* (New Albion Records), *Earth and the Great Weather*, and *Clouds of Forgetting, Clouds of Unknowing* (New World Records).

JOHN CAGE (1912–1992) was the one twentieth-century composer to have as much influence outside music as within it. Although celebrated (or berated) for his completely silent piece "4'33"," Cage should be most remembered as a musical and poetic philosopher who continually taught us to listen and to let go. His book *Silence* is among the most important books on music of the last century.

Taiwanese author and illustrator TSAI CHIH CHUNG's cartoons are world renowned. His books include a series of cartoon adaptations of classic Chinese writings by Zen masters, Confucius, Lao-tzu, Zhuangzi, and Sunzi.

DAVID JAMES DUNCAN is the author of *The River Why* (Bantam, 1988) and *The Brothers K* (Bantam, 1996). He lives, writes, and plays the tin whistle and piano on a Montana trout stream.

Composer, sound artist, and philosopher DAVID DUNN is the author of *Why Do Whales and Children Sing?* (EarthEar, 1999) and *Harry Partch: An Anthology of Critical Perspectives* (Harwood Academic Publishers, 2000). His CDs include *Angels and Insects* (oodiscs, 1998) and *Music, Language and Environment* (Innova, 1997). He is a professor of music at the College of Santa Fe's Contemporary Music Program.

EVAN EISENBERG has worked as a synagogue cantor, a music critic for *The Nation*, and a gardener for the New York City parks department. His writing on nature and culture has appeared in *The Atlantic*, *The New Republic*, and *Natural History*. He is the author of *The Recording Angel* (McGraw-Hill, 1986) and *The Ecology of Eden* (Knopf, 1998).

BRIAN ENO is "a mammal, a father, a European, an inventor, a celebrity, an improviser, an employer, a producer, a grumbler, a 'drifting clarifier.'" Combining sound, sculpture, and lighting effects, his installations of environmental soundscapes create ambient spaces within which music can reside.

STEVE ERICKSON is the author of the novels *Rubicon Beach, Days between Stations,* and *The Sea Came at Midnight*, along with the political campaign memoirs *Leap Year* and *American Nomad*.

STEVEN FELD is a professor of anthropology at New York University. He is the author of *Sound and Sentiment* (University of Pennsylvania Press, 1990) and *Music Grooves* (University of Chicago Press, with Charles Keil, 1994); the editor, with Keith Basso, of *Senses of Place* (School of American Research Press, 1996); and the recordist of *Voices of the Rainforest* (Rykodisc, 1991).

TIM HODGKINSON is a self-taught composer whose musical endeavors over the years have included involvement with the groups Henry Cow, The Work, and

Momes. *Pragma* (ReR) is his most recent CD of new works. His writing has covered topics ranging from music and shamanism, to technology in music, to aesthetics of improvisation, in publications including *Contemporary Music Review*, *Musicworks*, *Resonance*, and *ReR Quarterly*.

ALAN HOHVANESS (1911–2000) was a most distinctive and prolific composer who melded Western and Asian musical styles. He wrote more than 400 works, from pieces for various solo instruments and chamber ensembles, including Asian instruments, to large orchestras and choirs.

HAZRAT INAYAT KHAN (1882–1927) was born in India. A great Sufi mystic and musician, he gave up music to spread his spiritual teachings. Out of his lifework arose the International Sufi Movement, which takes care of his legacy and works in the service of the Message of Love, Harmony, and Beauty.

BERNIE KRAUSE has recorded natural soundscapes all over the globe and has fought tirelessly for their preservation. He has done sound design for over 135 Hollywood films and has produced or collaborated on over fifty recordings, one of which, *Bayaka*, is featured on our audio CD. His book and CD, *Notes from the Wild* (Ellipsis Arts, 1996), describes his life in the field.

ANATOLI KUULAR is one-fourth of the internationally known Tuvan ensemble Huun-Huur-Tu, which tours the world.

STEVE LACY, masterful improviser and composer in contemporary jazz music, has worked with such musical visionaries as Cecil Taylor and Thelonious Monk. His collaborations over the years have included myriad musicians and artists from diverse creative disciplines, many of whom are acknowledged in his book *Findings: My Experience with the Soprano Saxophone*.

JARON LANIER is a computer scientist, composer, visual artist, and author. He coined the term "virtual reality" and was a principal pioneer in the scientific, engineering, and commercial aspects of the field. As a musician, Lanier has been active in the world of new classical music since the late seventies. He is a pianist and a specialist in unusual musical instruments, especially the wind and string instruments of Asia.

RICHARD LERMAN is a composer and sound recordist and a professor of interdisciplinary arts at Arizona State University.

FRANCISCO LÓPEZ is a Spanish ecologist and electroacoustic composer who has for eighteen years been developing a body of sound matter based on environmental recordings that he has collected from all over the planet, "trying to reach an ideal of absolute concrete music." His catalog comprises over ninety sound works, which have been released by more than fifty record labels.

LUCKY PEOPLE CENTER is a Swedish performance group and artistic movement.

DAVID LUMSDAINE is a distinguished Australian composer who now lives in York, England. He has also made a series of recordings of Australian soundscapes, all available on the Tall Poppies label.

RAM SARAN NEPALI was a wandering Gaine musician in the Kathmandu valley, a virtuoso on the *sarangi*. He died in 1996.

MORGAN O'HARA divides her time between New York City and Europe. Her artworks, in solo and group exhibitions and installations, and her live performances have been presented internationally.

PAULINE OLIVEROS is one of America's most inspiring and interactive composers, focusing on meditative and ritual works that involve an approach she calls "deep listening" (find out more at www.deeplistening.org). In 1985, she established Pauline Oliveros Foundation, Inc., to support collaborations and all aspects of the creative process for a worldwide community of artists with residencies and international exchange.

MICHAEL ONDAATJE was a celebrated poet in Canada long before he wrote the best-selling novel *The English Patient*. He teaches at Glendon College, York University.

D. L. PUGHE is a writer and artist living in Berkeley, California. Her essay "Letter from the Far Territories" was published in *When Pain Strikes* (University of Minnesota Press, 1999), and passages from *A Philosophy of Clean* can be found in *Nest* magazine (1999) and *The New Earth Reader* (MIT Press, 1999).

DOUGLAS QUIN is a composer, naturalist, and wildlife sound recordist. His works have been performed at numerous festivals and venues, from the Netherlands to Antarctica. His CDs include *Forests* (EarthEar, 1999) and *Madagascar: The Fragile Land* (Miramar, 1998). He is the recipient of awards from the National Endowment for the Arts, the National Science Foundation, Meet the Composer, and the Pollack-Krasner Foundation.

RAINER MARIA RILKE (1875–1926) is considered one of the greatest lyric poets of modern Germany. In his poetry and prose, Rilke's main subject was the distance between himself and the rest of the world.

DAVID ROTHENBERG is a musician and philosopher. He is the author of *Hand's End: Technology and the Limits of Nature* and the upcoming *Sudden Music*. His latest CD is *Before the War* (EarthEar, 2000). He is an associate professor of philosophy at the New Jersey Institute of Technology and the founder of *Terra Nova*, now an annual book series on the culture of nature.

ERIC SALZMAN is a composer, critic, and widely published writer on natural history subjects. His writings have appeared in the *New York Times*, *The Kingbird*, and *Birder's World*.

LOUIS SARNO is a native of New Jersey who now resides in the Ituri forest.

PIERRE SCHAEFFER (1910–1995) was a pioneer of sound recording as an art form. In the 1940s, working as a broadcast engineer for the Radio-Television Française, he formulated the ideas and techniques of musique concrète and founded a studio for tape composition.

R. MURRAY SCHAFER, inventor of the word "soundscape," is one of the world's foremost composers committed to integrating music with nature. His book *The Tuning of the World* (Knopf, 1997), reprinted by Inner Traditions as *The Soundscape* (1995), is the standard work on the subject.

ROBERT SCHNEIDER is a novelist and playwright who has won numerous prizes for *Brother of Sleep*, including the prestigious Robert Musil Prize of the

City of Vienna and the French Prix de Medici. The book was made into a film by Joseph Vilsmaier, for which Schneider wrote the screenplay.

CLAUDE SCHRYER's electroacoustic and environmental compositions focus on spiritual, musical, and interdisciplinary aspects of acoustic ecology. A founding member of the World Forum for Acoustic Ecology (WFAE), he has given lectures, workshops, concerts, and conferences on acoustic ecology and electroacoustics in Europe and North America. He currently works for Canada Council.

RUSSELL SHERMAN is an internationally renowed pianist who has performed with the world's leading orchestras. He teaches at the New England Conservatory.

TORU TAKEMITSU (1930–1996) is generally regarded as Japan's most important contemporary composer. Although he originally considered himself a Western composer, later in life he blended traditional Japanese elements with a lush emotive style reminiscent of Olivier Messiaen. In addition to his most famous work — *November Steps* — and many other orchestral and chamber compositions, he composed the music to many of Akira Kurosawa's films, including *Ran*.

JUNICHIRO TANIZAKI (1886–1965) is one of the most world-renowned Japanese novelists of the first part of the twentieth century, known for his subtle investigations of the relations between men and women and of the conflict between modern notions of love and beauty and traditional values.

DAVID TOOP is a musician, composer, writer, and sound curator. He has worked with musicians including Brian Eno, John Zorn, Prince Far I, Jon Hassell, Derek Bailey, Talvin Singh, and Evan Parker. His articles have appeared in *The Wire*, *The Face*, *The Times*, *Spin*, and the *Village Voice*.

MARTA ULVAEUS is the associate director of continuing *Terra Nova* projects at the New Jersey Institute of Technology. She was previously an editor of *TDR: The Drama Review*, at New York University, where she did graduate work in performance studies. For years she could be heard spinning discs on radio stations KPFA and KDVS in California.

HANS WEISETHAUNET is an ethnomusicologist at the University of Bergen, Norway.

HILDEGARD WESTERKAMP's work since the mid-1970s, whether as a composer, educator, or radio artist, has centered primarily around environmental sound and acoustic ecology. She was a member of the original World Soundscape Project, has taught courses in Acoustic Communication at Simon Fraser University in Vancouver, Canada, conducts soundscape workshops, and lectures internationally. She is a founding member of the World Forum for Acoustic Ecology (WFAE).

RAFI ZABOR, music writer and occasional drummer, won the PEN Faulkner award in 1998 for his novel *The Bear Comes Home*.

PERMISSIONS

John Luther Adams, "The Place Where You Go to Listen," *Terra Nova* 2:3 (Summer 1997), reprinted by permission of the author.

John Cage, "Happy New Ears," and "Diary: Emma Lake Music Workshop 1965" reprinted from *A Year from Monday: New Lectures and Writings* (Wesleyan University Press, 1967) with permission from the publisher.

Tsai Chih Chung, "The Music of the Earth," from *Zhuangzi Speaks: The Music of Nature* © 1992 by Princeton University Press. Reprinted by permission of Princeton University Press.

David James Duncan, "My One Conversation with Collin Walcott" from *River of Teeth* by David James Duncan, © 1995 by David James Duncan. Used by permission of Doubleday, a division of Random House, Inc.

David Dunn, "Nature, Sound Art, and the Sacred," *Terra Nova* 2:3 (Summer 1997), © 1997 by the Massachusetts Institute of Technology and reprinted by permission.

Evan Eisenberg, "Deus ex Machina," adapted excerpt from *The Recording Angel* © 1986 by Evan Eisenberg. Reprinted by permission of the author.

Brian Eno, "Ambient Music," © 1979 by Brian Eno/Opal Ltd. and reprinted from *A Year with Swollen Appendices* (Faber and Faber, 1996) by permission of the author.

Steve Erickson, excerpt from *Rubicon Beach* © 1986 by Steve Erickson. Reprinted by permission of Melanie Jackson Agency, L.L.C.

Steven Feld, "Lift-Up-Over Sounding," adapted from "A Poetics of Place" © by Steven Feld, in *Redefining Nature: Ecology, Culture, and Domestication* (Oxford: Berg Publishers, 1996), edited by Roy Ellen and Katsuyoshi Fukui. Used by permission of the author.

Tim Hodgkinson, "An Interview with Pierre Schaeffer" originally appeared in *Re Records Quarterly Magazine*, volume 2, number 1, March 1987, and is reprinted with the author's permission.

Hazrat Inayat Khan, "The Music of the Spheres" reprinted from *The Mysticism of Sound and Music* (Boston and London: Shambhala, 1996), with permission from the International Headquarters of the Sufi Movement, Geneva.

Bernie Krause, "Where the Sounds Live" adapted excerpt from *Into a Wild Sanctuary: A Life in Music and Natural Sound* © 1998 by Bernie Krause. Used by arrangement with Heyday Books, Berkeley, CA, publisher.

Steve Lacy, "Sax Can Moo" from *Findings: My Experience with the Soprano Saxophone* © 1994 by Outre Mesure/Steve Lacy. Reprinted with permission from Éditions Outre Mesure, Paris, publisher.

Jaron Lanier, "Music, Nature, and Computers: A Showdown," *Terra Nova* 2:3 (Summer 1997), reprinted by permission.

[ 253 ]

Pauline Oliveros, "Sonic Images" and "The Poetics of Environmental Sound" from *Software for People* © 1983 by Smith Publications, Baltimore, MD. Used by permission.

Michael Ondaatje, excerpt from *Coming Through Slaughter* © 1976 by Michael Ondaatje. Used by permission of W.W. Norton & Company, Inc.; Ellen Levine Literary Agency, Inc.; and Knopf Canada.

Douglas Quin, "Toothwalkers," *Terra Nova* 2:3 (Summer 1997), © 1997 by the Massachusetts Institute of Technology and reprinted by permission.

Rainer Maria Rilke, "Primal Sound," from *Rodin and Other Prose Pieces* (London: Quartet Books, 1986), *Ausgewählte Werke II* © 1948 by Insel Verlag. Reprinted by permission.

Eric Salzman, "Sweet Singer of the Pine Barrens," *Terra Nova* 2:3 (Summer 1997), © 1997 by the Massachusetts Institute of Technology and reprinted by permission.

R. Murray Schafer, "Music and the Soundscape" from *Voices of Tyranny, Temples of Silence* (Indian River, Ontario: Arcana Editions) © 1993 by R. Murray Schafer. Used by permission.

Robert Schneider, excerpt from *Brother of Sleep* © 1992 Reclam Verlag, Leipzig; translated by Shaun Whiteside, © 1995 by The Overlook Press, reprinted by permission.

Russell Sherman, excerpts from *Piano Pieces* © 1996 by Russell Sherman. Reprinted by permission of Farrar, Straus and Giroux, LLC.

Toru Takemitsu, "Nature and Music" from *Confronting Silence* (Berkeley: Fallen Leaf Press, 1995). Reprinted by permission of the publisher.

Junichiro Tanizaki, excerpt from "A Portrait of Shunkin," in *Seven Japanese Tales*, translated by Howard Hibbett, © 1963 by Alfred A. Knopf, Inc. Reprinted by permission of Alfred A. Knopf, a Division of Random House, Inc., and Martin Secker & Warburg.

David Toop, excerpts from *Exotica: Fabricated Soundscapes in the Real World* © 1998 by David Toop. Reprinted by permission of Serpent's Tail, London.

Rafi Zabor, excerpt from *The Bear Comes Home* © 1979, 1980, 1997 by Rafi Zabor. Reprinted by permission of W.W. Norton & Company, Inc.

# INDEX

*Index*

MUSIC / CULTURE

*A series from Wesleyan University Press*

*Edited by Harris M. Berger and Annie J. Randall*

Complete list of series titles available at http://www.wesleyan.edu/wespress

# The Disc of Music and Nature

This is now a virtual CD available at http://www.wesleyan.edu/wespress/musicandnaturecd

1 **Dawn Solo from *Pied Butcherbirds of Spirey Creek***              4:07
Recorded by David Lumsdaine. From *Mutawinji* (Tall Poppies TP 091).
Used by permission.

2 **Making Sago**    Ulahi                                                4:15
Recorded by Steven Feld. From *Voices of the Rainforest* (Rykodisc RCD 10173).
Used courtesy of 360° Productions, Sebastopol, CA.

3 **The Butterflies of Jumla**    Ram Saran Nepali              4:29
Recorded by Hans Weisethaunet; mixed by Jan Erik Kongshaug. From *The Real Folk
Music of Nepal* (© 1997 Traveling Records TR 001-2). Used by permission.

4 **The Concert of Noises** (excerpt)    Pierre Schaeffer         3:21
Recorded fragments of an orchestra tuning and J. J. Grunewald, piano improvisations
From *L' oeuvre musical* (Musidisc 292 572). Courtesy of Jacqueline Schaeffer.

5 **Beneath the Forest Floor** (excerpt)    Hildegard Westerkamp       6:49
From *Transformations* (1996 Empreintes digitales IMED 9631). Used by permission.

6 **Ikebukoro/Madrid/4**    Brian Eno                                 5:56
© Upala Music (BMI). Courtesy of Opal Ltd.

7 **Women Gathering Mushrooms**    BaBenzélé Pygmies        4:06
Recorded by Louis Sarno and Bernie Krause. From *Bayaka* (Ellipsis Arts CD 3490).
Courtesy of Ellipsis Arts.

8 **And God Created Great Whales** (excerpt)    Alan Hohvaness      6:29
Seattle Symphony, conducted by Gerard Schwartz. From *Mysterious Mountain/
And God Created Great Whales* (Delos DE 3157). Courtesy of Delos International.

9 **Borbangnadyr: Overtone Song and Rushing Stream**    Anatoli Kuular      3:41
Recorded by Ted Levin and Joel Gordon. From *Tuva, Among the Spirits: Sound,
Music, and Nature in Sakha and Tuva* (Smithsonian Folkways SFW 40452).
Provided courtesy of Smithsonian Folkways Recordings.

10 **In the Wilderness**    Lucky People Center                     4:56
From the film *Lucky People Center International* (Stockholm: Memfis Films 1997).
Courtesy of Lucky People Center and Stockholm Records/Stockholm Songs.

11 **Sonora**    Richard Lerman                                    5:49
Richard Lerman, piezoelectric Sonoran desert field recordings. David Rothenberg,
bass clarinet. © 1998 Richard Lerman. Used by permission.

12 **La Selva** (excerpt)    Francisco López                            4:18
From *La Selva* (V2_Archief V228). © 1997 Francisco López. Used by permission.

13 **Visions, Part 1: Mystère**    Toru Takemitsu                  5:46
From *Takemitsu: Visions* (Denon CO-79441). Courtesy of European American
Distribution Corporation, Schott Japan.

14 **Toothwalking**    Douglas Quin and David Rothenberg        5:12
© Mysterious Mountain Music (BMI). Used by permission.

15 **Poem for Change** (excerpt)    Pauline Oliveros              4:11
From the CD that accompanies the book *Roots of the Moment* (New York:
Drogue Press, 1998) © 1998 Deep Listening Foundation. Used by permission.

Total Time: 73:35

This compilation © Terra Nova/Wesleyan University Press, 2001
Produced by David Rothenberg. Production management by Marta Ulvaeus.